LIBERAL EUGENICS

For Laurianne

LIBERAL EUGENICS

In Defence of Human Enhancement

Nicholas Agar

Blackwell
Publishing

© 2004 by Nicholas Agar

BLACKWELL PUBLISHING
350 Main Street, Malden, MA 02148-5020, USA
108 Cowley Road, Oxford OX4 1JF, UK
550 Swanston Street, Carlton, Victoria 3053, Australia

The right of Nicholas Agar to be identified as the Author of this Work has been asserted in accordance with the UK Copyright, Designs, and Patents Act 1988.

First published 2004 by Blackwell Publishing Ltd

Library of Congress Cataloging-in-Publication Data

Agar, Nicholas.
    Liberal eugenics : in defence of human enhancement / Nicholas Agar.
       p. cm.
    Includes bibliographical references and index.
    ISBN 1–4051–2389–3 (hardback : alk. paper) — ISBN 1–4051–2390–7 (pbk. : alk. paper)
 1. Eugenics. I. Title.

    HQ755.A29 2005
    363.9′2—dc22

                                                                   2004007788

A catalogue record for this title is available from the British Library.

Set in 10.5/13pt Minion
by Kolam Information Services Pvt., Ltd, Pondicherry, India
Printed and bound in the United Kingdom
by MPG Books Ltd, Bodmin, Cornwall

The publisher's policy is to use permanent paper from mills that operate a sustainable forestry policy, and which has been manufactured from pulp processed using acid-free and elementary chlorine-free practices. Furthermore, the publisher ensures that the text paper and cover board used have met acceptable environmental accreditation standards.

For further information on
Blackwell Publishing, visit our website:
www.blackwellpublishing.com

Contents

Preface and Acknowledgements

Many of my friends and colleagues were somewhat incredulous when I told them that I was writing a book defending eugenics. The word 'eugenics' has acquired some ugly associations since it was coined in the late nineteenth century. Francis Galton defined it as the science of improving human stock. The suggestion that we should be making humanity better may not sound particularly objectionable, but any semblance of innocuousness was removed by the actions of Galton's most thorough disciple, Adolf Hitler. Although other twentieth-century eugenicists killed far fewer people than Hitler, they did not hold back on imposing their visions of human improvement on others.

The improvement of human stock is no business of the eugenics that this book preaches. Indeed, I do not presume to make any judgements about what to count as such an improvement and how it might be accomplished. Twentieth-century eugenicists thought that bettering humanity would require the strict regulation of reproduction. The eugenics defended here differs in being primarily concerned with the protection and extension of reproductive freedom. Reproductive freedom as it is currently recognized in liberal societies encompasses the choice of whether or not to reproduce, with whom to reproduce, when to reproduce, and how many times to reproduce. What I call *liberal eugenics* adds the choice of certain of your children's characteristics to this list of freedoms. At the book's centre are powerful genetic technologies that will enable prospective parents to make such a choice.

There seems to be a big difference between a programme of eugenics that radically restricts reproductive freedom and one that would dramatically extend it. Some distinctions are clearer in principle than they are in practice, however. We will need to ensure that the differences between liberal eugenics and its authoritarian precursor run deeper than rhetoric while remaining alert to new dangers brought by liberal eugenics. Individuals can make bad eugenic choices just as surely as states can. Our understanding of the harms that such choices may lead to is handicapped by a lack of historical examples of societies committed to giving prospective parents free access to genetic technologies. Writers of novels and screenplays have used their imaginations to fill the gap. They see a host of moral dangers. In the movie *GATTACA*, free access to enhancement technologies has created a society divided into genetic haves and genetic have-nots. What you can be and whom you can marry are set by the enhancements your parents have purchased for you. In Margaret Atwood's 2003 novel *Oryx and Crake*, a free market in human biotechnology leads to the end of human civilization.

Do I think that the fears provoked by these imagined futures are groundless? It would be glib to just assert that the new genetic technologies turn out to be entirely morally unproblematic. While I am confident of rebutting the objections that many opponents of eugenics take to be decisive, I recognize that unprecedented power brings unprecedented dangers. This book does not propose that individuals be given an unrestricted choice of characteristics for their children. Indeed, the same arguments that I use to establish the freedom to make eugenic choices will also set its limits.

I hope at a minimum that this book encourages people to take the idea of liberal eugenics seriously. Hitler and *GATTACA* have made eugenics an unpopular idea. However, being unpopular is not the same as being wrong. Philosophers lack the experimental apparatus that enables physicists to test unpopular hypotheses. The only way to make the thesis of liberal eugenics fit for trial in the court of moral opinion is to vigorously argue for it. How the new genetic technologies should be used on human beings is likely to be a defining moral question of the coming decades. Although there can be no one-off vindication of a view with implications as far-reaching as liberal eugenics, I hope at least to establish it as one of the major alternatives.

This book has benefited from the comments and criticisms of colleagues and friends at every stage in its writing. A number of people gave me written feedback. David Wasserman provided probing, sceptical comments on every chapter. A significant part of the process of writing the book was my responding to his searching inquiries. Stuart Brock, Joseph Bulbulia and Jessica Hammond read and commented on near complete drafts, forcing me to re-examine and strengthen the book's exposition of ideas and argument in many places. Ruth Anderson, Nick Bostrom, Diana Burton, Tony Fielding, Caroline ffiske, Bette Flagler, Jeff McMahan, Laurianne Reinsborough and Katzen Schlect provided philosophical and stylistic pointers on many chapters. I profited also from feedback of a less formal nature. This was provided by my colleagues in presentations of some of the book's ideas to the Victoria University of Wellington philosophy programme seminar and by students in my Ethics and Genetics class. Special thanks must go to Nick Bellorini for his enthusiasm about the project. He both excellently discharged his duty as editor and offered insightful criticisms. I benefited also from the advice of anonymous referees for the press.

CHAPTER 1

Genius Sperm, Eugenics and Enhancement Technologies

In 1978, Robert K. Graham, millionaire inventor of shatterproof eyeglasses, set up the Repository for Germinal Choice on the grounds of his Southern Californian estate.[1] The Repository would offer the sperm of exceptional men to women unable, or unwilling, to become pregnant by their husbands. Graham's initial ideas about where to find his 'genius sperm' led the media to rebaptize the Repository, the 'Nobel Prize sperm bank'. However, Nobel laureates proved reluctant donors. Only one of the couple of dozen Californian prize winners approached by Graham ended up contributing his germinal fluid. Therefore, Graham relaxed his criteria. He petitioned the younger scientists who he predicted would be the Nobel laureates of the future. He also took sperm from Olympic athletes and successful businessmen. The Repository did a better job of attracting the attention of journalists than it did customers, and it was shut down in 1999, two years after Graham's death. At the end of its twenty years of operation, the Repository's tally stood at just over two hundred children.

Graham's customers were prepared to pay for the sperm of men who excelled in science, business and sports because they hoped to have children who would also excel in science, business and sports. But what was in it for him? There must have been more lucrative paths open to the successful inventor. Graham was chasing a dream. He hoped that the Repository would be followed by other genius sperm banks, and that jointly they would arrest a calamitous decline in the quality of human genetic material. In his 1970 book, *The Future of Man*, Graham argued that twentieth-century healthcare systems and social welfare programmes were preventing natural selection from purging the feeble and preserving the strong. He feared that, unless checked, the welfare state would lead to universal mediocrity and communism. Anecdotal evidence suggests that Graham had a small degree of success. When David Plotz, a journalist with the online magazine *Slate*, matched some of the Repository children with their donors, he found that at least a few were taking after their high-achieving fathers. Three children of an Olympic gold medallist were very athletically talented. The sperm of science and mathematics professors had given rise to children gifted in these areas. Children conceived with the sperm of donors described as having happy temperaments were reported to be habitually upbeat.

This book investigates the idea of human enhancement that motivated Graham to establish the Repository for Germinal Choice. I defend the liberal view suggested by the Repository's full name. More specifically, I will argue that prospective parents should be empowered to use available technologies to choose some of their children's characteristics.

A sperm bank is a clumsy tool of choice. Graham's customers may have attributed the intelligence or happiness of their children to their selection of sperm, but how they raised them is likely to have made at least as significant a difference. Prospective parents may soon have technologies that give them greater power to choose what kinds of children to have. In the future, a woman who wants a brilliant child will not be restricted to the random selection of a genius's genes in the sperm that happens to fertilize her egg. She might choose to get pregnant with a genetic copy, or a clone of the genius. Alternatively, she may be empowered to search out the specific genes linked with genius, and have these engineered into her embryo.

If cloning and genetic engineering come anywhere near to meeting the expectations of writers of science fiction they will enable choices quite unlike those humans have made in the past. In chapter 2 I will address the question of what we can realistically expect of human genetic engineering and cloning as technologies of enhancement. I will argue that we should prepare ourselves for futures in which science fiction expectations are met. This presents us with the problem of how to make good moral choices about the technologies. The *method of moral images*, which I describe and defend in chapter 3, achieves this end by reducing the strangeness of the technologies of enhancement. There are not yet any human beings who have been genetically engineered to be very intelligent; nor have any geniuses been cloned. Nevertheless, we can understand the morality of these undertakings by constructing moral images of them. The activities referred to by moral images must have two properties. First, they must resemble the practices at issue in relevant respects. Second, we should have secure moral intuitions about them. Under these circumstances, we are justified in transferring moral judgements from familiar to unfamiliar practices. Exploring the limits of the freedom to choose children's characteristics will involve testing many moral images. The liberal position I defend is defined as much by what it bans as by what it permits. The very same moral images that establish the freedom to choose children's characteristics will also help us to understand why some choices should not be permitted.

TWO KINDS OF EUGENICS

Human cloning and the genetic engineering of human embryos are technologies of the future. But the idea of human improvement has a past. Graham was practising *eugenics*, defined by its nineteenth-century inventor, Francis Galton, as 'the science of improving stock, which is by no means confined to questions of judicious mating, but which . . . takes cognisance of all influences that tend in however remote degree to give the more suitable races or strains of blood a better chance of prevailing speedily over the less suitable than they otherwise would have had.'[2] Galton thought he knew how this improvement in human stock was to be achieved. He shared with his cousin, Charles Darwin, a fascination for human evolution. But while Darwin's main interest was in describing the forces that have shaped us and other living things, Galton was intent on harnessing them to human improvement. He dreamed of a social system that would not hinder natural selection, but would instead help it to make better humans.

Galton could not have foreseen the evil that would be done in eugenics' name.[3] This evil took its most concentrated form in the racist doctrine of human perfection promoted by the Nazis. Hitler's *lebensborn* or 'life spring' project was supposed to increase the number of blue-eyed, blond Aryans by mating racially screened women with SS men and officers in the German regular army. Room had to be created for these superior beings and their purified blood-lines protected from taint. In the early part of the Nazi era, enforced sterilization and legal bans on the intermarriage of superior and inferior humans were the preferred means of excluding bad hereditary material. Later, death camps were judged more expedient.

Some of Graham's rhetoric seems disturbingly similar to that of the Nazis. He appears to have been a racist, a believer in the superiority of Europeans. Notably, all of Graham's sperm donors were white. Among them was the notorious William Shockley, Nobel laureate co-inventor of the transistor. Upon his death in 1989, Shockley's wife reported that he considered his most important work to be, not his enormous contribution to the computer revolution, but his investigation of race differences in intelligence. Shockley thought that bad hereditary factors were disproportionately located in the genomes of black people. He also argued that any successful American eugenics programme would need to address the fact that the people least well equipped to survive had the highest reproductive rates.

But the name of Graham's business, the Repository for Germinal *Choice*, signals an important difference between him and the Nazis. The Nazis' eugenic template was inflexible. 'Nordic bearing', being of good build without 'disproportion between the lower leg and the thigh or between the legs and the body', freedom from alcoholism, 'absence of the Mongolian fold (inner epicanthic eyefold)' and 'reproductive capability' appear on a list of traits sought for entry into Hitler's SS.[4] They were also the goals of Nazi race science. Graham may have bemoaned the dysgenic tendencies of the modern welfare state, but he did not actively seek to prevent the reproduction of the hereditarily poor. The genius sperm went only to women who wanted it. Graham himself was a fan of the hard sciences, and the men he first approached for sperm reflect this bias. The reluctance of Nobel laureates to part with their germinal fluid was certainly one reason he cast his net wider. But customer demand was another. Women came to the Repository with their own ideas about the kinds of children they wanted. Some were after scientific genius, but others sought athletic talents or good looks, and still others sunny temperaments. Graham is reported to have approached Prince Philip of Britain for a sample of his genetic material. Apparently, the prince rebuffed this particular attempt to add breadth to the Repository's offerings. Moreover, Graham did not appear to hold ordinary folk in complete contempt. Among the maths prodigies and business successes on the Repository register is a man reassuringly nicknamed 'average guy'. 'Average guy' turns out to have had a better reproductive record than any of Graham's Nobel laureates. There was never a successful insemination using sperm from a Nobel laureate, but 'average guy' sired a dozen children.

Those whose vision of human enhancement emphasizes individual choice tend to avoid the term 'eugenics'.[5] They want language that clearly distinguishes them from the Nazis. But this smacks of Orwellian redefinition. Both approaches are broadly true to Galton's original conception of human improvement. Anyone advocating such a programme must demonstrate an awareness of the errors of the past. To adapt a saying of the philosopher George Santayana, those who do not learn from the history of human enhancement may be doomed to repeat it. And it is not enough to avoid Nazism. Eugenics was practised in other parts of Europe and in the United States.[6] In all of these places, race and class prejudice was permitted to dictate whose reproductive efforts would be encouraged, and whose would be hindered. While some Americans were competing for the titles of 'fittest family' and 'best baby', the courts were forcibly sterilizing other Americans on the grounds of congenital stupidity or criminality.[7] Retaining the label 'eugenics' makes obvious our obligation to show how what we are contemplating differs from the programmes of Galton's twentieth-century disciples.

Hitler showed us exactly where eugenics in pursuit of a racial ideal could lead us. However, I will argue that switching attention from races and classes of humans to individuals provides a version of eugenics worthy of defence. We would be rejecting *authoritarian eugenics*, the idea that the state should have sole responsibility for determining what counts as a good human life, in favour of what I will call *liberal eugenics*. On the liberal approach to human improvement, the state would not presume to make any eugenic choices. Rather it would foster the development of a wide range of technologies of enhancement ensuring that prospective parents were fully informed about what kinds of people these technologies would make. Parents' particular conceptions of the good life would guide them in their selection of enhancements for their children.

The freedoms that define liberal eugenics will be defended in the same fashion as other liberal freedoms. Liberal societies are founded on the insight that there are many different, often incompatible ideas about the good life.[8] Some seek huge wealth, others enlightenment; some devote themselves to their families, others to their careers; some commit to political causes, others to football teams; some worship God(s), others would rather go fishing. And this is only to begin to describe the variation in the kinds of lives that people choose for themselves. Living well in a liberal society involves acknowledging the right of others to make choices that do not appeal to us. John Robertson defends a procreative liberty, which he understands as individuals' freedom to decide whether or not they become parents and to exercise control over their reproductive capacities.[9] His arguments are motivated by the recognition that one of the most significant choices that people make about their lives concerns whether or not, with whom, when, and how often they reproduce. We have invented a range of technologies to assist us in making these choices. Contraceptive technologies help those who want sex without reproduction. Infertility treatments help those who want reproduction but cannot use sex to achieve it. Genetic technologies currently being developed may give us the power to choose some of the characteristics of our children. Nazi eugenicists would have used these technologies to dramatically curtail reproductive choice. Only a narrow range of human beings would have been deemed worthy of cloning; genetic engineering would have been imposed on couples whose reproductive efforts were deemed incapable of producing children sufficiently close to the Nazi ideal. But liberal eugenicists propose that these same technologies be used to dramatically enlarge reproductive choice. Prospective parents may ask genetic engineers to introduce into their embryos combinations of genes that correspond with their particular conception of good life. Yet they will acknowledge the right of their fellow citizens to make completely different eugenic choices. No one will be forced to clone themselves or to genetically engineer their embryos.

The fact that eugenics has its strongest associations with one of the most illiberal regimes of the twentieth century makes the term 'liberal eugenics' seem an oxymoron. Showing that the differences between liberal eugenics and Nazi eugenics run deeper than rhetoric will require careful attention to how the social and economic realities of liberal societies may subvert individual enhancement choices.

TECHNOLOGICAL POSSIBILITIES

One difference between liberal and Nazi eugenics is that between pluralistic and monistic views of human excellence. Another lies in the technological means available to mid-twentieth-century Nazi eugenicists and the liberal eugenicists of the future.

Suppose that the Nazi programme of human enhancement had not been terminated by Germany's military defeat. Hitler could never have realized his eugenic ideals, simply because the Nazi science of human heredity was hopelessly wrong. A text called *Human Genetics*, written jointly by geneticists Fritz Lenz and Erwin Baur, and an anthropologist, Eugen Fischer, served as a repository of Nazi wisdom about heredity. According to this work, genetics would explain why it was that Jews are prone to 'fraud and the use of insulting language', why Negroes were lazy, and why 'the Mongolian character...inclines to petrifaction in the traditional'.[10] The race scientists hoped that an understanding of heredity would enable programmes that would replace these vices with the Nordic virtues. However, it is wrong to think that the biological distinctions between people of different ethnicities mark a distinction between vice and virtue. One of the most salutary lessons of the new genetics has been the biological closeness of people who look very different. Humans share 99.99 per cent of their genetic material.[11] That leaves room for about 2.1 million genetic letters to vary from individual to individual. But the pattern of even this comparatively small amount of variation is a disappointment for scientific racists. In the early 1970s, the geneticist Richard Lewontin showed that only a small part of overall human genetic variability is between what we think of as different races.[12] From the standpoint of genetics, the differences between Africans, Asians, Europeans and the members of other races are almost invisible. All of this shows that a programme of depressing the reproductive rates of the members of some cultures and boosting that of others could not achieve the end of encouraging virtue, whatever one's conception of it.

Our understanding of human heredity has come a long way since the Nazi era. The experts on human genetics consulted by the prospective parents of tomorrow's liberal societies will give vastly better scientific advice than that given by Hitler's scientific lackeys. A collection of technologies that I will call *enhancement technologies* will enable the selection and manipulation of human traits by selecting and manipulating the hereditary factors that contribute to them.[13]

The most topical of these technologies is cloning. A clone is a genetic copy of another organism. The modern history of cloning begins on 5 July 1996 with the birth of a sheep called Dolly. Dolly was the first mammal successfully cloned from an adult cell, produced by a method known as *somatic cell nuclear transfer*. Her embryo was made by transferring the nucleus of an adult body cell into an egg whose nucleus had been removed. This procedure rejuvenated the genes of the adult cell, enabling them to start life all over again. Before Dolly, this rejuvenation was thought to be a biological impossibility. This is part of the reason for the surprise that greeted her. But even those not at all concerned about science had some idea about where Dolly could lead. The register of cloned mammals now includes sheep, cows, cats, goats, mice, pigs, horses and mules. Although each of these species has presented its own technical challenges experimenters have overcome them. As biologists like to remind us, humans are just another species of mammal. We are just another challenge for cloners.

Advocates of the technology give a range of reasons for cloning humans. Some tout cloning as a means of creating human embryonic stem cells. This so-called 'therapeutic' cloning would involve the creation of a clone embryo from the cell of a patient requiring transplant tissue. The clone would be allowed to develop to the blastocyst stage, at which point it consists of some two hundred cells. The embryonic stem cells that would now be harvested combine two remarkable powers. Their pluripotency means that they can, in theory, be turned into any type of tissue that the patient might require. The fact that they come from an embryo cloned from the patient should make the new tissue a perfect immunological match. If all goes according to plan, doctors will acquire the powers of automotive mechanics. Mechanics replace a seized gearbox with one up to the standard of the original on the day the car was driven out of the factory. Doctors practising 'regenerative medicine' will provide brand new kidneys, pancreases and hearts that are perfect matches for their recipients. Therapeutic cloners must overcome many scientific obstacles before they open an era of regenerative medicine. In addition, they must also overcome moral obstacles. As we will see in chapter 3, opponents challenge the label 'therapeutic cloning', arguing that it obscures a dark side of the procedure. What they would call 'research cloning' necessarily involves the destruction of human embryos, and so the killing of very young human beings.

While therapeutic or research cloners would stop the development of the embryo well before it has any recognizable human features, others hope to turn clone embryos into clone babies. Dolly's presentation to the world in early 1997 triggered a race to create the first human clone child. The most enthusiastic public advocates of what is known as reproductive cloning are an organization known as CLONAID. In late 2002 and early 2003 CLONAID announced, but refused to confirm, the births of three human clones.

Creating a human clone baby would be a scientific coup. But is there a reason for doing it other than to demonstrate that it can be done? Some see reproductive cloning as a treatment for kinds of infertility intractable by other means. Men who produce no sperm and women left without eggs have nothing for practitioners of in vitro fertilization to work with. However, cloners could make children for them out of cells taken from almost any part of their bodies. Those behind CLONAID have more exotic ambitions. The organization was founded by the Raelians, a UFO cult whose creation myth describes aliens' invention of humanity by cloning. They are vague about what the human species was cloned from. For the Raelians cloning is something more than a means of treating infertility. It is the technology of eternal life. The CLONAID website announces: 'Once we can clone exact replicas of ourselves, the next step will be to transfer our memory and personality into our newly cloned brains, which will allow us to truly live forever.'[14] Much of their funding comes from people sufficiently enticed by this vision to pay the asking price of US $200,000.

Cloning by somatic cell nuclear transfer might also serve the purpose of enhancement. In the wake of the first successful cloning of frogs in the early 1960s, the distinguished British biologist J. B. S. Haldane suggested that we select the most talented human beings for cloning.[15] He thought it wise in most cases to wait until candidates were in their fifties so as to be sure that their genomes really warranted repetition. Haldane allowed that athletes and dancers might be cloned younger, and suggested that if we were aiming to boost longevity we should clone healthy centenarians. He thought that this measure might 'raise the possibilities of human achievement dramatically'.[16] A programme for the mass improvement of human stock sounds like something of which Hitler would approve, something inimical to reproductive freedom. But it is not hard to imagine how cloning might promote individual enhancement agendas. The technology presents an option that will appeal to those with the right combination of humility and commitment to a eugenic ideal. While combining your egg or sperm with the sperm or egg of a talented person may offer some chance of having a talented child, cloning improves the odds. You could choose an embryo that would be a genetic duplicate of a certified genius or sports star, and thereby not dilute high-quality genes with your own more lowly genetic material. Were Graham to have opened the Repository for Germinal Choice in the year 2078 he might have collected a Nobel laureate's skin cells rather than his sperm. He might have extracted the nucleus of one of these cells, placed it in an enucleated egg, and put the resulting embryo in the womb of a woman in pursuit of Nobel excellence.

Cloning can serve the end of human enhancement so long as the traits that parents want for their children are influenced by genes. Replicating all of a person's genome reproduces, in a new person, all of the genetic influences that helped shape her. Another biotechnology might enable more precise choices of hereditary influences. This is the biotechnology of genomics, whose task is to describe hereditary material. On 26 June 2000 the publicly funded Human Genome Project and the private Celera Genomics announced the completion of drafts of the collection of all human DNA, the human genome.[17] Work continued and on 14 April 2003 members of the International Human Genome Sequencing Consortium, an organization combining the research efforts of eighteen institutions, believed they had progressed to the point of 'completing' the map.[18] The human genome had been described to 99.99 per cent accuracy. The job of identifying all the human genes and determining their functions remains.

The technique of Pre-implantation Genetic Diagnosis (PGD) enables parents to put genomic information to use. PGD involves the fertilization by IVF (in vitro fertilization) of a number of a woman's eggs. One or two cells are separated from the embryos that result, and are tested for the presence of particular genetic variations. Doctors then introduce only embryos that lack the genetic variants the woman is trying to avoid or that possess the variants that she is seeking.

PGD allows parents-to-be to choose from the variation provided by nature. Genetic engineers may allow them to improve on nature. They would insert genes linked with traits valued by parents into the genomes of their future children. Although diseases have been the early focus, the most morally challenging uses of genetic engineering are driven by an ambition that reaches beyond treating disease.

Consider Doogie, a breed of mouse whose genome has an extra copy of a gene called NR2B[19] The breed's name signals a resemblance between it and the television teen genius, Doogie Howser MD. Joe Tsien, Doogie's Princeton University creator, tells us that the mice acquire new knowledge twice as fast, and retain it for around four to five times as long as their normal counterparts. Doogie's creators offer an explanation for the breed's cognitive talents. Memory involves establishing links between bits of information stored in different parts of the brain and the additional copy of NR2B appears to make brain tissue more connective. The greater number of connections allows the mouse to lay down memories more easily, and to hold on to them for longer. Some researchers at Harvard, more concerned with muscles than brains, have created Schwarzenegger mice.[20] This feat was achieved by adding an additional copy of the gene that produces a protein associated with muscle growth known as insulin-like growth factor type 1 (IGF-1). Mice with additional IGF-1 not only gain muscle with little exercise, but seem immune from the muscle wasting normally associated with aging.

NR2B and IGF-1 exist in humans. Both research teams speculate about what might be achieved by giving humans additional copies of these genes. Tsien hopes that genetic engineers might one day insert additional NR2B genes into human brain cells to repair the damage done by Alzheimer's and Parkinson's. The Harvard team speculates that IGF-1 offers a biotech solution to muscular dystrophy, a condition characterized by fatal muscle wasting. It is easy to see why scientists fighting for research funding should emphasize the less controversial, therapeutic potential of their work. But there is nothing in nature, no stop sign built into the human genome, limiting these techniques to the treatment of disease. Tsien says that Doogie 'points to the possibility that enhancement of learning and memory or even IQ is feasible through genetic means, through genetic engineering'.[21] The Harvard scientists' choice of the nickname 'Schwarzenegger' indicates an awareness of one potential use of their technique. If you can make Doogie and Schwarzenegger mice, then why not go ahead and make real Doogies and replacement Schwarzeneggers?

Although this brief discussion of enhancement technologies makes us aware of their potential power, we should also be aware of their limitations. Some limitations are inherent in the science on which the technologies rely. Journalists tend to describe the possibilities of human biotechnology as if they are only a few experiments away from being realized. In chapter 2 I will describe some of the obstacles in the way of cloning geniuses or inserting additional NR2B genes into human embryos. Other limitations have more to do with us, or at least with our expect-ations of the technologies. The popular imagination tends to oversimplify the new technologies to make more apparent their potential perils and dangers. We are encouraged to think that all biotechnologists have to do to make a genius is to find the right genes and insert them into a suitable embryo, and that Einstein's clone would, of necessity, achieve scientific breakthroughs on a par with those of Einstein. This is *genetic determinism*. It is based on a misunderstanding about the significance of genes in making persons that overstates what enhancement technologies can achieve. Genes certainly influence intelligence, but they are not the only influence. We will not arrive at sensible moral guidelines for enhancement if we rely on the cartoon representation of human development presented by genetic determinists. I will investigate the issue of what enhancement technologies can achieve in chapter 2.

MORAL PERPLEXITIES

Suppose we do put enhancement technologies in the hands of prospective parents. The Nazis taught us how badly states can go wrong in implementing their ideas about human improvement. But there are also many ways in which individuals can err.

A contemporary case points us towards the kinds of moral perplexities that liberal eugenics will confront. Although few would go as far as the Repository's customers in pursuit of academic, sporting and business success, these are things that we tend to want for our children. Contrast the choices made by the Repository's customers with a choice that Graham would definitely not have countenanced. Sharon Duchesneau and Candace McCullough were a lesbian couple who wanted a child.[22] In an earlier era the notion of two women starting a family together would have caused scandal; however, what provoked public anxiety was not that the two wanted a baby, but the kind of baby they wanted. Duchesneau and McCullough, both deaf since birth, wanted a baby who would resemble them in this way. Said Duchesneau about their quest, 'A hearing baby would be a blessing. A deaf baby would be a special blessing.'[23] The couple's request for a congenitally deaf donor was turned down by several sperm banks. So Duchesneau and McCullough approached a friend with an impeccable pedigree of deafness – he was not only deaf, but had five generations of deafness in his family. At four months of age Gauvin McCullough was perhaps not quite the perfect baby – he had a slight amount of hearing in one ear.

Consider how the technologies I have just been describing might have helped Duchesneau and McCullough in their quest for a deaf child. Some deaf people perceive a threat to their community from genetic technologies. It is true that our current maps of the human genome point to a number of mutations linked with deafness, and that congenital deafness is a condition that many parents-to-be will want to avoid. But any test that helps them do this would also help Duchesneau and McCullough in their quest for a deaf child. They would choose the embryos that others would discard. The clone of either Duchesneau or McCullough may have a greater chance of turning out deaf than a child produced from an egg of one of them and the sperm of another person. Their clone child could have other advantages. She would certainly be female and, to the extent that genes influence female sexual orientation, would have a higher chance of being gay.

Duchesneau's and McCullough's choice seems bizarre. Isn't choosing to have a deaf child choosing to have a disabled child? Ever since J. S. Mill, liberals have distinguished sharply between decisions concerning oneself and those concerning others. While the former kind of decision is morally protected, the latter kind must address the interests of the people it affects. The burden of the deafness Duchesneau and McCullough created falls most directly on Gauvin. Critics wonder what separates what they did from the intentional deafening of a hearing child. At least Duchesneau and McCullough can point to a clear difference between them and the Nazis. Hitler's race hygiene laws dictated sterilization for the hereditarily deaf.

The recognition that some choices are harmful, regardless of what parents say in their defence, sets moral limits on the realization of their values in the lives they will create. What grounds should be used to decide whether, their protestations notwithstanding, Duchesneau and McCullough's choice actually harmed Gauvin? The analysis of harm we arrive at must explain how it is that one can ever be harmed by being brought into existence in a certain way. Gauvin may be hard of hearing, but had Duchesneau and McCullough been forced to choose different sperm they would have had a different child. How can deafness harm Gauvin, if the alternative for him is not a hearing existence but no existence at all?

We must also ask whether what Duchesneau and McCullough did is really so different from what others do without any need for justification. Suppose Sharon Duchesneau had not been a lesbian. Instead of being with Candace McCullough, she falls for the profoundly deaf man who in fact donated the sperm used to conceive Gauvin. They have a child together. This sounds like a conventional story about a man and woman who fall in love and decide to start a family. But the procreative consequences of this counterfactual decision could be identical to those of Duchesneau's and McCullough's actual decision. Perhaps Duchesneau and her male partner don't think of themselves as deliberately having a deaf child, but they do confess that their mutual attraction has a great deal to do with their deafness, and the fact that they have faced and overcome similar hurdles in life. It is possible that Duchesneau and McCullough and the Repository's customers are just consciously doing what everyone else has always done subconsciously. We tell ourselves that we take an interest in the intelligence of our mates so we can converse with them about Martin Amis novels or be guided through the process of setting the time on the VCR. However, evolutionary psychologists tell us that, deep down, the intelligence of a mate matters to us because we see it as influencing how intelligent our offspring will be.

The deaf couple had a ready response to the allegation that they had ignored the welfare of their child. They had taken Gauvin's welfare into account, indeed it was their primary concern. Duchesneau and McCullough argue that their deafness makes them better parents of a deaf child. Furthermore, they reject the description of their actions as the intentional creation of a child with a disability. According to them, there is a sense in which hearing people are disabled. Hearing people are, after all, unable to fully participate in the rich and distinctive culture evolved by the deaf. It is true that our societies are not properly set up to meet the needs of deaf people and this makes their lives more difficult than they would otherwise be, but McCullough says that 'black people have harder lives'. She asks, 'Why shouldn't parents be able to go ahead and pick a black donor if that's what they want?', answering, 'They should have that option. They can feel related to that culture, bonded with that culture.'[24] Duchesneau and McCullough point out that should Gauvin reject his parents' plans for him, he will have the option of a hearing aid.

We can describe what the Repository's customers and the deaf couple did in ways that make them seem self-centred. People living in liberal societies express their views about the good life by way of their choices about what music to listen to, what clothes to wear, where to live, and what political parties to support. Choosing the characteristics of one's future child appears to be just another mode of self-expression, one that involves not CDs, clothes, apartments, or voting ballots, but instead the lives of the people one brings into existence. This seems to trivialize the having of children. However, the Repository's customers and the deaf couple do not see their choices as motivated by vanity. They present themselves as merely trying to give their children the best possible starts in life. Choosing the best sperm is, for them, much like choosing the best school. Uncharitable people might describe a Catholic parent's selection of Catholic schooling for her child as just the expression of the parent's commitment to her faith, whereas she would insist that her choice was motivated by what is best for her child. She will point to her own morally legitimate conception of the good life to justify the view that a Catholic education is better than any alternative.

There will surely be some eugenic choices that are beyond the pale. Uses of enhancement technologies that display a callous indifference to a child's future welfare or that are motivated by racism seem clear-cut examples. In his critique of liberal eugenics, Jürgen Habermas argues that the logic of liberalism militates against limiting the choices that individuals can make. He says that from the standpoint of liberal eugenics 'it virtually goes without saying that decisions regarding the genetic composition of children should not be submitted to any regulation by the state, but rather should be left to the parents'.[25] On the face of it, this seems an unlikely claim. Liberal freedoms are always freedoms within limits; no freedom is absolute. The presumption in favour of the freedom of speech does not stop us from banning incitements to commit race crimes or false bomb alerts by passengers on 747s. Therefore, it would seem that liberal eugenicists should be open to the idea that some uses of enhancement technologies are just wrong and should be banned.

However, perhaps there is something about enhancement technologies that rules out interference by the state in individuals' choices. Consider the attempt to transfer to procreative choices the laws that make it illegal for employers to be influenced by racism in their hiring choices. When one chooses a mate one is often also choosing what kind of person will contribute genes to one's children. We accept that racist people can refuse to have children with members of a race they despise because we think that who one is attracted to and repelled by is beyond state regulation. Our negative judgements about their characters do not lead us to force them into relationships with people for whom they claim no attraction. By analogy, perhaps no moral reason could be sufficiently strong to justify the state's intruding on individuals' eugenic choices. Insisting that racism be no motive for the use of enhancement technologies would, in effect, be like insisting that people be sexually attracted to others regardless of skin colour.[26]

Nevertheless, liberal eugenics does permit the state to regulate the use of enhancement technologies. These technologies separate the purely personal choice of what kind of person one will spend one's life with from the choice about what characteristics one's child will have. Prospective parents will be looking to some third party, perhaps the state or perhaps some private organization, to facilitate the second kind of choice. The third party can and should impose conditions on this co-operation, refusing to assist reproductive choices that are morally defective in some significant way. In the era of human enhancement, it should often withhold assistance. Racists may view the colour of their children's skin as a characteristic chosen by means of their selection of partner, but the results of this eugenic choice are no different from those achieved by those who fall in love with people who just happen to share their skin colour. Enhancement technologies give individuals greater powers to implement their procreative ends, and in doing so magnify the potential harms. The method of moral images will help us to recognize when the providers of enhancement services should withhold their services; the same moral images that motivate a parental prerogative to use enhancement technologies will also establish the prerogative's limits.

HITHER POSTHUMANITY?

It would be blinkered to suppose that enhancement technologies prompt no questions not already raised by the selection of a mate because of the perceived quality of his sperm or her eggs. If they fulfil their potential, cloning by somatic cell nuclear transfer, genetic engineering and genomics will grant an unprecedented power over the future of the human species. We must look beyond the first, cautious attempts at enhancement to consider where liberal eugenics will eventually take us.

Attempts to describe both the perils and the promise of enhancement technologies have crystallized around the concept of *posthumanity*. The Transhumanist FAQ is the manifesto of an organization called the World Transhumanist Association, established to advocate the enhancement of human beings. It defines a posthuman as 'someone or an entity whose basic capacities so radically exceed those of unaugmented humans as to be best thought of as constituting a new kind of being'.[27] Posthumans will be anticipated by the intermediate stage of transhumans, beings who have benefited from enhancement technologies to some extent, but remain recognizably human.

The transhumanist writer Mark Walker gleefully imagines the benefits that would follow from doubling our cranial capacities from an average of 1,300 cc to 2,600 cc, producing a being who exceeds 'humans in intelligence by the same margin as humans exceed that of chimpanzees'.[28] Geneticists have identified a gene whose manipulation might achieve this.[29] The ASPM gene on chromosome 1 is thought to play a significant role in the growth of the brain. Scientists have identified a part of this gene whose length seems to dictate how many times neuronal stem cells divide. This part of the fruit fly ASPM gene is shorter than its analogue in mice, which is in turn shorter than the human analogue. It is conceivable, though far from proven, that lengthening this part of the human gene might produce a larger brain. Many questions remain before such a thing could be attempted. Posthuman babies, like human ones, will need to be born. If there were not a correlative widening of the birth canal, this process would become a much greater ordeal for women than it currently is.

Enhancers may not be limited to stereotypically human traits. Lee Silver, a Princeton geneticist whose best-selling book on human biotechnology was published in the wake of the announcement of Dolly the sheep, notes that '[i]f something has evolved elsewhere, then it is *possible* for us to determine its genetic basis and transfer it into the human genome.'[30] He imagines future humans with the ability to detect ultraviolet light and with the olfactory powers of dogs. Silver wonders if we might one day give our children powers not found anywhere in nature, for example, radiotelepathy, the capacity to 'send and receive information as radio waves'.[31]

This sounds like the stuff of science fiction. Why should we want to replace ourselves with beings that seem as close to us as the movie aliens often depicted as intent on our destruction? Nick Bostrom presents the potential pleasures of posthumanity as justification for taking this step.

> We can conceive, in the abstract at least, of aesthetic and contemplative pleasures whose blissfulness vastly exceeds what any human has yet experienced. We can imagine beings that reach a much greater level of personal development and maturity than current human beings do, because they have the opportunity to live for hundreds or thousands of years with full bodily and psychic vigor. We can conceive of intellects that are much smarter than our own, that read books in seconds, that are much more brilliant philosophers than we are, that can create artworks, which, even if we could understand them only on the most superficial level, would strike us as wonderful masterpieces. We can imagine love that is stronger, purer, and more secure than any human has yet harbored.[32]

Transhumanists allow that we may have difficulty relating to the inhabitants of the biotechnological future, but if they are free of disease, super-intelligent, and routinely compose symphonies whose brilliance surpasses that of Beethoven's Ninth, this failure of identification is our problem, not theirs. Or is it?

On one of my first attempts to visit the Transhumanist FAQ I found that its website had been hacked. Rather than being taken to a site that would inform me of posthumans' various virtues, I was taken to a webpage advertising products that would enlarge my penis. The hackers may have been working on behalf of the penis enlargers – happy to find a way of advertising their product other than spam e-mail. But there is another possibility. The hackers may have intended their diversion as a criticism of the transhumanist ethos, the idea that once we identify something as good it must always be better to have more of it. Why be content with an IQ of 100 when you might have one of 180, or 70 years of life when you might have 120, or six inches when you might have...?[33]

The opponents of enhancement technologies say that we need a less simplistic understanding of the impact of enhancement on human beings. We should be asking not whether enhancement technologies will make human beings 'better', but whether they will make humans 'whole'.[34] These opponents are an ideologically disparate group. They include Francis Fukuyama who, in his book *The End of History and the Last Man*, forecasts a liberal democratic future for all of humanity. There is also the environmentalist writer, Bill McKibben.[35] Leon Kass, a conservative social critic, provides the group's intellectual leadership from his position as the chair of President Bush's Council on Bioethics. Kass initially achieved prominence as a critic of IVF in the 1970s and early 1980s.[36] He has since become the most vociferous opponent of human cloning.[37] For simplicity's sake I will refer to these critics of enhancement technologies as 'conservatives'. Like the transhumanists, they use the concepts of humanity and posthumanity to make their moral points. Elsewhere conservatives are people who seek to preserve established customs and social arrangements. However, these thinkers are conservative in a more fundamental sense. Rather than striving to protect some manner of acting, they see themselves as preserving both humanity and human meaning.

Both Kass and Fukuyama appeal to Aldous Huxley's *Brave New World* to explain why we should be horrified by biotechnology's propensity to make us posthuman. In giving us what we ask for, biotechnology empties our lives of meaning. Here is how Kass describes Huxley's imagined technological dystopia:

The Brave New World has achieved prosperity, community, stability and near-universal contentment, only to be inhabited by creatures of human shape but stunted humanity. They consume, fornicate, take 'soma,' enjoy 'centrifugal bumble-puppy,' and operate the machinery that makes it all possible. They do not read, write, think, love, or govern themselves. Art and science, virtue and religion, family and friendship are all passé. What matters most is bodily health and immediate gratification: 'Never put off till tomorrow the fun that you can have today.' No one aspires to anything higher. Brave New Man is so dehumanized that he does not even realize what has been lost.[38]

Kass wonders what is the point of freeing ourselves of biological limitations if doing so leaves nothing worth wanting.

Although they share an interest in posthumanity, the moral visions of the transhumanists and the conservatives are starkly opposed, drawing on very different views about what makes humans morally special and how enhancement technologies impact on these things.

The liberal eugenics that I defend occupies a location between these extremes. Against the conservatives, I argue that enhancement is not incompatible with a meaningful human life. But against the transhumanists, I offer no unconditional endorsement of the idea that we should use technological means to increase the psychological and physical vigour of our descendents. The transhumanist vision of a seamless fusion of humanity with technology may appeal to some prospective parents, but it will certainly not appeal to others. Furthermore, the onus will be on those with very ambitious visions of enhancement to show that they do not harm those they bring into existence.

In the next chapter I address the issue of how we should characterize enhancement technologies so as to enable good moral choices about them.

CHAPTER 2

A Pragmatic Optimism about Enhancement Technologies

Almost everyone has opinions about enhancement technologies. We readily respond to depictions of them and their results in movies such as *GATTACA, Star Wars: Attack of the Clones* and *Star Trek: Nemesis*. Our responses would be excellent raw material for moralizing but for the fact that the movies misrepresent the technologies. In *Star Wars: Attack of the Clones*, clones are carbon copies of each other. They form an army whose regimentation matches that of the opposing android army. The idea of human clones as emotionless zombies who will inevitably be bred in military quantities has filtered through to more earnest discussions. In his recent pessimistic analysis of human nature, *Straw Dogs*, John Gray opines that if 'it becomes possible to clone human beings, soldiers will be bred in whom normal emotions are stunted or absent'.[1] Popular presentations also oversimplify the biotechnology of genomics. In the movie *GATTACA* characters present a single hair of a potential mate for DNA sequencing. All of the hair's genetic information is represented in a few-page print-out, which is in turn summarized by a single number indicating overall eligibility. Uma Thurman's character is told '9.3, quite a catch', as she is being handed the genetic sequence of Jude Law's character.

There is just enough truth in these representations of cloning and genomics to seriously mislead. Clones created by somatic cell nuclear transfer have identical nuclear DNA to the organism that donated the body cell from which they sprang. However, that does not make a clone an exact copy. Unless it is reared identically, a clone is bound to differ from the donor of its DNA. There is no reason to follow John Gray and the writers of the screenplay of *Star Wars: Attack of the Clones* in thinking that the genes responsible for the development of human emotions would be systematically deactivated in clones. A general in charge of a clone army would face the same kinds of difficulties as his counterpart commanding an army of conventionally conceived soldiers. Both would envy the general of the robot army. Turning to *GATTACA*, genomics may provide information about some of the influences that shape our personalities. But even in an era in which genomic information is properly understood, those hunting for the ideal boyfriend would still be advised to rely on conversation rather than on a DNA read-out. It is nonsense to think that a single number could capture even the genetic factors, let alone all the factors, relevant to being a good partner or parent.

Hollywood gives bad moral advice about enhancement technologies precisely because it gets the facts about them wrong. We could rectify this problem by insisting that our moral evaluation proceed from full and accurate representations of cloning, genetic engineering and genomics. But here we face another difficulty: enhancement technologies are complex. The accounts provided in chapter 1 only begin to explain how they will work and what kinds of human beings they will bring into existence. The people who know most about human biotechnologies are those who develop them. If grasping every last detail about cloning, genetic engineering and genomics were a prerequisite for sound moral opinions we would have to bow to the moral assessments of scientists. Some biotechnologists would clearly prefer this state of affairs to the current situation in which democratically elected officials presume to have a say. Michael West of Advanced Cell Technology (ACT), one of the companies trying to develop therapeutic cloning, resents the attempt by some members of the US Congress to ban the necessary experiments. He says: '[I]t's disgusting to me when members of Congress propose legislation and the author of the bill can't even demonstrate that he knows what he is trying to criminalize.'[2]

Non-scientists may not grasp every last fact about human biotechnology, but we know perfectly well that it raises serious moral issues. We should not cede our moral authority to scientists. Although human genetics itself pushes no moral agenda, influences from without genetics have opened up a moral gap between value-neutral science and the people who produce it. In Dolly's wake, President Clinton barred federal support for human cloning research. Rather than ending experimentation, this opened the door for privately funded research. Scientists working for corporations like ACT have different incentives from those employed by universities. The editors of journals such as *Nature* and *Science* will happily publish articles on cloning pitfalls. However, investors in cloning research want lucrative successes, not interesting failures. The November 2001 announcement that ACT had cloned human embryos should be considered in this light. These embryos were presented as a great scientific breakthrough, but it soon became apparent that there was more to this story than just science. The most advanced of ACT's human clones had got only as far as six cells before it stopped growing. Ian Wilmut, Dolly's creator, belittled the achievement, pointing out that an embryo's growth up to the six-cell stage is driven by factors external to the nucleus, rather than by its own genetic material.[3] If he is right, then the ACT embryos were not even a first step towards the 100- to 200-cell blastocysts that might furnish embryonic stem cells. Cynics argued that the announcement was more about politics and raising funds than the advancement of our understanding of human cloning.[4]

There is another reason why we should not put scientists in sole charge of humanity's future. They simply do not have the whole picture. An ethic of enhancement technologies must draw together scientific knowledge and moral wisdom. While the procurement of scientific knowledge often telescopes to minute empirical detail, morality's focus must be broad. We need to be aware of a new technology's effects not only on human organisms, but also on human persons and on the communities that would permit the use of enhancement technologies. CLONAID, the human cloning company founded by the Raelians, is ample evidence that the first kind of understanding does not necessarily bring the second. The organization's reluctance to provide evidence should make us suspicious of its claim to have created three clone babies, but it is almost certain that they have experimented on human embryos. If their pronouncements are any guide, CLONAID's close contact with the science of cloning humans has not conduced to a deeper understanding of the morality of this undertaking. They seem to have a keen sense of cloning's publicity value, but little interest in its potential to transgress moral norms.

We can avoid arguing from Hollywood misrepresentations or taking scientists' pronouncements on faith if we find descriptions of enhancement technologies that make them morally transparent. Morally transparent descriptions reveal moral effects, effects that occur at the points of contact between a technology and morally valuable beings. Doctors routinely satisfy the requirement of moral transparency. Although the science of disease cannot be conveyed to newly diagnosed patients in all of its complexity, doctors must do more than say 'Never again eat butter', or 'We are going to have to operate on your brain', or 'Take these twenty-seven pills daily'. A morally transparent explanation of a disease condition and proposed treatment makes clear how the condition threatens the patient and how the proposed change in lifestyle, surgery or onerous treatment regime treatment meets this threat. This explanation may give only an impressionistic account of the disease state's biochemistry, for example, but it must at least gesture towards the deeper scientific truth. Providing patients with this information gives them the real power to consent to or reject the treatment that they are being offered.

Morally transparent descriptions of enhancement technologies enable those whom they will affect to better understand both what results they will produce and how they will produce them. Advocates of enhancement have a duty to furnish such descriptions. However, these descriptions impose reciprocal obligations on people suspicious of enhancement. They must show that their criticisms are properly directed at the technologies, not merely at caricatures of them. We can safely ignore opponents of reproductive cloning whose only fear is John Gray's: that 'soldiers will be bred in whom normal emotions are stunted or absent'.

Enhanced intelligence appears at the top of most lists of imagined improvements to human beings; it was the primary motivation behind the foundation of Graham's Repository for Germinal Choice. To help put enhancement technologies in moral context I now consider some ways in which enhancement technologies might make humans more intelligent.

The popular science of human enhancement tends to give the impression that clones of Einstein and children whose memories have been boosted with additional NR2B genes will be enrolling at schools within a generation. In a recent address to President Bush's Council on Bioethics, Steven Pinker poured cold water on these and other ambitious forecasts about biotechnology. He stressed the immense technological obstacles in the way of 'designer babies', likening predictions that they would be with us very soon to predictions made early in the twentieth century that we would be making nuclear-powered vacuum cleaners by 1965 and growing ready-for-the-table chicken parts by 1982.[5] Pinker identifies four reasons for the excess of optimism of futurologists and other forecasters of technology:

First, there's a habit of assuming that technological progress can be linearly extrapolated. If there's a little bit of progress now, there will be proportional progress as we multiply the number of years out.... Secondly, there's a tendency to underestimate the number of things that have to go exactly right for a given scenario to take place. Most technological changes don't depend on a single discovery, but rather on an enormous number of factors, scores or even hundreds, all of which have to fall into place exactly right.... Third, there's a widespread failure of futurologists to consider the costs of new technologies, as well as the benefits, whereas in reality the actual users faced with a particular technology consider both the benefits and the costs.... Finally, there is an incentive structure to futurology. Someone who predicts a future that's radically different from our own, either to hype it or to raise an alarm against it will get the attention of the press and the public.[6]

Closer investigation of how enhancement technologies might produce super-intelligent humans seems to bear out Pinker's warning.

WILL WE BE ABLE TO CLONE GENIUSES?

Cloning involves making organisms that are genetic copies of other organisms. Given that human cloners are working only with existing human genomes, it may seem difficult to see how they could enhance human intelligence. Cloning's success as a stand-alone enhancement technology would require judicious selection from among the human genetic variation that nature provides. Random recombinations of genetic material do occasionally make people of exceptional intelligence. In chapter 1 I described J. B. S. Haldane's proposal that human stock be improved by the systematic cloning of exceptionally talented fifty-year-olds.

Whether or not this proposal could ever be put into practice depends on the viability of human reproductive cloning. At the end of 2002 and the beginning of 2003, CLONAID claimed to have brought three human clones into existence. The Raelians gave only sketchy details about the identities of the people to whom the clones were born, refusing to allow the genetic tests that could confirm that any babies that they might be talking about were in fact clones. There are, however, a number of reasons for scepticism about their claims. At the time of their announcement, primates had been cloned by embryo splitting, a process involving the division of an early embryo into two or more embryos, but there was no well-documented case of anyone getting to full term a primate embryo created by somatic cell nuclear transfer.[7] Many laboratories have been seeking to produce the 100- to 200-cell embryos that will provide the stem cells required for therapeutic cloning. By early 2003, the time of the Raelian announcement, there had been rumours, but no confirmed success. In February 2004 researchers at Seoul National University announced that they had created thirty cloned human blastocysts.[8] This advance certainly brings the era of regenerative medicine closer. If the Raelians are to be believed, then their scientists must not only have beaten the Korean researchers in the race for a clone blastocyst but also have overcome many further obstacles. Scientists working on sheep and cattle have been made painfully aware that there are many places on the track from blastocyst to live birth at which a clone's development can derail.

Suppose Raelian scientists have produced clone babies. If so, we should be suspicious of the claim that the three babies are perfectly healthy. Opponents of reproductive cloning argue that the technology is likely to produce children with various handicaps.[9] Many mammal clones suffer from a condition known as large offspring syndrome. Clone foetuses can be up to a third larger than normal foetuses, their bloated bodies filled with enlarged internal organs. The additional length and burden of pregnancy can have fatal consequences for surrogate mothers. There is a favourite among the many candidate scientific explanations of large offspring syndrome. The creation of Dolly from a differentiated cell was only possible because scientists worked out how to take a cell whose genes were set up to produce only proteins appropriate to mammary function and turn it into a cell whose genes behaved as if they were yet to have been activated at all. The procedure essentially tricked them into beginning a new life. Incomplete reprogramming of the nuclear genes may explain large offspring syndrome and other maladies. It is not surprising that reprogramming might be incomplete. Practitioners of somatic cell nuclear transfer expect DNA to be ready to start a new organism within minutes or hours of being extracted from a differentiated cell, yet mammalian eggs can take years to ripen in ovaries. Large offspring syndrome is thought by some to result from the incomplete reprogramming of genes whose function is to regulate foetal growth.[10]

Advocates of reproductive cloning give reasons for thinking that human foetuses may avoid large offspring syndrome. They point out that while cattle created by IVF suffer from the condition, it is entirely undocumented in human IVF. Perhaps clone humans would be spared this particular consequence of incomplete genetic reprogramming. However, we need also to take into account the other 30,000 or so genes necessary to make a healthy human being. Unless the process of reprogramming is completed for them, too, human clones are likely to suffer in ways that humans resulting from sexual reproduction do not.

There may be other reasons that cloning by somatic cell nuclear transfer can not do what enhancers of intelligence want. Consider Haldane's plan to clone fifty-year-old geniuses. The choice of the age of fifty reflects the realization that intelligence is a complex trait. We would require histories of intellectual achievement to be sure that we have not chosen to clone intellectual flashes in the pan. But the biology of cell division and DNA replication may make this plan unfeasible.[11] Each time a cell divides, its DNA must be copied. It so happens that this copying process is astonishingly accurate – there is only a minute chance that any given nucleotide, or letter of DNA, will be copied wrongly. On the other hand, the human genome is very long – it is made up of over three billion base pairs of DNA. The various proof-reading and error-correcting mechanisms cannot prevent many nucleotides from being incorrectly copied. It is inevitable that the DNA of the sperm and egg that made me carried mutations accumulated throughout the lifetimes of my parents. Many of these errors make no difference to me – they occur outside of my genes, which cover only a small percentage of the total length of my genome or, if they do occur in a gene, do not affect its functioning. Of those mutations that affect gene functioning, some may even count as improvements. But the vast majority of changes to gene function will be harmful. This is because random changes to a complex system that is already working well will almost certainly make it work less well. Throwing a brick at a computer will make many random changes to it, but only rarely will any of these changes fix a minor software glitch. The phenomenon of DNA copying error is something that we may all confront, but the problem could be more pronounced for someone whose genome comes from the somatic cell of a fifty-year-old man or woman. It is theorized that there are mechanisms that weed out heavily mutated sperms and eggs, preventing them from starting new life, but no such mechanisms help cloners to select correctly from the skin cells of a fifty-year-old. This may mean that the beneficial effects of genius genes are cancelled by the harmful effects of fifty years of cell divisions. Similar obstacles may stand in the way of Haldane's proposal that centenarians be cloned for their longevity. By the time someone has been able to demonstrate conclusively how well suited her genome is to a long life, the DNA of her somatic cells may have accumulated sufficient mutations to make it unusable for this purpose. Perhaps the only way to overcome this problem would be to freeze everyone's embryonic cells.

However, there is an obstacle in the way of the replication of genius by cloning that is more basic than genetic mutation and cell division. The idea that my clone would resemble me in every significant respect relies on one of the most pervasive contemporary misunderstandings of biology. This misunderstanding is genetic determinism, the view that our genes dictate all but superficial aspects of our phenotypes, or visible traits.[12] Genetic determinism lies behind many of the misguided hopes and fears about the new genetic technologies. People find human clones creepy because they think their exact genetic resemblance to other human beings means that they must resemble them in every respect down to the smallest skin blemish and the most shameful sexual fantasy.

Monozygotic twins provide swift refutation of genetic determinism. These twins are genetically identical to one another. While the similarities between some monozygotic twins are the stuff of legend, it is clear that they are not exactly psychologically and physically identical.[13] The differences between them must result from differences in the environments that they have encountered. The twin or clone of a genius might easily miss out on the precise combination of early educational or nutritional influences required for the making of great intelligence.

How genes help to make human beings has a significant bearing on the results enhancement technologies can achieve. It will receive a good deal of attention in this book.

HUMAN GENOMICS AND THE SEARCH FOR SMART GENES

Haldane's plan would give someone the chance to have a genius child by replicating all of the hereditary influences operative in making an Einstein or a Picasso. Another biotechnology may further extend the range of procreative choice by allowing the parents of the future to select specific genetic influences.

The ultimate goal of human genomics is a complete account of human genes, which traits they influence, and how they influence them. This information will enable genetic engineers and practitioners of pre-implantation genetic diagnosis to target their efforts. Under a liberal scheme, practitioners of PGD would use only embryos that have genes linked with the traits parents have requested for their child, or are free of genes linked with traits that they are seeking to avoid. Once the methods of moving genes from one organism into another are perfected, genomic information will enable humans to become designers of humans. Practitioners of PGD are restricted to the combinations that nature provides. Genetic engineers will combine in a single organism the traits found in a variety of organisms by creating a single genome that combines genes for these traits.

There is certainly ample evidence that differences in genes are part of the explanation of why some people are smarter than others. In 2001, scientists at the University of California, Los Angeles published a study that set out to separate the influence of genes on intelligence from the various environmental influences.[14] The research involved a comparison of monozygotic and dizygotic twins. Monozygotic twins are genetically identical because they result from a single fertilized egg that splits, creating two embryos from one. Dizygotic twins come into existence when two eggs happen to be fertilized by different sperm at roughly the same time, and hence are no more genetically similar to one another than are any two siblings conceived at different times. These twin comparisons proceed from the assumption that the environments of dizygotic twins are equalized to the same extent as are the environments of monozygotic twins. The finding that monozygotic twins are more similar to one another in respect of a certain trait than are dizygotic twins, points to genes. The University of California researchers scanned the brains of monozygotic and dizygotic Finnish twins born between 1940 and 1957. They focused in particular on Broca's and Wernicke's areas, parts of the brain whose functions bear on language use, and the frontal region, known to influence general cognitive competence. Although these regions were extremely similar in monozygotic twins, the Wernicke's areas of dizygotic twins were only quite similar, and the other parts even less so. The differences carried through to the results of intelligence tests. The scores of monozygotic twins were more similar than were the scores of dizygotic twins. Researchers concluded that differences in genes account for at least some of the variation in human intelligence.

What should we call these genes? The label 'intelligence genes' smacks of genetic determinism – the idea that there are genes that will make someone intelligent regardless of her environment. We should stick with the label, but understand that it describes influences rather than determining causes. Compare genes with other inputs into human development. Even if they were an influence in that direction, the French lessons that I attended in my childhood did not succeed in turning me into a French speaker. As it is with French lessons, so it is with intelligence genes. One can certainly be born with the 'high intelligence' variant of a gene and not turn out to be at all intelligent.

While it is one thing to know that there are intelligence genes somewhere on the human genome, it is quite another to identify the specific genes that genetic enhancers of intelligence will need to manipulate.[15] Intelligence is a polygenic trait – a large number of genes influence it. To further complicate matters for genetic engineers, many of these genes are likely to be pleiotrophic; they affect traits other than intelligence.

Those hunting for intelligence genes work in an area that has come to be called behavioural genetics. The quest for correlations between genetic variants and behaviours is made possible by technological advances that enable DNA to be described and the invention of statistical techniques capable of separating the small influences of a particular gene from a host of environmental and other genetic influences. However, behavioural geneticists confront an obstacle not faced by others seeking to link traits with genes. There are agreed-upon criteria for conditions like Alzheimer's or cystic fibrosis. Geneticists investigating these conditions start with a straightforward means of identifying those who have the disease. This is not the case when dealing with psychological traits.

There is deep controversy over what kind of characteristic intelligence is. Some scientists hold that there is a cognitive ability called general intelligence or g. This g is said to explain performance across a very wide range of tasks, including mathematics, music and reading comprehension, making it a convenient target for enhancers of intelligence.[16] But Howard Gardner defends an alternative theory of multiple intelligences.[17] He argues that there are distinct intelligence modules each accounting for performance in a relatively circumscribed area. The bases of musical intelligence differ from those of mathematical intelligence, which, in turn, differ from the bases of social intelligence, and so on. If Gardner's view is correct it would be too simple to describe a genetic engineer as just enhancing intelligence. We will need to ask which intelligence is being enhanced, looking out for the effects of this enhancement on other intelligences. Further controversy concerns how we would decide that we have achieved the goal of enhanced intelligence. Higher IQ test scores can only be counted as evidence of success if we allow that they really measure intelligence, rather than, as some have suggested, conformity with the cultural norms of the writer of the test.[18]

Suppose we can agree both on what kind of attribute intelligence is and a way to decide whether it has been enhanced. Genes of use to would-be enhancers are likely to be hard to find. The fact that the construction of intelligence involves so many genes explains why there seem to be many genetic variations linked to disruptions in normal human cognition. The year 1993 saw the discovery on chromosome 4 of the genetic variant responsible for Huntington's disease, a neurodegenerative disorder characterized in its early stages by impaired motor control and leading, over the course of ten or more years, to death. Genes linked with Alzheimer's disease have been traced with varying degrees of certainty to chromosomes 3, 12, 14, 19 and 21.[19] There are candidate genes for disorders such as autism and schizophrenia. With so many genes influencing intelligence, it is unsurprising that there are many ways in which genetic error can disrupt cognitive function. However, the aspiring enhancer of intelligence is not as interested in these as she is in genetic variants that explain the difference between normal and superior cognition.

Progress in the search for such genes has been faltering. In 1998, a team led by Robert Plomin claimed to have discovered a genetic variation associated with approximately 2 per cent of the difference between two samples of high-IQ children and a group whose intelligence was in the normal range.[20] The difference between the high-IQ and the average-IQ children was in a gene on chromosome 6 called IGF2R, or the insulin-like growth factor 2 receptor gene. There is a gap between showing that a genetic variation is associated with a difference in intelligence and showing that the variation causally explains the difference; Plomin's finding was consistent with IGF2R merely occupying a spot on the genome near a genuine intelligence gene. However, the science writer Matt Ridley did propose one way in which IGF2R might influence intelligence.[21] There is some evidence that the gene plays a role in the burning of sugar. Ridley connected Plomin's finding with research indicating that people with higher IQs metabolize more sugar than those with lower IQs when performing cognitive tasks.

Although its effect appeared small, variation in IGF2R would certainly have been of value to those seeking to enhance intelligence. However, in late 2002 Plomin retracted his claim in a letter to the journal that published the original finding.[22] A study based on a larger sample than that of the 1998 research failed to find any association between different versions of IGF2R and differences in intelligence.

Plomin's announcement and retraction are emblematic of the history of the study of genetic influences on behaviour. If one follows the history of research on genes for psychological traits through the science journals one notices a pattern. Announcements of significant discoveries are followed either by failures by other scientific teams to replicate the claimed result, or, as in the case of IGF2R and intelligence, by the original team's retraction.[23]

DOOGIE'S DOWNSIDE

Perhaps we do not need cast-iron conclusions in behavioural genetics before we attempt to enhance intelligence. Joe Tsien enhanced the intelligence of mice without having to locate all of the genes that feed into mouse intelligence, or even to come up with a precise definition of what it was that he was seeking to enhance. He achieved his result by the simple expedient of inserting an additional NR2B gene into mouse genomes. The effect that Tsien achieved would be invisible to behavioural geneticists, who could only discover a connection between two copies of NR2B and enhanced memory if they found individuals with an extra copy of the gene in the populations they studied. But mouse populations contained no individuals with extra copies of NR2B in advance of Tsien's experiment.

It is possible that providing humans with additional NR2B genes might enhance memory and the capacity for learning. However, there are significant obstacles that need to be traversed before we allow genetic engineers to create Doogie humans.

Producing a genetic arrangement that occurs nowhere in nature brings risks that the substitution of one naturally occurring arrangement for another does not. Novel genetic arrangements can have unanticipated effects. Continuing the story of Joe Tsien's Doogie mouse sounds a warning for genetic engineers who want to innovate. Most of the experiments that Tsien's team conducted involved pain or frightening situations – one was conducted in a chamber flooded with water, and in others the mice were given electric shocks. People remember the breaking of a bone but not the stubbing of a toe suffered earlier on the same day because of differences in the intensity of the pain. Perhaps Doogie's enhanced memory was purchased at the price of greater pain. A team led by Min

Zhou, a medical researcher at the Washington University School of Medicine in St Louis, conducted experiments on Doogie mice that appeared to support this hypothesis.[24] Zhou injected a noxious substance into the hind paws of Doogie and normal mice. He observed that Doogie mice continued to lick and bite the affected paws long after the experimental controls had stopped. The pain seemed worse for them. Zhou thinks that Doogie mice may remember pain simply because an extra NR2B gene makes it more intense. If pricking a finger feels like sticking it in a naked flame, it is not surprising that the mishap stays longer in the memory. A life of intense pain is a high price to pay for an expanded memory. Tsien contests Zhou's explanation. He argues that better memory of pain need not mean that pain is necessarily more intense. Tsien compares Doogie mice with a child who 'may start to cry once he realizes that he [has] come back to the doctor's office, even before seeing the syringe and needles...the context of the doctor's office reactivates those unpleasant experiences'.[25]

Tsien's and Zhou's disagreement centres on a difference between having enhanced pain and having an enhanced capacity to remember pain. It is difficult to resolve partly because of science's awkwardness about pain. Most of us think of pain as a subjective experience. The capacity for pleasant and unpleasant subjective states is held by some philosophers to mark the boundary between beings that matter morally and those that do not.[26] However, scientists have long treated subjective phenomena with suspicion, focusing instead on their objective behavioural or neurological correlates. This means that they have an at best indirect interest in the pain and pleasure states of uppermost concern to many moral philosophers. It is worth noting that even if Tsien is right, and Doogie mice merely remember pain longer, there may be cause for concern – especially if painful experiences are more likely to be remembered than non-painful ones. The child in Tsien's analogy may not actually be feeling pain upon returning to the doctor's office, but its memory does seem to cause him a degree of suffering.

NUCLEAR POWERED VACUUM CLEANERS OR NUCLEAR BOMBS

There are a number of reasons for scepticism about what enhancement technologies might do. This scepticism may seem to make ethical speculation pointless. Consider Pinker's examples of comical overconfidence about technology. We are not cleaning our homes with nuclear-powered Electroluxes, nor are we eating chicken genetically engineered to be exactly the right shape for the plate. Those who laboured to design codes specifying safe use of the nucleo-lux, or the ethical raising of walking chicken breasts, would have been wasting their time. In her discussion of procreative liberty and its limits Onora O'Neill concedes that scientists may one day present us with technologies capable of enhancing human attributes, but she thinks that the current primitive state of these technologies reduces the urgency of moral debate about enhancement.[27] We should instead concentrate on evaluating reproductive technologies that are here now.

O'Neill is wrong to think of human enhancement as something that will only be possible in the distant future. I have argued that technologies that we currently have, such as PGD, or may soon have, such as reproductive cloning, permit people to choose some of their children's characteristics. Furthermore, we should not forget science's propensity to present us with moral surprises. In the 1930s it was thought that the immense energy locked within the atom could not be put to destructive ends. Hiroshima and Nagasaki were not long coming. Another example is both more recent and more pertinent to the moral concerns of this book. In the early 1980s the biologists Davor Solter and James McGrath conducted an exhaustive series of experiments in which they attempted what seemed like every possible permutation and variation of putting the nuclei of differentiated mouse cells into fertilized eggs that had had their nuclei removed.[28] Each attempt met with failure. Solter and McGrath concluded that 'the cloning of mammals, by simple [somatic cell] nuclear transfer, is biologically impossible'.[29] The paper was published twelve years before Dolly's birth.

These best guesses of the scientific establishment had the effect of making ethical speculation about nuclear weapons and human cloning seem frivolous, activities best restricted to philosophy lecture halls. As a consequence, Hiroshima and Dolly arrived largely morally unannounced.

Suppose that prior to 1997 there had been a wide debate about human cloning, with contributions from representatives of many different moral traditions. We might now have reached some kind of moral consensus about the various uses to which the technology should be put. Advocates of human cloning might not be demonstrating their commitment to the idea by trying to make clone babies in secret. Opponents of therapeutic cloning would have been able to present their arguments without appearing to be wilfully prolonging the suffering of people whose Alzheimer's or diabetes might be cured if research on human embryonic stem cells were to proceed unhindered.

A PRAGMATIC OPTIMISM ABOUT ENHANCEMENT TECHNOLOGIES

It is better to have principles covering situations that turn out to be impossible than to have no principles for situations in which we suddenly find ourselves. Acquiring moral insurance against the many different futures that enhancement technologies might make requires that we think beyond the limits of current science. We need principles for situations that might never eventuate, but whose possibility can not be ruled out given our current state of knowledge. Finding such principles requires what I will call a *pragmatic optimism* about cloning, genomics and genetic engineering. The pragmatic optimist considers a wide range of possibilities about the developmental trajectory and potential limits of enhancement technologies. Answers to questions about what would be right or wrong in these technologically ideal scenarios tell us about the 'in principle' obligations governing the technologies and about the 'in principle' liberties opened up by them.

Pragmatic optimism intentionally abstracts from considerations of risk and feasibility to focus on the goals motivating the development of enhancement technologies. It permits the kind of moral discussion we must have before technologies are thrust upon us. When scientists tell us that they have isolated intelligence genes and have perfected techniques for transferring them we will need to engage in a different kind of moral inquiry, one informed by the risks associated with the technologies as they currently stand and estimates of how likely they are to achieve the ends set for them.

Consider how this distinction in moral discussions about biotechnology applies to the debate over reproductive cloning.[30] Earlier in this chapter I described some of the technological obstacles in the way of this undertaking. CLONAID should explain how it can overcome these obstacles before they set about making clone babies, but in advance even of this they need to defend the very idea of human cloning. When conducting this defence they are permitted to imagine away limitations specific to current cloning protocols. They can suppose that somatic cell nuclear transfer creates humans with the same odds of physical disability as conventionally conceived humans. Consideration of this technologically ideal scenario should not be seen as biasing discussion in favour of reproductive cloning. Rather it prompts both opponents and advocates to formulate arguments whose soundness is not affected by refinement of the technology. Would the mere fact of having identical nuclear DNA to the person you call your father make a happy life impossible or unlikely? Pessimistic answers to this question will not be deflected by scientists' success in perfecting human somatic cell nuclear transfer.

Pragmatic optimism is not moral optimism. For example, pragmatic optimists about biological warfare will imagine agents that once introduced into a population infect everyone they come into contact with, and that kill 100 per cent of infected people. We can be grateful that this technologically ideal scenario will probably never be realized. Nevertheless, it provides a standpoint from which to assess the research efforts of those seeking to develop biological weapons. Pragmatically assuming that their experiments will go as well as possible enables criticism of the research and the ideals behind it. It also offers the chance of moral insurance against scientists' realization of our worst fears.

Although pragmatic optimism encourages a wide view of scientific possibilities, it is not an 'anything goes' approach to technology. We should dismiss from moral consideration proposals that transcend logical or metaphysical limits. For example, the ambitions of the Raelian religious sect for human reproductive cloning go beyond the treatment of infertility, or even human enhancement. Consider the following statement on the website of the sect's commercial offshoot, CLONAID:

> Once we can clone exact replicas of ourselves, the next step will be to transfer our memory and personality into our newly cloned brains, which will allow us to truly live forever. Since we will be able to remember all our past, we will be able to accumulate knowledge *ad infinitum.* (www.clonaid.com)

The hope that cloning by somatic cell nuclear transfer might be the technology of eternal life runs into obstacles that are more metaphysical than technological. Imagine that the technology is perfected to the point of being able to turn any human somatic cell into the starting point of a new human person with 100 per cent efficiency. No philosophically coherent view of personal identity enables us to think of the clone as the same person as the donor of the somatic cell. Philip Kitcher is right to emphasize that 'here is no hope of ensuring personal survival by arranging for cloning through supplying a cell nucleus. Megalomaniacs with intimations of immortality need not apply.'[31]

Philosophers have pursued three broad strategies in attempting to explain personal identity over time. According to one account, somewhat out of fashion in these materialist times, my survival is a matter of the persistence from second to second of some non-physical substance – a soul.[32] This account faces off against two different materialist theories of the metaphysics of personal identity. *Physical continuity theorists* hold that my survival over time is a matter of my body, or at least significant parts of it, continuing to exist over time.[33] *Psychological continuity theorists* insist that it is not the physical material of my body that counts, but instead the preservation of the psychological patterns currently realized by this material.[34] On this last view, my survival over time is a matter of my psychological characteristics – memories, beliefs and hopes – continuing on.

None of these accounts allows us to make sense of the Raelian proposal. Consider the soul theory. Does cloning transfer not only DNA, but also a soul, from one person's body into the body of a clone? It is unlikely that this could be the case. Remember that all that somatic cell nuclear transfer requires from me is a single cell. I shed millions of cells every day in brushing my hair, drying myself with a towel, and rolling around in my sheets. If nuclear transfer can move my soul from my current body to my clone's body, then we would have to say that my soul somehow adheres to each of these cells until their DNA has degraded to a point that it is useless to would-be cloners. Such a possibility seems so bizarre as not to warrant further consideration. What about the physical continuity theory? According to this view, my survival over time is a matter of the ongoing survival of my body, or at least something physically continuous with that body. There is a physical link between me and my clone – the clone begins from a cell taken from my body. However, no physical continuity theorist will think that such a tenuous physical link could suffice to ensure my survival as my clone. Otherwise, why isn't the loss of a hair rather more than part of a process that may one day lead to my baldness, and instead part of a gradual winnowing away of my identity – a small step towards my death? If so, people will need to view having a haircut, clipping toenails and sneezing in an entirely different light. The psychological continuity theory also fails to make the Raelian aspiration intelligible. The transfer of DNA does not transfer memories, the most significant elements of identity according to psychological continuity theorists. Doubtless, the Raelians will protest that an indispensable element of their plan for eternal life is the device that would transfer the psychological states of the DNA-donor to the clone. This brain-state-transfer machine would be a fabulous piece of technology – up to the task of recording all the information about a person's psychology and then configuring another brain accordingly.[35] If the psychological continuity theory is right, this piece of technology alone could secure my survival after the destruction of my current body. In societies with this technology, those seeking eternal life would be well advised to select a brain and body that might improve on their current one, rather than cloning themselves.

I conclude that no plausible account of human existence over time can make sense of the idea of cloning as the technology of eternal life. Those who formulate moral principles governing human cloning must take account of the fact that many people will see the technology as a means of self-perpetuation, but they can safely ignore the hypothesis that anyone will actually be able to use the technology to achieve this end. In this way, the metaphysics of persons sets limits on pragmatic optimism about cloning by somatic cell nuclear transfer.

The label 'enhancement technologies' groups human biotechnologies in terms of a particular end to which they might be put. However, we must avoid being too one-eyed about biotechnological ends. In chapter 1 I acknowledged that 'enhancement technologies' is a somewhat contentious label for cloning by somatic cell nuclear transfer, embryo selection and genetic engineering. The scientists who work on these technologies and those who fund their work are an ideologically disparate collection. Many, indeed most of them, do not see the technologies as means of enhancing humans; in some cases they explicitly reject this goal. I chose to present the Doogie mouse as a precursor of humans that acquire new knowledge twice as fast, and retain it for around four to five times as long as normal humans, but most of the scientists behind Doogie envisage the technique being used to treat neurodegenerative disorders. Human cloning has proved so morally fraught in part due to the diversity of ends that would-be cloners are pursuing. Suppose we discount the outlandish aims of the Raelians. The goals of therapeutic and reproductive cloning are frequently confused. For example, an issue of *The Atlantic Monthly* carrying a discussion of Advanced Cell Technology's efforts to make therapeutic cloning a reality bore, as cover art, the picture of a young boy.[36] This picture, together with the article's title 'Cloning Trevor', gave the impression that ACT wanted to make clone babies – but this is precisely what they do not want to do. A full moral evaluation of cloning requires different ideal scenarios corresponding with the many different ends to which somatic cell nuclear transfer might be put.

I can now describe the technologically ideal scenario that will enable us to evaluate liberal eugenics. In this scenario genomics has identified all the human genes and informed us of their functions and exactly how these functions are carried out. Genetic engineers are able to transfer genes from one genome to another with their functional properties intact. Further, enhanced pregnancies have the same rate of mishap as natural pregnancies. A person whose intelligence has been genetically boosted is as likely to suffer from any form of ill-health as a conventionally conceived person. This scenario is not a forecast. Perhaps we will never understand the myriad ways in which human genes interact with one another and their very complex environments to produce human traits. Genetic engineers may never possess tools capable of introducing genes from one organism into the genome of another with any certainty that the new gene will both perform its original function and not interfere with other genes. But on the other hand, we cannot tell how many Dollys geneticists have in store for us. Consideration of technologically ideal scenarios can prepare us for the many different futures that enhancement technologies might make.

CHAPTER 3

Making Moral Images
of Biotechnology

It is one thing to describe enhancement technologies, but quite another to defend their use. Here we face a problem. The moral principles that guide us well enough in our dealings with people whose existence is not at issue seem ill-equipped to help us to decide who to create and how to create them.[1]

I present the *method of moral images* to help us to make decisions about enhancement technologies. The moral image of an unfamiliar practice is another practice chosen both for its similarity to the problematic practice and the fact that it elicits moral reactions of which we are confident. If we have chosen our image well, consistency will demand that we react to the unfamiliar practice in the same way that we react to the familiar one. Conservatives' images of enhancement prompt negative judgements. The images I favour will expose some of the dangers of enhancement, but they will support a more favourable evaluation.

The method of moral images is not designed to displace moral principles; it does not pretend to systematize and justify our moral intuitions in the way that moral principles do. Rather its purpose is practical, to direct us to the wide variety of moral concerns provoked by enhancement technologies. The method makes no decision ahead of time about which kinds of considerations are to be properly viewed as moral ones. It gives the representatives of different moral traditions a way to express their distinctive concerns about human enhancement. They will propose different moral images, each of which can be assessed in terms of its closeness to the practice of enhancement.

UTILITARIAN AND KANTIAN ADVICE ABOUT ENHANCEMENT

Before presenting the method of moral images, I describe some problems that confront two of the most widely advocated moral principles when they are applied to enhancement technologies. My discussions of utilitarianism and Kantian morality are far from exhaustive; we are, after all, talking about enormously rich moral traditions rather than simple, straightforwardly specifiable principles. However, they do provide some incentive to find other ways to orient our moral intuitions towards questions about the people we might create.

The principle of utility directs that we maximize global happiness and minimize global suffering. When we face a choice, utilitarians think we should choose the best outcome once the costs of suffering are subtracted from the benefits of happiness. The most straightforward application of utilitarianism to human genetic engineering would have us inserting genetic variants judged most likely to make both the subject of the procedure and others happy. Such genes are not a philosopher's fantasy. Behavioural geneticists claim to have identified a sequence of DNA linked with different levels of subjective well-being.[2] A region on chromosome 17 known as 5-HTTLPR regulates the activity of a gene called 5-HTT. People who inherit at least one copy of the short version of the regulatory region are apparently more prone to anxiety, depression, anger and hostility than those who inherit two copies of the long variant. Although it is not well understood why the sequence should have this effect, different versions of it are linked with different rates of the re-uptake of serotonin, the neurotransmitter acted on by the antidepressant, Prozac.

The claim that 5-HTTLPR influences temperament is controversial. However, suppose it is true. The question that interests me is how utilitarians would put this information to use in deciding what kinds of people to bring into existence. First, consider the responses of utilitarians who advocate a hedonistic conception of human ends. According to them, the greater the number of pleasurable experiences and the fewer unpleasant ones, the better the life. Defenders of this view would make it mandatory for parents to engineer the longer versions of the 5-HTTLPR sequence into the embryos of their future offspring. They would accuse the parent-to-be who withheld this therapy of inflicting an unequivocally worse existence on her child. The same reasoning would be applied to any other DNA sequence with predictable effects on human subjective states. If, by chance, genetic engineers were to find a human genome in conformity with their moral ideal they would be obliged not to change it. This utilitarian approach would allow parents discretion only in respect of genes that have no expected bearing on happiness.

The notion that we must genetically engineer every human being to be as emotionally upbeat as possible is absurd. A personality that behavioural geneticists may describe as anxious, depressed, angry and hostile, others might consider cautious, sombre, sceptical and intolerant of fools. We all know people leading perfectly worthwhile lives, but whose characters correspond with the second list, and it is hard to believe that their very existence would be immoral in the era of human enhancement. The abandonment of a hedonistic conception of human ends offers one way to escape this implication. Preference utilitarians think that instead of maximizing the number of pleasant sensations and minimizing the number of unpleasant ones we should be trying to maximize the satisfaction of preferences and minimize their frustration.[3] This theory comports better with our intuitions about the way we should live. Most of us do not set the accumulation of units of pleasure as life's single aim; rather we pursue goals involving family, careers and friends and we consider a good life to be one in which many of these significant goals are achieved. Preference utilitarians can readily grant that being naturally sombre does not stand in the way of a satisfactory existence; many people who have sunny temperaments nonetheless fail to satisfy their most important desires, something that many of the less temperamentally buoyant achieve. This variant of utilitarianism also gives strongly counterintuitive answers to questions about human genetic engineering. For example, Helga Kuhse and Peter Singer wonder whether it would be 'possible – and desirable? – to attempt to genetically engineer people whose capacities and goals, while possibly truncated, are in harmony with their limited passions?'[4] The goal of designing humans who are both limited to easily satisfiable preferences and meet the criteria for personhood is likely to pose technological difficulties for enhancers. But the claim that if feasible it should be mandatory seems even more absurd than the idea of compulsory 5-HTTLPR therapy.

The most obvious way for utilitarians to avoid these conclusions is by limiting their principle's application. What are known as person-affecting moral views restrict the domain of moral discourse to individuals whose existence and identities are not at issue.[5] Our actions can harm such individuals; we harm them when we make them worse off than they would otherwise have been. But it is hard to see how someone could be harmed by being brought into existence as a human clone. Had he not been created by somatic cell nuclear transfer, he simply would not have existed at all. The question of the impact of embryonic genetic interventions on identity is one that I address at greater length in chapter 4. But suppose that one's identity is partly constituted by which versions of 5-HTTLPR one has. Utilitarian lawmakers who accepted a person-affecting condition on moral discourse could avoid making 5-HTTLPR therapy compulsory by pointing out that their moral principle simply does not apply to the countless different kinds of people we could bring into existence. The problem is that person-affecting utilitarianism avoids the aforementioned absurd conclusions only by offering no guidance on how we should use enhancement technologies.[6]

Kantians also seem forced to choose between absurdity and silence when they confront enhancement technologies. According to the version of Kant's Categorical Imperative most often used to resolve bioethical dilemmas, one should never treat another person exclusively as a means to an end. People are rational beings, and their wishes and needs must be taken into account in our dealings with them. Kantian bioethicists have used this idea to illuminate problems that arise from the differences in power between doctors and medical researchers on the one side, and patients and experimental subjects on the other.[7] It seems to capture the complaints of many critics of human biotechnology. These critics think that genetically modifying one's offspring reduces them to the status of mere things. They imagine twenty-second-century parents seeking the same manner of redress from genetic engineers who fail to provide their child with an additional NR2B gene, that people now seek from technicians who fail to upgrade their computer's memory. Some of the advocates of reproductive cloning appear particularly guilty. The Raelians would create special kinds of human beings merely to satisfy the vanity of those who misguidedly see somatic cell nuclear transfer as a means of perpetuating their own existences.

But first appearances are deceptive. People have always had selfish motives for reproducing. They want kids to save marriages, to ensure pampered retirements, or to find some new purpose in life. This selfishness in respect of individuals who do not yet exist seems perfectly compatible with proper parental concern once children's lives are under way. The fact is that it is hard to have non-instrumental motives in respect of a person who does not yet exist. Compare the aforementioned instrumental motives with the absence of motive that anticipates the existence of children whose parents were just too drunk or drugged to remember to use contraception. These children don't seem better off simply in virtue of the fact that there were no instrumental reasons for their existence.

There is some reason to think that enhancement technologies will forever elude Kantian morality's focus. Kant identifies rationality as a human constant. However, as David Heyd recognizes, it is precisely this assumption that new reproductive technologies call into question:

> [W]e may raise the question why we should create *rational* humans if we can choose to engineer nonrational robots? We might have perfectly rational grounds for creating nonrational beings; we might equally choose to create rational beings on the grounds that we want 'them' to become ends in themselves. But we cannot say that being potentially ends in themselves creates a claim on the part of our potential children to be born.[8]

Philosophers have thought hard about whether potentially rational human embryos have a moral entitlement to be born.[9] Later in this chapter I will discuss the moral status of potential in the context of the debate about therapeutic cloning. The advent of enhancement technologies raises the issue of whether human embryos have any moral claim on a *rational* existence. Those who argue against any right to rational existence would point out that the discovery of human intelligence genes and the invention of techniques for transferring them into non-human embryos may herald an era in which every mammalian embryo is potentially a rational being. Kant seems to have little to contribute to this particular exchange on enhancement technologies beyond the idea that if we do deliberately create non-rational beings in place of rational ones, our treatment of them will not be constrained by the Categorical Imperative.

MORAL IMAGES AND MORAL CONSISTENCY

Utilitarianism and Kantianism orient our intuitions about right and wrong towards certain kinds of moral problem – those involving people whose existence is not at issue. We can use these theories to help us to decide whether or not we are permitted to end someone's existence, but not to decide whether or not someone should *ever* exist. The fact that these theories do not cope well with such choices does not indict the intuitions about right and wrong that lie behind them. In what follows, I show how to redirect these intuitions towards problems about how to bring people into existence.

The method of moral images makes use of one of our most familiar moral ideas – that of consistency. Being consistent involves treating morally like cases alike. Suppose you hold that foxes should not be hunted because foxes are sentient beings and that sentient beings should never be deliberately harmed. You would be guilty of inconsistency if you were also to claim that the benefits to human beings of medical experiments on chimpanzees necessitate painful experiments on them. One can not consistently believe both that sentient beings should be intentionally harmed and that they should not. Inconsistencies of this type fall foul of the principle of rationality that specifies that one should not hold both that P is the case and that P is not the case. Reason demands abandonment or qualification of either the view about fox hunting or the view about medical experimentation on chimpanzees.

Utilitarians and Kantians have their own specific interests in the idea of consistency. Utilitarians tell us that we should be consistent about the consequences of our actions or inactions for beings capable of experiencing happiness or suffering. Peter Singer is a utilitarian who has argued vigorously that it is inconsistent to strive to reduce human suffering while having no regard for the suffering of chimpanzees, dogs and other sentient beings.[10] Kantians demand consistency not about consequences but instead about intentions. According to one version of Kant's Categorical Imperative, a condition for my acting on a certain intention is that there be no contradiction in everyone's acting on that intention. Suppose that Raël, leader of the Raelian religious sect, is deciding whether or not it would be right to lie about having cloned a human being. He seeks to universalize the lie, but finds that he can not do so consistently. Lying whenever deemed convenient to do so undermines the activity that it presupposes, that of communication.

The question of this book is simple. Does consistency demand the banning, the mere toleration or the encouragement of enhancement technologies? Simple questions do not always have simple answers. I have just pointed out that the choices that enhancement technologies enable are quite unlike those that concern people whose existence is not at issue, the kinds of moral choice that we are used to making. How does one recognize a consistent approach to something unprecedented and unfamiliar?

We can work out what would count as a consistent approach to enhancement technologies only if we find a way to establish connections between familiar and unfamiliar practices. Moral images can help us to do this.

The debate about the appropriate response to the 11 September 2001 attacks on the United States allows me to illustrate how a moral image can help us towards moral understanding of something that seems entirely unfamiliar. It is an early twenty-first-century truism that these attacks were unprecedented in terms of scale, target and means. Their novelty made it especially difficult to decide what was the appropriate way to respond to them. Two competing moral images of the attacks emerged. The image that came to dominate was that of an act of war – a recent historical analogue being the Japanese attack on Pearl Harbor on 7 December 1941. Both the 1941 and the 2001 events were surprise attacks, both caused great loss of life, both were directed by people hostile to the policies of the United States. There is another image of the attacks, however. According to this second image, the attacks were not acts of war, but instead great crimes. The terrorists should be compared not with the Japanese carrier pilots, but instead with multiple murderers like Jeffrey Dahmer and Jack the Ripper. Defenders of this moral image point out that, although they killed many people, the attacks did not seriously affect the United States' capacity to implement its foreign policy or to project military power. The Pentagon was struck, but the effect of that blow was much less militarily significant than was the destruction of a large part of the US fleet by the Japanese pilots. The attackers certainly saw themselves as striking a blow against the USA. But mass murderers can have a variety of delusional motivations – they sometimes see their murders as the striking down of demons, or doing God's will. Although the terrorists may not have been clinically insane, examination of their training literature did reveal a wide gap between their view of the world and the way it actually is.

The choice between these two moral images, call them ACT OF WAR and CRIME, dictates how the attacks are best responded to. Opting for ACT OF WAR makes military action the appropriate response. ACT OF WAR legitimizes the attack on the al Qaeda bases in Afghanistan and the regime that supported them. A different response is appropriate if we opt for CRIME. Suppose Jeffrey Dahmer had escaped from police custody to a foreign country. This foreign country meets requests that he be returned for trial with the claim that there is no extradition treaty between it and the USA. It refuses to negotiate Dahmer's return. Under these circumstances the courts should continue to seek Dahmer's extradition, but we would be unlikely to see a military assault as justified.

Only rarely will we find an image of an apparently unfamiliar practice that resembles it in every moral respect. Neither ACT OF WAR nor CRIME corresponds precisely with the September 11 attacks. Unlike most mass murderers, the terrorists acted in concert and under orders but, unlike soldiers, they were not members of armies representing states. The most obvious approach would be to look for guidance to the image that we judge to be *more* similar. This apparently reasonable proposal faces an argument by the philosopher, Nelson Goodman, that no sense can be made of the idea of two things being more objectively similar to each other than either is to a third thing.[11] The fact that any two things share an infinite number of properties makes it impossible to say that either one possesses more properties in common with the third than the other. According to Goodman, talk of similarity can only make sense relative to an interest that provides a frame of reference. There is no objective measure that makes dogs and domestic cats more similar to each other than either is to leopards. If we classify them in terms of their suitability as pets they are similar, while if we are attempting a biological classification they are not.

It might seem that we have a straightforward answer to Goodman. When comparing an unfamiliar act or practice with a collection of candidate images we are concerned not with similarities *simpliciter*. The practice we are comparing to enhancement technologies must resemble them in the morally relevant factual respects. It must both involve some choice or process that leads to human improvement, and clearly support the moral judgement we are trying to pass.

A difficulty with this response to Goodman is that it presupposes an agreement on which respects are moral ones. Those with Kantian moral intuitions will find genetic enhancement very similar to one collection of familiar practices, while utilitarians will find stronger connections between enhancement and a completely different collection.

I take this indecision about which similarities are the moral ones to be a reflection of the plurality of human interests in morality. In chapter 2 I emphasized the need for morally transparent descriptions of new technologies. Pragmatic optimism brings enhancement technologies within the understanding of the advocates of the many different moral viewpoints expressed in contemporary liberal democracies. Investigation by means of moral images is also open to a plurality of approaches to moral questions. In this respect it differs from investigation driven by a moral principle. When one decides to examine a moral problem from a utilitarian standpoint one has already decided to dismiss purported moral reasons that can not be understood in terms of changes to global happiness or suffering. Those seeking consensus on the new genetic technologies should acknowledge that this moral resolution comes at a cost. People who find that their distinctive moral concerns are accorded no weight at all in the calculus of consequences are unlikely to accept the utilitarian solution. The method of moral images offers a way for the advocates of a wide range of moral approaches to say how the new practice impacts on what they value. Some moral images will compare the consequences of a familiar act with the consequences of an unfamiliar one; others will compare the intentions behind familiar and unfamiliar acts; still other images will focus on similarities between the characters of actors in familiar and unfamiliar situations. Utilitarians insist that one arrives at the end-point of moral consideration once one has accounted for all of a technology's morally significant consequences. The approach that I am describing allows that we can always construct images that illuminate hitherto hidden moral aspects of new technologies.

This concession to the diversity of moral interests would come at too high a price if it made moral progress impossible. For example, we could make no progress on the question of liberal eugenics' acceptability if, whatever your intended use of enhancement technologies, you could always find a moral image that would provide the requisite endorsement. The important thing to note is that not all moral images are created equal. This book evaluates the images of liberals and conservatives in terms of how well they represent individuals' enhancement choices and how clearly they vindicate the moral evaluation that is being argued for.

The method of moral images will clearly not settle the big debates between advocates of different moral principles. Utilitarians, Kantians and Virtue Ethicists can all construct images that make their distinctive moral concerns salient. Most of us think that you should lie to the would-be murderer at the door. But few think that your plan to give all the money to charity would justify your theft of a friend's bank card and the emptying of her accounts. The heterogeneity of our untheorized moral intuitions poses problems for those who hope to use moral images to demonstrate the global superiority of one of these traditions. I take this to be the lesson of two hundred years of debate between utilitarians, Kantians and the advocates of other moral principles. But those with practical concerns have no need to explain away the apparent moral diversity. Instead, they want to work out which approach to human genetic engineering and cloning is consistent with the values of the citizens of contemporary liberal democracies. To do this they need to test the bearing of a wide range of moral intuitions specifically on enhancement technologies.

My defence of a liberal policy of enhancement turns on finding images supporting liberal eugenics that are closer in relevant respects than are images which would recommend a ban – hence my conclusion that liberal eugenics is consistent with our widely accepted moral beliefs. But the images I construct do not support an unconstrained prerogative to enhance. They also help us to see that some uses of enhancement technologies do not pay proper heed to the welfare of genetically engineered humans, or infringe their autonomy, or manifest bad character on the part of enhancers.

MIDGLEY'S SCEPTICISM ABOUT CONSISTENCY

Mary Midgley is sceptical about appeals to consistency in the moral debate about biotechnology.[12] She sees them as abetting the intrusion of technology into new areas of human existence. According to Midgley, those who use consistency arguments to defend biotechnology are effectively urging that, since we have already begun the taming of wild nature and the refashioning of our own human natures, we can not object to any biotechnological proposal. Midgley says:

> [c]onsistency... is notoriously not always a virtue, as the public is uneasily aware. The fact that you have cut off somebody's arm is not always a reason why you have to cut off his leg as well. It is one thing to have drifted into having faulty institutions that one doesn't yet see how to change. Deliberately adopting an ideology that entirely obscures what is bad about them is quite another.[13]

Midgley challenges consistency's having too central a role in moral thinking, yet her example does not bear this out. We recognize the forcible severing of a leg as straightforwardly wrong. This should surely lead us to question our earlier endorsement of the severing of the arm, unless, that is, we can show that there is a relevant difference between the two severings – that the arm was gangrenous, for example.

Consistency arguments never compel us to accept any particular moral claim. Instead, they present us with a choice. We can endorse the unfamiliar practice, or we can undertake a radical critique of the quotidian and commonplace. I have been speaking as if our views about right and wrong will be transferred from a familiar practice to an unfamiliar one, but comparison with the unfamiliar may, on occasion, lead us to retract our hitherto unquestioned endorsement of the familiar. Familiarity is sometimes just moral complacency; the immoral tendencies of everyday practices are easy to overlook. Consider the way that a contract killer's moral sensibilities are dulled by repeat assignments. Suppose the killer remembers how difficult his first job was. It would be wrong for him to infer from the ease with which he now performs his executions that his earlier reluctance was misguided.

The biotechnological refashioning of humans and nature might exaggerate immoral tendencies to make them more clearly visible. Farmers have long engaged in crop selection, a practice that has, over the thousands of years of agriculture, enhanced the qualities of plants that humans value. Remarkable transformations have been achieved. The tomato has been converted from a small, yellow member of the same botanical family as the poisonous weed, black nightshade, into the large, lusciously red fruit found today on supermarket shelves. The gradualness of this transformation has given little opportunity for moral questioning. However, agricultural biotechnology brings the idea of the intentional refashioning of nature into starker relief; the introduction of transgenes, genes from other species, enables the radical transformation of a crop species within a single generation. Defenders of agricultural biotechnology often run a consistency argument that appeals to crop selection. But those who start with a strong intuition, provoked by the proposal to introduce fish antifreeze genes into tomatoes, that it is wrong for us to treat nature as modelling clay to be moulded into any shape we prefer, are being no less consistent if they argue in the opposite direction. According to them, the immoral tendency will be less pronounced in selective planting than it is in genetic engineering, but it will be present nonetheless.

If we do not find some morally significant difference between adding transgenes to tomatoes and planting seeds from tomatoes that have favourable traits, we face two options. We can move from endorsement of the familiar practice of crop selection to endorsing genetic engineering; or our suspicion of agricultural biotechnology can expand to encompass selective breeding. How do we decide between these alternatives? I have no simple algorithm to recommend. However, sometimes we recognize that thinking about an unfamiliar practice makes apparent hitherto ignored aspects of familiar practices. In such cases, we may need to change traditional views. On other occasions, contemplation of a novel practice will not expose anything unexpected about accepted practices. Here the direction of justification will run from the familiar to the unfamiliar.

HARVESTING STEM CELLS: RESEARCH OR THERAPY?

My next example of the use of moral images to illuminate the unfamiliar comes from a debate within human biotechnology. The potential of human embryonic stem cells to develop into any human cell has inspired hopes for a new era of regenerative medicine in which diseased or worn-out body parts are replaced with perfect replacements. If doctors make these parts from cells cloned from patients then there would be no need for the immunosuppressive drugs that increase susceptibility to cancer and infectious disease. It is far from clear that this use of cloning will cure any human disease; practitioners of regenerative medicine must do more than just make an immunologically matched replacement body part. The new part must be properly integrated into the patient's body. There is no point in giving Alzheimer's patients new neurons if they can not combine with existing brain tissue in the storage and retrieval of memories. The procedure would be far from risk free. Cancer cells' loss of differentiation is part of the explanation for their propensity to divide without limit. The process by which therapeutic cloners make stem cells also involves reversing cellular differentiation. If the process of respecialization is not fully complete when the replacement tissue is returned to the patient, cancer may be a consequence.[14]

There are also distinctively moral obstacles. Embryonic stem cells are harvested from embryos that will be destroyed in the process. We must balance possible cures for ailments including Alzheimer's, insulin-dependent diabetes and Parkinson's against the intentional sacrifice of very young human beings.

The debate over human embryonic stem cells has provoked what a *New York Times* reporter describes as a 'word war'.[15] Proponents indicate an alignment of the harvesting of stem cells from clone embryos with conventional medicine by labelling this practice 'therapeutic cloning'.

Charles Krauthammer, one of the members of President Bush's Council on Bioethics, challenges this term, noting that the procedure 'is not therapeutic for the clone – indeed, the clone is invariably destroyed in the process – though it may be therapeutic for others. If you donate your kidney to your brother, it would be odd to call *your* operation a therapeutic nephrectomy. It is not. It's a sacrificial nephrectomy.'[16]

While opponents of the harvesting of human stem cells for medicinal purposes challenge the word 'therapeutic', some proponents have argued that the word 'cloning' be excised. They reason that people do not really understand the distinction between reproductive cloning, in which the goal is a human baby, and somatic cell nuclear transfer used to create an embryo that is never introduced into a womb, nor allowed to grow beyond a couple of hundred cells. The substitution of 'nuclear transplantation' for 'cloning' would clearly separate what they are attempting from what CLONAID claims to have done. Irving Weissman, a Stanford scientist investigating the technology, recommends 'nuclear transplantation to produce human pluripotent stem cell lines'.[17] Doubtless, the extreme wordiness of this label would deflect some criticisms. The President's Council on Bioethics stoutly opposes this terminological strategy, arguing that labels that omit the word 'cloning' mislead because they 'fail to convey the nature of the deed itself, and ... hide its human significance'.[18]

The report of the President's Council makes the following plea for language that describes the procedures involved but does not prejudge the moral issues:

> Advisors to decision makers should strive not only for accuracy, but also for fairness, especially because the choice of name can decisively affect the way questions are posed and, hence, how answers are given. The issue is not a matter of semantics; it is a matter of trying fairly to call things by names that correctly describe them, of trying to fit speech to fact as best one can. For the sake of clarity, we should at least stipulate clearly the meanings we intend by our use of terms. But we should also try to choose terms that most accurately convey the descriptive reality of the matter at hand. If this is well done, the moral arguments can then proceed on the merits, without distortion by linguistic sloppiness or chicanery.[19]

The Council proposes terminology that it hopes will serve as a morally neutral starting point for debate about the various uses of cloning by somatic cell nuclear transfer. What is widely known as reproductive cloning, the use of cloning to provide a child with identical nuclear

DNA to another human being, would be called 'cloning-to-produce-children'. Uses of the technology that create human embryos without the intention of turning them into human children are to be called 'cloning-for-biomedical-research'.[20]

However, it is not possible to cleanse the language we use to describe cloning of any morally contentious elements. Neutral language has the habit of absorbing colouration from associated moral reasoning, without regard to the quality of this reasoning. The term 'clone' suggests, and will continue to suggest, armies of zombie soldiers, regardless of experts' attempts at clarification. Hollywood has seen to this. 'Therapeutic cloning', 'research cloning', and 'nuclear transplantation to produce human pluripotent stem cell lines' all take some manner of moral stand; there are some elements of the process to which they draw attention, and elements on which they are silent. It is better that we are honest about the moral connotations of our terms, acknowledging that in choosing them we have made a move in the game of morally evaluating and justifying. Candour about moral assumptions allows them to be properly questioned. This candour is part and parcel of the methodology of moral images.

Those who prefer 'therapeutic cloning' are appealing to the moral image of therapy. This image highlights the intended beneficiaries of stem cells taken from clone embryos. It signals the source of the cells as less morally interesting. Krauthammer suggests the label 'research cloning', connecting the harvesting of stem cells with the moral image of research.[21] This image highlights the sources of the cells – the human beings that must be created and destroyed to provide them. It also emphasizes the speculative nature of the procedure; the fact that there is no conclusive evidence that any human disease could ever be treated by this method. The authors of the Council report allow that the substitution of 'research cloning' for the more familiar 'therapeutic cloning' may in itself send a moral message. 'Because it appears to be a deliberate substitution for "therapeutic cloning" it may seem to imply that scientists have abandoned the pursuit of medical cure in favor of research as an end in itself. . . . [T]hese critics of the term "research cloning" want to avoid giving the impression that scientists want to experiment on new life just to satisfy their curiosity.'[22] This is why the Council appends 'biomedical', giving their preferred 'cloning-for-biomedical-research'. This term does indicate the medical goals of the research, but it, together with its associated image, BIOMED-ICAL RESEARCH, still takes a moral step, continuing to suggest that most or at least many of the significant moral issues arise in connection with the beings that are researched upon rather than intended recipients of the medicine. Mice that serve as experimental models for disease therapies are often killed after their procedures so that researchers can get a better idea of the effects of treatments on them. The infamous Auschwitz doctor Josef Mengele took this approach to many of the human subjects of his 'biomedical research'. The moral image of biomedical research prepares the way for the allegation that researchers are being wrongfully indifferent to the embryos that must be destroyed to furnish stem cells.

We should recognize that highlighting of the source of the cells takes a controversial stand on moral worth. The clone blastocyst has not developed to the point of having any body parts at all; it is made up of entirely undifferentiated cells. There is no intrinsic difference between the cells that would, if the blastocyst were to find itself in a womb, divide to form the central nervous system, and those that would go on to form toenails. Since it lacks a central nervous system, the clone is no more capable of suffering than are the collections of cells that vigorous scratching separates from the skin. Advocates of RESEARCH and BIOMEDICAL RESEARCH encourage us to place the interests of these beings above or on a par with the interests of sentient, rational human persons, individuals whose suffering may be alleviated by the therapy.

Is the stance on moral worth that advocates of RESEARCH or BIOMEDICAL RESEARCH assume defensible? The main way for opponents of the harvesting of stem cells to express the moral specialness of embryos is in terms of their *potential*. What marks off embryos from other collections of human cells is that they can become human persons.

Scientific information has a habit of muddying the clear vision of moral philosophers. In particular, information about the science of cloning should lead us to question their commitment to the moral significance of potential. The invention of cloning by somatic cell nuclear transfer profoundly alters the potential of biological things. Before Dolly a human skin cell could only ever be a skin cell, but now it must be acknowledged as having the potential to become a human person. Defenders of the moral significance of potential will insist that we distinguish the kind of potential possessed by embryos from that possessed by skin cells. One way to do this is to say that the human embryo possesses the *natural* potential to become a human person. In its normal environment, a human womb, it stands a fair chance of turning into a person, without any need for intervention. In contrast, something quite extraordinary must be done to the skin cell to turn it into a person.[23]

Opponents of the harvesting of stem cells maintain that this morally distinct natural potential is destroyed by therapeutic or research cloners.

Again, biological details prove awkward for clearly stated philosophical principles. Somatic cell nuclear transfer requires the fusion of two cells – the somatic cell that provides the nuclear DNA, and a cell whose nucleus is dispensed with to make way for the nucleus of the somatic cell. Earlier researchers used zygotes, fertilized eggs, as recipients for the somatic cell nucleus. They reasoned that their experiments would have the greatest chance of success if they chose as the recipient a single cell that was as far down the path leading to a fully-grown organism as a single cell can get before it becomes two cells. However, subsequent researchers switched to late-stage unfertilized eggs or oocytes. Their contrary reasoning was that the material outside of the nucleus (known as the cytoplasm) of an oocyte, but not of a zygote, might retain some of the factors necessary to the reprogramming of DNA taken from differentiated cells. This switch from zygotes to oocytes appears to have been crucial to the successes that followed.[24]

The switch from zygotes to oocytes was not made for any moral reason. Early cloning researchers were working on mice, sheep and cattle oocytes and zygotes, and they cared even less about harming potential sheep by experimenting on them than they did about harming actual sheep. But the switch is significant for anyone who thinks that the potential to be a person matters morally. Were human somatic cell nuclear transfer to require zygotes, then researchers would be experimenting on something that has the natural potential to become a human person, but oocytes have only the same kind potential to become human persons as each one of the millions of sperm in an ejaculate. Although unfertilized eggs do occasionally go through a few divisions, these parthenogenic embryos never get very far. It would be biologically impossible for them to get as far as birth. Therapeutic or research cloners encounter potential for personhood only later – at the point at which the somatic cell nucleus is added to the enucleated oocyte. There seems a difference in our moral reactions to the potential that ordinary human embryos have, and this recent, artificially created potential to become a person.

Margaret Atwood's novel *Oryx and Crake* depicts a nightmarish future that current biotechnological research might lead to. Scientists are now working on ways to genetically modify pigs so that their organs can be transplanted into humans. The main obstacle to this transplantation between species, also known as xenotransplantation, are markers on the cells of pig organs that would prompt an immediate and massive immune reaction from their human recipients. Genetic engineers are learning how to modify the genes responsible for these problematic markers.[25] Atwood extrapolates this technology to arrive at the pigoon, a pig genetically modified so as to be a perfect donor of tissue for humans. She describes the next generation of pigoons produced as part of the 'neuro-regeneration project'.[26] These pigoons would be genetically engineered to produce human brain tissue for transplant into stroke victims. The makers of pigoons are on the verge of crossing a moral boundary. A pigoon that could provide neural tissue for the full range of diseases of the brain may itself be a person, qualifying for the kind of moral protection that our combination of sentience and rationality earn for us. Suppose scientists were to create a pigoon embryo with the potential for personhood. Having done this they decide that it was wrong to create a pig-person after all. It strikes me that the fact that the embryo's potential for personhood is both recent and artificial legitimizes the use of artificial means to thwart it. Two extraordinary interventions in nature would, in effect, be cancelling each other out. Those who harvest stem cells would be doing the same thing. Rather than destroying the potential generated when a human egg and sperm meet in a natural setting, they would be destroying only laboratory-created unnatural potential.

The line of argument just presented shows one moral respect in which the image of THERAPY is closer than RESEARCH to the harvesting of human stem cells. But this does not bring the moral debate to an end. Advocates of RESEARCH are free to explore the technology to find respects in which their image is a closer match, and to argue that these respects are more salient to moral evaluation. Perhaps they will propose new moral images that highlight aspects of the use of cells taken from clone embryos that none of the existing images do. The method of moral images morally elucidates without generating moral full stops.

Consideration of the full range of means by which humans will be enhanced requires a correspondingly wide range of moral images. The following three chapters explore three images of enhancement. However, the purpose of my first moral images specific to these technologies is not to urge a positive view of enhancement; instead, they counter two conservative arguments that, if successful, would demonstrate the moral impossibility of liberal eugenics. First, I examine the argument that human cloning and genetic engineering are wrong because they violate some deep, inchoate sense of what is right for us. This line of thinking has come to be called the 'yuck' argument. It is most closely associated with Leon Kass. The second conservative argument is that enhancement should be banned because it would take the meaning out of human existence.

ARE ENHANCEMENT TECHNOLOGIES WRONG BECAUSE THEY ARE 'YUCKY'?

Kass is very impressed by the queasiness that typically accompanies contemplation of the possibility of cloning humans. He proposes that this unease is 'the emotional expression of deep wisdom, beyond reason's power to fully articulate it'. Kass continues: 'We are repelled by the prospect of cloning human beings...because we intuit and feel, immediately and without argument, the violation of things that we rightfully hold dear.'[27] In chapter 2 I argued that we must make the new genetic technologies morally transparent. According to Kass, significant parts of morality itself are not transparent. We often know that we are disgusted by a certain practice without understanding precisely why we are disgusted. Kass asks of other abhorrent activities such as 'father–daughter incest (even with consent), or having sex with animals, or mutilating a corpse, or eating human flesh, or even just (just!) raping and murdering another human being' whether 'anybody's failure to give full rational justification for his or her revulsion at these practices make that revulsion ethically suspect.'[28] The contention that there is no decisive argument against human cloning should be understood not as support for cloning, but instead as an expression of rationality's impotence when faced with an issue that bears on human existence in such a fundamental way. Instinctual disgust is the only reliable guide.

Kass's 'yuck' argument sounds like cheating. Placing the conservative's conclusion about biotechnology beyond reason's reach goes against the grain for those who are used to rationally justifying their moral conclusions. Consider one of Kass's examples. You may not pause to justify your disgust at a rape murder, but you are confident that, were you to be called on to do so, you could. Yet the 'yuck' argument is designed for reactions of disgust that lack an obvious rationale. Those who are not instinctually repelled by human cloning will complain that Kass is even worse than people who refuse to reflect on why they find biotechnology disgusting. Kass is presuming to foist his revulsion on others.

In what follows, I argue that Kass's 'yuck' argument has a place in the moral debate about biotechnology. Seeing where it belongs requires us to separate the two major contemporary moral debates about biotechnology. While we are at the very beginning of the era of genetically modifying ourselves, the era of genetically modifying our food is well under way. The multinational company Monsanto has genetically modified canola to withstand its proprietary herbicide, Roundup. Genetic engineers have inserted DNA from the bacterium *Bacillus thuringiensis* into other crops; plants modified in this way produce a toxin effective against insect pests. These first-generation GM crops are currently planted throughout North America and in other parts of the world. Agricultural biotechnologists talk with great enthusiasm about the power of genetic engineering to end starvation and improve the health of all. Environmentalist and anti-globalization organizations oppose their plans with equal vigour. Although I am suspicious of Kass's deployment of it against human biotechnology, I argue that 'yuck' belongs in their argumentative armoury of those who argue against genetically modified crops. It should be no great revelation that 'yuck' is better deployed against those who would put strange food on our plates than against those who defend new ways to bring people into existence.

The moral images of racism and homophobia show why we should not accept uncritically the message of our guts about the moral status of other people. There are those who are made uncomfortable by the idea of people whose skin colour or sexual orientations differ from their own. It is not surprising that we sometimes feel this way about those who differ from us; an attitude of suspicion towards people who are unfamiliar would have served our Pleistocene ancestors well. However, there is a gap between explaining a widespread attitude and justifying it. Most of us have an idea of moral progress that involves subjecting our subrational urges and aversions to rational scrutiny. Consider the people who refuse to convert the discomfort they feel when in the company of people whose skin colour differs from their own into a negative moral judgement about them. Is what they are doing ignoring the message of their guts – or, put more eloquently, ignoring the 'the emotional expression of deep wisdom, beyond reason's power to fully articulate it'? Surely these people are not to be chastised but, instead, applauded for allowing reason to guide them.

Kass might deny that he is passing a negative moral judgement on clones, insisting that the 'yuck' reaction is specific to the process that brought them into existence. The distinction between condemning a class of people and condemning the means by which they were brought into existence seems lost outside of the philosophy classroom; it is only a small consolation to be informed that the hate is not directed at you, but at the means by which your kind is created. Suppose, however, that we can play up the moral significance of this difference. The moral image of IVF shows the inadmissibility of instinctual suspicion about the way in which a person is made. Kass's 'yuck' argument against reproductive cloning is a direct descendant of his earlier disgust for IVF, disgust that now appears misguided.[29] We should not interpret the growing acceptance of IVF as a decline in the understanding of how humans should be. This is not to say that IVF is not a worthy target for moral questioning. Recently there has been concern about intracytoplasmic sperm injection (ICSI), a technology sometimes combined with IVF. ICSI involves the injection of individual spermatozoa into eggs. One study found a higher rate of malformation in the urogenital systems, guts, muscles, bones and skin of children conceived in this way.[30] It is one thing, however, to use a scientific finding as a premise in an argument for more tightly regulating IVF, but quite another to ban IVF because we just can not get the erroneous image of foetuses growing in test tubes out of our minds. We should take exactly the same attitude to cloned or genetically engineered human beings. If we lack a rationally persuasive reason to find their existence wrongful, we should not translate queasiness into moral condemnations.

WHY FOOD IS DIFFERENT

In his defence of genetically modified food Gregory Pence complains that his opponents think that they can offer 'yuck' in the place of a rational argument.[31] He is right that many of the reasons people give for rejecting GM food are silly. When told that a gene that prevents the freezing of the blood of arctic fish may be introduced into tomatoes, people fear that their tomatoes will taste fishy. They forget that genetic engineers will be introducing into tomatoes only one among the tens of thousands of fish genes. Fish and sheep are both vertebrates and hence share many more genes with each other than either does with the genetically modified tomato. But those commenting on the fishiness of the lamb you have served them are much more likely to be passing judgement on your cooking than to be reflecting on the collection of tastes that gives lamb its distinctive flavour.

Such mistakes notwithstanding, 'yuck' can support the rejection of GM food. Although people shouldn't go with their guts in condemning people of different races, they can in deciding which food to eat and which to spurn. Imagine the waiter who refused to take your order for vanilla ice cream because you present him with nothing more than an expression of disgust for other flavours. A simple preference is a bad reason for choosing to hire a white rather than a black person, but it can justify choosing vanilla over chocolate ice cream.

What is involved in the judgement that one food tastes better than another? Call the properties of a food that influence what it is like to eat, its taste properties. Other important properties of a food, such as how it contributes to human well-being, or the environmental impact of its cultivation, do not count directly towards its taste. However, I will argue that these properties, or at least how these properties are perceived, may contribute indirectly towards its taste. To see this we must distinguish between what we can call *narrow* and *wide taste properties*. The properties of food that make an immediate difference to the experience of eating it are its *narrow taste properties*. Chocolate and vanilla ice cream differ in ways that are directly detectable by our taste buds and this means that there is a difference in their narrow taste properties. A cursory survey demonstrates that our experience of eating food is influenced by a variety of factors beyond its narrow taste properties. People prefer some brands of Scandinavian vodka because they believe them to contain glacial water. They like to hear that they are eating fresh rather than dried basil in their pesto pasta even when there is no immediately detectible difference. The knowledge that meat was slaughtered in a religiously prescribed way can make a difference between food's being delicious or disgusting. I call these determinants of taste *wide taste properties*.

Preferring one food to another because of a difference in wide taste properties may not seem entirely rational, but liking or loathing food has never been limited to its immediate impact on our taste buds. It is hard to think of a culture that has come close to complying with a prescription to take into account only narrow taste properties when describing the experience of eating. The basics of human physiology are likely to set limits on the variation in people's perception of narrow taste properties, but there is considerable relativity in wide taste properties; our perception of them is influenced by aspects of culture, such as our histories or religious beliefs. Relativity does not imply ease of modification. The broad taste properties of Western foods may be tweaked by marketing jingles – Ronald

McDonald can help us to like food that might otherwise taste bland or bad. But even in the West, influences on the difference between good and bad food are linked to central elements of culture. We really are a long way off the science fiction scenarios in which people happily take their food in tablet or toothpaste form.

The distinction between narrow and wide taste properties helps us to understand some of the complaints about GM food. Consider food made out of crops genetically modified to contain the gene from the *Bacillus thuringiensis* bacterium, otherwise known as Bt crops. Although there is unlikely to be any difference in the narrow tastes of ordinary tacos and tacos made from Bt corn, there may be wide taste differences between them. If religious people can think that meat tastes better because of its means of slaughter, then others can prefer tacos made from natural ingredients. This difference in taste need not be dispelled by pointing out the falsehood of some of popular beliefs about transgenic corn. Muslims wavering in their faith may still prefer the experience of eating meat slaughtered in the traditional way. So too, opponents of GM food may have many of the factual errors in their arguments pointed out to them, but still feel as justified in saying that natural food tastes better. It is no more incumbent on them to produce a complete rational explanation for their food preferences than it is on the person who prefers vanilla to chocolate ice cream.

The anti-GM activist, Vandana Shiva, was pilloried when she argued against accepting GM food sent as aid after a cyclone in the Indian state of Orissa.[32] The approach to taste that I am recommending can help us to understand her position. One could imagine that some people with no moral objection to eating the body parts of their dead friends would, when faced with starvation, refuse to do so because they found the idea so disgusting. Given that the alternative is certain death, this response may not be sensible, but it wouldn't have been irrational for them to accept some risk of starvation in the hope that rescuers would find them before they had to eat human flesh. Returning to Shiva's argument, she may have been speaking up for cyclone victims prepared to accept a heightened risk of death to avoid consuming food that they find repellent. Of course, we should pass a different judgement on Shiva if she was mistaken about the cultural values that the people of Orissa associate with food. She might then be trying to prevent people from eating food that both could have saved their lives and that they did not find at all repellent. If this is the case, then Shiva's 'yuck' reaction should no sooner prevent them from eating

GM food than should my dislike for bananas prevent you from eating them.

Kass's opponents are right to criticize him for transferring to thinking about humans language whose proper place is the evaluation of food; just because some people can not stomach the idea of human clones does not show that we should think of them as a morally inferior brand of humanity. But they should grant 'yuck' its proper place in our moral evaluation of genetically modified food. Although it may not be the deciding moral consideration, it should be given some weight.

ARE ENHANCEMENT TECHNOLOGIES WRONG
BECAUSE THEY WILL DESTROY MEANING?

Conservatives do not rely only on their guts to protect them against reproductive technologies. They object that these technologies give us what we say we want, but only in a form purged of its proper human significance. Kass explains that biotechnologists pay 'little attention to what it means to begin to change the deep structure of human activity, severing performance from effort or, in other cases, pleasure from activity that ordinarily is its foundation'.[33]

The argument from meaning plays out in different ways in respect of different biotechnologies. Those who argue for reproductive cloning represent this use of somatic cell nuclear transfer as satisfying hitherto unsatisfiable desires. People suffering from infertility resistant to other therapies could use it to become parents. Reproductive cloning could also help someone who wants a child whose genome does not contain some other person's nuclear DNA. This book considers it principally as a means of choosing the characteristics of one's children. Kass thinks that in giving people the reproductive options that they ask for, cloning takes something less tangible away from them – it destroys the meaning that sexuality brings to human lives:

Sexuality brings with it a new and enriched relationship to the world. Only sexual animals can seek and find complementary others with whom to pursue a goal that transcends their own existence. For a sexual being, the world is no longer an indifferent and largely homogeneous *otherness*, in part edible, in part dangerous. It also contains some very special and related and complementary beings, of the same kind but of opposite sex, toward whom one reaches out with special interest and intensity.[34]

Kass makes the same kinds of points against human genetic engineering. The embryo that a couple offers to a genetic engineer for modification may contain nuclear DNA from both of them. But the attempt to improve upon sex's power to provide the kinds of children we want threatens the meanings of love and of making families that we humans have layered on to the biological functions of sex and reproduction.

Transhumanists deny that enhancement technologies destroy meaning. They speak of 'aesthetic and contemplative pleasures whose blissfulness vastly exceeds what any human has yet experienced' and 'love that is stronger, purer, and more secure than any human has yet harbored'.[35] Deciding who to believe requires moral images constructed from other cases in which a technology has separated the satisfaction of a desire from its customary foundation. We can use our judgement about whether this separation has destroyed meaning as a guide to what to say about the similar propensity of enhancement technologies.

Consider the moral image of food finding. Finding, cultivating and preparing food were the most difficult and time-consuming of our distant ancestors' activities. The hunting of certain animals required teamwork and entailed a risk of death; crops would be planted only to fail. Technology has transformed the significance of food and of the methods historically used to procure it. Although many people fish and hunt recreationally, these activities are travesties of the fishing and hunting of our ancestors. We get food in other ways. But putting a jar of pasta sauce in a supermarket trolley has little of the significance of a successful hunt on the African savannah; it is a comparatively meaningless activity for us. To use Kass's language, modern supermarkets and fishing rods sever the satisfaction of desires from the activities that have historically been their foundations. The question we must ask is whether their advent has taken meaning from our lives.

An affirmative answer to this question ignores the propensity for the human mind to invest things with meaning. Technology has *displaced* – but not destroyed – the meaning associated with procuring and preparing of food. One doesn't greet one's dinner guests with 'I have meat.' Instead, one prepares beef Wellington. The food one presents to them is superior to – or at least interestingly different from – the food one could have bought, ready-made, at the supermarket. Its style of preparation and presentation bears the stamp of the host. We use some of the time that our ancestors would have spent finding and preparing food to read novels, watch movies and reflect on the meaning of life. Or we go fishing, which is usually much more about spending time with nature than bringing it home for the cooking pot.

Supermarkets and fishing rods seem to have displaced, but not destroyed, the meanings associated with finding and preparing food. Kass needs to give us a reason why enhancement technologies will not merely displace, but destroy the meanings associated with sex. Contraception allows people to have sex without risking reproduction. Cloning may complete this separation by allowing people to have children without sex. One does not have to be a transhumanist to imagine that in societies that endorse enhancement technologies, people will still reach out to others and derive great joy from their relationships with them. Sex will continue to be fun in the era of reproductive cloning. And sex with someone you love will continue to be even more fun.

FOOD FINDING shows that we should not rush to condemn a technology simply because it severs an activity from its customary foundation. However, I do not present this moral image as decisively resolving the debate with those who think that enhancement technologies void human lives of meaning. In chapter 5 I will consider Fukuyama's argument that these technologies take meaning out of human lives by taking the 'human' out of them.

CHAPTER 4

The Moral Image of Therapy

In chapter 1 I alluded to a very potent moral image of enhancement, one that points in a direction diametrically opposed to the liberal view I defend. This is image is NAZI EUGENICS. We are accustomed to thinking of the Holocaust as an entirely singular event, standing apart from the other horrors of the Second World War. However, those who study the history of eugenics view it as the most terrible element of the Nazi programme of human enhancement.[1] The death camps were supposed to rid Europe of lesser peoples, clearing space for the purified population of Aryans that the other arm of Nazi eugenics would produce. Defenders of liberal eugenics must find moral images that clearly distinguish their programme from what the Nazis attempted. In the last chapter we saw how the moral image of therapy was called upon to justify the harvesting of stem cells from clone embryos. In this chapter I consider how THERAPY might apply to human biotechnology more broadly.

THE BIOTECHNOLOGICAL SOLUTION TO DISEASE

October 1990 marked the formal start of the Human Genome Project, an international effort to identify the three billion base pairs that constitute the human genome and to discover all of the 30,000 to 40,000 human genes. The project was sold to the public on the basis of two ideas. One of these was the somewhat metaphysical notion that deep truths about the human condition would be revealed once we had the complete map of our genome. Gene sequencers would fill the cultural role recently vacated by

Freudian psychologists, who had, in their turn, displaced priests as the experts on that significant part of us hidden from self-reflection. I will have something to say about this metaphysical idea and its allied thesis of genetic determinism in this chapter.

The other marketing idea was more practical. James Watson's fame as co-discoverer of the structure of DNA made him the obvious choice as inaugural director of the Human Genome Project. Watson is no retiring, white-coated sage. In an address given at the University of California at Berkeley in 2000, he showed a slide of a pouting supermodel to demonstrate that thin people are miserable, and therefore ambitious. Watson said of happy but unambitious fat people, 'Whenever you interview fat people, you feel bad, because you know you're not going to hire them.'[2] Comments like these have made Watson and the study of human genetics many enemies. However, Watson also knows how to make friends for genetic research. He said: 'What the public wants is not to be sick, and if we help them not to be sick, they'll be on our side.'[3] Marketers of the Human Genome Project presented genes as the root causes of disease. Addressing them, therefore, promised the most complete cures. A great sense of expectation accompanied the discoveries of genes linked with Huntington's, Alzheimer's and breast cancer. It was hoped that there would soon be therapies for these conditions as miraculous as the methods that were unearthing their causes. At a press conference called to announce that the Human Genome Project and the privately funded Celera Genomics had completed a draft of the human genome, Craig Venter, Celera's CEO, proclaimed that the rough, gappy record represented 'a new starting point for science and medicine, with potential impact on every disease'. He continued, 'There's at least the potential to reduce the number of cancer deaths to zero in our own lifetimes.'[4] President Bill Clinton offered a more poetic expression of the same sentiment, conjecturing that it 'is conceivable that our children's children will know the term Cancer only as a constellation of stars'.[5]

With the turning of the millennium, rhetoric is beginning to be matched by therapies. Severe Combined Immune Deficiency is otherwise known by its acronym SCID, or more widely still as 'bubble boy disease'.[6] People with SCID lack two crucial elements of the immune system, leaving them fatally vulnerable to infection. In 2002, French doctors announced that they had used gene therapy to cure four young boys of X-linked SCID. This form is found almost exclusively in males because it results from a defective gene on the X chromosome. Males do not have the insurance possessed by females, whose second X can compensate for a defective gene on the first one. The gene therapy involved removing bone marrow cells and infecting them with a virus modified to carry the good version of the gene lacked by the boys. The replacement gene was taken up by the bone marrow cells, which, when returned to the boys, appeared to provide them with perfectly normal immune systems.

However, the story of this biotech breakthrough does not end here. Two of the recipients of the gene therapy have developed leukaemia.[7] This is unlikely to be a coincidence. Leukaemia results from a breakdown in the bone marrow's regulation of the production of white blood cells, and the bone marrow was the target of the gene therapy. Defenders of the trial urge that we balance the great harm of leukaemia against the even greater harm of SCID. This kind of response seems less satisfactory when offered by gene therapists as a plea in mitigation for their part in the fate of a young man suffering from a different disease. In 1999, 18-year-old Jesse Gelsinger died after receiving gene therapy for ornithine transcarbamylase deficiency, a serious liver disorder that causes ammonia to build up in the body.[8] He appears to have been killed by the supposedly harmless virus used to insert the gene he required into the cells of his liver.[9]

These cases make it clear that late twentieth-and early twenty-first-century gene therapies should not be likened to the medicine practised by most doctors. EXPERIMENTAL THERAPY is a more precise moral image for early twenty-first-century gene therapy than plain THERAPY. The former image aligns gene therapy not with insulin shots or surgery to remove infected tonsils, but instead with artificial hearts and treatments for epilepsy that involve the cutting of the corpus callosum. EXPERIMENTAL THERAPY carries some of the negative moral associations of the moral image of research discussed last chapter. Artificial hearts are so experimental that they are suitable only for those with heart disease intractable by more conventional methods. The same reasoning applies to twenty-first-century gene therapies.

It is important not to confuse the qualified approbation implied by EXPERIMENTAL THERAPY with the more robust endorsement of THERAPY. I will not make too much of the difference between the two images, however. The pragmatic optimism about genetic technologies that I recommended in chapter 2 idealizes about their development and efficacy so that we can scrutinize the motives behind them. Pragmatic optimists about gene therapies will ask what moral conclusions we should draw about them in an era in which they are no more dangerous than today's conventional remedies.

The most philosophically thorough advocates of viewing gene therapy as an extension of conventional medicine are Allen Buchanan, Dan Brock, Norman Daniels and Daniel Wikler.[10] They coin an expression, 'the colonization of the natural by the just', to describe a new set of duties accompanying the emergence of genetic technologies.[11] Previously we had to accept genetic predispositions to disease as natural givens. We were limited to indirect moral remedies that, at best, would reduce disease's impact on equality of opportunity. The new genetic technologies will enable us to tackle the causes of some natural misfortune directly. Buchanan et al. offer the same manner of justification for gene therapy as they do for conventional medicine. Gene therapies, like conventional medicine, bring persons up to a baseline of capabilities that enables them to pursue a wide range of ways of life with realistic chances of success. The state has an obligation to make conventional medicines available to citizens. It must also provide gene therapies.

In this chapter I focus on two areas of uncertainty concerning the application of the moral image of therapy to enhancement technologies. The first concerns the individuals who receive treatment. It seems an important part of the idea of therapy that it can benefit those who receive it. Yet in many uses of genetic medicine it is difficult to identify a candidate for benefits. A second kind of uncertainty concerns the conditions that gene therapy will remedy. According to conventional wisdom, the limits of the therapeutic domain are set by the notion of disease. A procedure can be called a therapy only when it is directed at a disease state, yet it is hard to find definitions of disease suitable to serve as a moral guideline for genetic technologies.

WHO BENEFITS FROM GENE THERAPY?

The big money in human biotechnology leads to frequent suggestions that the real beneficiaries of experimental therapies are not patients but investors.[12] There is, however, a deeper philosophical puzzle about the benefits of certain kinds of gene therapy. The replacement of a defective gene with a good version in the cells of a child suffering from SCID exhibits the same pattern of relationships between patient, disease and doctor as found in ordinary medicine. However, this is not how some biotech cures will work.

In some cases, the intervention will predate the existence of any individual who might be identified as a patient. For example, Pre-implantation Genetic Diagnosis enables parents to avoid using embryos that have genes linked with SCID, and other serious conditions such as fragile X syndrome and Tay–Sachs. Although it is clear that PGD helps people to have children who do not suffer from these conditions, it is less obvious that anyone is treated by the procedure. Talk of curing or treating assumes the existence of an individual to be cured or treated. PGD merely substitutes one person who has a high chance of suffering from a given condition with another person less likely to be afflicted.

These conclusions may also apply to the genetic modification of embryos. According to the necessity of origin view expounded by the philosopher Saul Kripke, each of us necessarily has the origin that we in fact had.[13] Changing facts about my origin would not have the effect of bringing me into existence in a different way, rather it would bring a different individual into existence in my stead. The view that my actual beginning is necessary to me is frequently conjoined with a view about the event that marked my beginning. Kripke thinks that I originated with the meeting of a particular sperm with a particular egg.[14] This thesis has direct implications for gene therapy that occurs at or near the point of conception. Both eggs and sperm are essentially packages of DNA, designed by natural selection to begin a new organism upon en-countering complementary gametes. Changing the DNA of a sperm would seem to change the sperm's identity. This makes the event of the modified sperm meeting an egg a different one from the event of the unmodified sperm meeting the same egg. The same point applies to the genetic modification of an early embryo. The replacement of a disease gene in an egg, a sperm or an embryo does not benefit the person who emerges. It merely enables that person to take the place of another. The inadmissibility of talk about benefits places these uses of enhancement technologies outside of the scope of THERAPY. Doctors seek to cure their patients, not to replace them with numerically distinct healthy people.[15]

I offer two lines of response to this challenge. The first response questions the connection between THERAPY and the provision of bene-fits. Although in many cases therapy has the goal of benefiting someone, I argue that we also apply the concept to cases in which there is no identifiable beneficiary. The second line of response is that exchanging a good for a bad version of a gene in an early embryo can often be seen as benefiting the individual that emerges.

Kass presents the use of genetic technologies to treat disease 'by eliminating the patient' as a 'peculiar innovation in medicine'.[16] But he is wrong. Consider the following example. Women who drink during pregnancy sometimes give birth to children suffering from foetal alcohol syndrome, a condition characterized by abnormal facial features, stunted growth and central nervous system problems. Suppose a woman who is currently drinking heavily asks her doctor for advice about whether or not she should get pregnant. He responds that she should not get pregnant until she has cut down on her drinking – in effect advising that she substitute the child she would have while not drinking for the one she would have while on alcohol. Does the fact that the healthy child would not exist at all had his mother become pregnant earlier make him a beneficiary of therapy? If we count his existence as a benefit conferred by the doctor, then we should be similarly generous to a sceptical father who postpones his daughter's marriage, thereby delaying the birth of her first child. This does not seem right. The important point is that, however we understand the case of the doctor advising his patient to cut down on her drinking before getting pregnant, it is not medical malpractice. We would not accuse the doctor of recklessly straying outside of the therapeutic domain. Perhaps no one is benefited, but disease is still prevented, and if so, the moral image of therapy can encompass PGD and gene therapy on gametes or early embryos.[17] Both conventional doctors and gene therapists act morally in allowing a healthy baby to be born in place of an unhealthy one.[18]

The conclusion that genetic engineering can be vindicated by appeal to THERAPY even if it does not confer benefits skirts around the philosophical riddle of benefits and genetic technologies. I now argue that many ways of altering the genes of early embryos do not interfere with the identities of the individuals involved. In such cases, we can understand gene therapists as benefiting the individuals they help into existence.[19] The discussion that follows is perhaps the most philosophically involved in the book. Readers happy to concede that someone can be benefited or harmed by the genetic modification of her embryo can jump ahead to the discussion of the concept of disease later in this chapter.

ARE WE ESSENTIALLY HUMAN BEINGS
OR ESSENTIALLY PERSONS, AND DOES IT MATTER?

There is a dispute that intersects with the one concerning my relationship with my origins. Two views about what kind of being I am lead to different answers to the question of when it was that I originated. If I am essentially a *human being* then my existence begins with the meeting of a sperm and an egg. This is the point at which there is a genetically human organism. According to an alternative position, I am essentially a *person*; my beginning is marked by the onset of complex psychological traits deemed constitutive of personhood. Although this line coincides with popular views about what makes me morally significant, it has some strikes against it. Eric Olson plays up the implausibility of denying that I was ever an embryo or indeed a new-born baby.[20] If I am essentially a human being then person-hood may mark me off in moral terms from wildebeest and cockroaches but, like toddler and university student, it is a property that I start without, acquire and then, possibly, lose.

I propose to bypass this debate. We can address the issue of which events are necessary for me without resolving the question of when it was that I began and whether I am essentially a human being or a person. The analysis I present remains neutral on the issue of whether I am essentially a human being, something that comes into existence with the meeting of a sperm and an egg, or whether I am essentially a person, something brought into existence at the onset of self-awareness. We reduce the significance of the debate about what kind of being I am if we clearly distinguish the necessity of origin view from the stronger thesis that the sameness of origins is both necessary *and sufficient* for the preservation of my identity in an alternative situation.[21] The pure necessity view allows that factors beyond my origins can also be necessary to my existence. This means that my being essentially a person does not prevent the joining of a particular sperm and egg from being necessary to me; although misla-belled as my origin, this event may still be one without which I could not have existed. The view that I am essentially a human being allows an analogous separation of facts about origins from facts about what is necessary to my existence. For example, the evolution of the human species would be necessary for my existence while pre-dating it.

In what follows, I argue that regardless of whether we are essentially human beings or persons, we have no good reason to privilege the formation of my embryo. Believing in the special significance of the meeting of my sperm and egg is tacitly tied to a genetic determinist view of development. Interpolating the true view of human development into our thinking about our origins has important implications for THERAPY's application to gene therapy. It will allow us to think of quite significant genetic changes as benefiting the individual that results.

GENETIC INFLUENCES, ENVIRONMENTAL INFLUENCES AND THE FORMATION OF HUMAN IDENTITIES

Genetic determinists make the formation of a person's embryo an extremely significant event for her identity. According to them, the formation of a person's genome causally necessitates her every significant characteristic. In chapter 2 I suggested that genetic determinism fails to take account of the important role of the environment. The question of the relative significance to human beings of environmental and genetic influences has occasioned many an academic spat. Genetic determinism finds its ideological counterpart in *environmental determinism*. According to environmental determinists, our educational and nutritional environments fully determine who we are, while genes make no contribution, beyond perhaps fixing our membership of the human species. Defenders of this view often express optimism about the power of the education system to achieve almost any reworking of human beings.[22] We should avoid the impulse to transpose the struggle between the advocates of genes and the advocates of the environment into our picture of the relationship between gene and environment. While their advocates may be fundamentally opposed, hereditary influences and environmental influences are not. According to the *interactionist* conception of development, traits are both essentially genetic and essentially environmental.[23] A person's intelligence, athletic skill and emotional sensitivity result from the intermingling of genetic influences with uterine, nutritional and cultural influences.

Richard Dawkins has argued that for most evolutionary processes we have a choice of whether we adopt a gene's view, thinking of evolution as essentially the struggle between genetic lineages, or an individual's view, thinking of evolution fundamentally as a struggle between different individuals.[24] We have a similar choice when it comes to development. Some descriptions make genes the active forces in the construction of human beings. Others present the environment as active. Viewed one way, genes make human beings, but they rely on environmental influences to determine when they get turned on, when they get turned off, and what kinds of biological structures they end up building. Viewed from the environmental standpoint, protein-rich food builds strong and healthy bodies and excellent teaching makes knowledgeable minds, but only by working in conjunction with genes.

Consider Dean Hamer's announcement in 1993 that he had found a genetic marker indicating the existence of a gene that influences male sexual orientation.[25] The media baptized this discovery 'the gay gene', but it is more accurately described as a sexual-orientation gene, with heterosexual and homosexual variants. Hamer's evidence pointed towards a location at the end of the long arm of the X chromosome in a region designated q28. This evidence came from the analysis of the DNA of forty pairs of gay brothers. Thirty-three of these pairs of brothers were found to share a version of a highly variable stretch of X chromosome DNA. This is a much greater number than the approximately twenty that one would expect to share versions of this genetic marker by chance. Hamer reasoned that the only statistically possible explanation was that the marker was near a gene linked with something the brothers had in common: their homosexuality.

The research on Xq28 and male homosexuality subsequent to Hamer's announcement has followed a similar pattern to that exhibited by the behavioural genetics of intelligence described in chapter 2. At the time of the publication of his results, Hamer thought he had narrowed the location of the sexual-orientation gene to a five million base pair region flanked by two markers on the X chromosome.[26] He hoped that his discovery would lead swiftly to the isolation and sequencing of the gene. This is yet to happen. There was a setback when one study failed to confirm the finding.[27] However, what perturbs Hamer most is the indifference displayed by the scientific establishment towards the genetics of sexuality. He complains that in the seven years since his result 'only three experimental studies of the topic have been undertaken, and only two of those were published'. Hamer hypothesizes that 'perhaps sexuality is still considered too private, too controversial, and too embarrassing to be studied scientifically'.[28]

In what follows, I take Hamer's finding at face value, using it to make a series of points about the relative contributions of genes and environments to human identities. Hamer was widely understood as showing that a man's sexual orientation is entirely fixed by his genes – that being born with the homosexual version of the gene at Xq28 would ensure a gay future, and that the heterosexual version of the gene would guarantee a straight future. But he certainly did not show this. Some pairs of gay brothers displayed variation in the marker at Xq28, and therefore could have had different versions of the claimed sexual-orientation gene. Furthermore, some heterosexual brothers of Hamer's target group of gay siblings were concordant for the marker at Xq28 – they, in all likelihood, had the same sexual-orientation gene as their brothers who had turned out gay.

Properly understood, Hamer's genetic strategy does not conflict with attempts to explain homosexuality by pointing to events in gay people's environments. Only an extreme environmental determinism, according to which genes made no contribution at all to sexual orientation, would preclude Hamer's conclusion. But few of the accounts offered by those interested in environmental explanation of differences in sexual orienta-tion are of this type. Take the strategy of environmental explanation pursued by Toronto-based psychologist Ray Blanchard. Blanchard found that when he compared a random sample of 302 gay men with a group of heterosexual men, the gay men had greater numbers of older brothers than did the straight men.[29] The average number of older brothers for the gay men was 1.31, while the figure for the heterosexual men was 0.96. He observed that for each older brother, a man's chances of being gay increased by a third. Why this effect? According to Blanchard, it may result from a maternal immune reaction prompted by a Y chromosome protein on the surface of cells. He hypothesizes that this reaction may affect foetal brain cells in such a way as to influence sexual orientation. With each male child, and each new exposure to the Y chromosome protein, the strength of reaction increases, and so its impact on the sexual orientation of male children becomes more pronounced.

This explanation mentions genes, specifically a Y chromosome gene that places a protein on the cells of male foetuses. However, Blanchard's is not a genetic explanation. To see this we must appreciate that Blanchard's theory is consistent with all Y chromosomes producing the protein that prompts the maternal immune response. Therefore, differences in Y chromosome genes are not being called upon to explain differences in sexual orientation. Rather, an environmental difference is key. Later-born sons face a uterine environment crucially different from that encountered by their older brothers.

Hamer and Blanchard are clearly looking in different places for influences on male sexual orientation. But their explanations are not mutually exclusive – they may just be focusing on different parts of the complete story about why some men are gay and others are straight. Hamer demonstrates appropriate modesty about the Xq28 gene when he suggests that it 'plays some role in about 5 to 30 percent of gay men'.[30] This clearly leaves a great deal of room for the environmental influence of birth order. It is possible that Hamer's genetic factor and Blanchard's environmental factor sometimes work in tandem to shape men's sexuality. Perhaps male babies with a specific variant of a gene at Xq28 aggravate the immune response initially provoked by the Y chromosome protein.

So, are genetic determinists right about the effects of any genes? Consider Huntington's disease, a condition sometimes presented as a proof of genetic determinism. Huntington's is an inherited neurodegenerative disorder that progressively destroys a person's cognitive faculties and her control over her muscles, leading eventually to death. The normal age of onset is the forties, though the disease may strike as early as adolescence. Huntington's results from a dominant gene that has been mapped to chromosome 4. While a recessive gene can cause disease only if it is paired on a genome with another copy of itself, a dominant gene can cause disease regardless of whether it is paired with another bad copy. At first glance, there are similarities between the notions of genetic dominance and genetic determinism. The Huntington's variant of the gene seems to produce the effect for which it is named regardless of its genetic and environmental context. Anyone who has the gene, supposing they live long enough, eventually manifests symptoms. However, thinking of Huntington's in a genetic determinist way seems to preclude any possibility of a cure that does not involve modifying genes. Although no one should doubt that preventing the ruinous effects of this gene will be immensely difficult, it is surely a mistake to think that a cure that does not involve genetic engineering is in principle impossible. Researchers may never find a drug that prevents Huntington's disease, but their goal is not the metaphysical impossibility that genetic determinism threatens to make it. Suppose this cure were to be discovered and made widely available. An environmental change would have made it the case that the Huntington's variant of the gene is present in the genomes of many human beings without ever producing Huntington's symptoms.

The preceding discussion of the relationship is important for understanding the effects of enhancement technologies. It prepares the way for the moral image of nurture that compares the effects of genetic and environmental enhancements in chapter 6. My principal purpose here, however, is to explore the implications of changes to genetic and environmental influences for human identities.

INTERACTIONISM'S IMPLICATIONS FOR IDENTITY

Interactionism about development puts pressure on any view of how human identities are formed that privileges the meeting of sperm and egg. Although a person's genes perform their part of the developmental double act from within his cells, this does not bind his identity any more intimately to his genome than to his environment. His genes, like the nutrients provided in his mother's womb and the first words he heard, stand at one causal remove from his distinctive properties.

Perhaps a person's genes matter more than his environment to his identity because of when he acquires them. If we exclude, for the time being, the possibility of genetic modification, he gets his distinctive genome when his embryo comes into existence. Environmental influences, by contrast, can only operate after his embryo is formed. This difference may explain why even small changes to a person's genes at, or before, the time that he comes into existence, replace him with a numerically distinct individual, while quite substantial changes to his environment could not have this effect. He has not begun to exist, or is on the point of coming into existence, in the former case, while he already exists in the latter. The possibility of someone failing to exist after his embryo has come into existence has the air of self-contradiction, especially for those who think that we are essentially human beings. However, this possibility is compatible with the facts about human development. It is a direct consequence of rejecting a neat separation of genetic, identity-relevant changes from environmental, identity-irrelevant changes.

Compare the possibility of someone failing to exist because of a change after his origin with another case. Suppose we reach agreement on the event that marked the beginning of the First World War. Consider an alternative history in which everything happens identically right up until a point one week after this event. Events now unfold very differently. A peace is reached, German soldiers withdraw from Belgium, and there are no further hostilities. Despite the fact that the events that actually marked the First World War's beginning are included in this alternative history, I think we have described a possibility in which the First World War never happened, rather than one in which it happened very differently. Whether or not we count the beginning of a conflict in an alternative history as the beginning of the First World War depends, in part, on events subsequent to that beginning. The brief skirmish in this alternative history lacks too many of the First World War's properties to be counted as the same event as it.

As it is with wars, so it is with human individuals. It is a mistake to think that changes to embryonic DNA are necessarily connected to an individual's origin in a way that changes to her environment are not. An inclusive approach to the influences that shape human identities allows us to count events subsequent to a person's origin among those that are necessary to him. This means that changes to events after my origin might have made it the case that I never existed at all.

What matters in development is not so much the time at which a person acquires a given gene, but instead the timing of the gene's *influence*. Many changes to DNA will have their significant effects only much later than the formation of the genome. For example, geneticists think that a mutation to the APP gene on chromosome 21 gives one an elevated risk of early-onset Alzheimer's.[31] The first symptoms of this form of the disease can strike in the sufferer's thirties or forties. Suppose we exchange an embryo's high-risk version of APP for the normal version. This seems a significant change, but regardless of its significance, the embryo's initial developmental stages will proceed as if no change had occurred. Two cells will become four and four eight in much the same way. The effects of the different gene will become apparent only some time after the recipient of the therapy comes into existence. This is also true of our example in chapter 2 of the genetic enhancement of intelligence. Although the modification of the DNA may pre-date or coincide with an individual's coming into existence, the major effects of this change take place only well after an individual comes into existence. This distinction between the time at which the causes of an influence are put in place, and the time at which the influence operates, applies also to the environment. Suppose a community introduces a programme of universal vaccination of children against tuberculosis. We can trace the origin of the influence – immunization against TB – back to the original decision by the community leaders to establish the programme. This event pre-dates the birth of people who are now immunized, but the influence affects a child's distinctive properties only once her primed immune system encounters tuberculosis.

Failing to separate changes to genes from changes to the environment in terms of their relevance to our identities forces some difficult choices. The extreme options of saying either that *any* or *no* counterfactual change to a person's environment or genes would have resulted in a numerically distinct individual seem equally implausible. The first option requires us to say that my parents' choosing a different brand of baby food would have resulted in an entirely different person taking my place. According to the second, changes to every single distinctive base pair of my genome and the freezing of my embryo so that it would give rise to a human being born one thousand years after my actual birth would not have resulted in a different individual.

We can avoid these extremes if we say of both genetic and environmental influences that some are necessary and some are not. Although this seems sensible, it presents a conundrum. Deprived of the distinction between genetic and environmental influences, we need to find some other way to separate the necessary from the accidental elements of the processes that brought me into existence. Otherwise, we can not say which changes would substitute someone else for me and which would not.

There is unlikely to be a hard and fast rule distinguishing identity-altering changes from ones that do not disturb the identities of individuals involved. However, two factors do seem relevant. One is the magnitude of the change. Changes to many genetic influences, or significant parts of the environment in which someone is raised, are more likely to bring a numerically distinct individual into existence than are more minor ones. The second factor is the timing of the change. I have argued that changes to influences that operate after an individual's origin can make it the case that that individual never existed. Nevertheless, we should acknowledge that the modification of an early influence is more likely to result in a numerically distinct individual than is the modification of a later influence. It is important that we show no genetic or environmental bias in sorting early or significant changes from late or relatively inconsequential ones. The effects of a genetic fix for cystic fibrosis may be sufficiently significant, and manifest early enough, to produce an individual numerically distinct from the one who would have existed without the therapy. But perhaps the same should be said of surgery conducted immediately after birth to correct a serious heart defect. Both changes could be of the requisite magnitude to alter the identities of individuals who had come into existence before them.[32]

This book is chiefly concerned with a goal that reaches beyond the restoration of health – that of enhancement. Perhaps the use of genetic technologies to enhance is more likely to disrupt identity than is their use to treat disease. An affirmative answer would mean that while gene therapy often confers benefits, enhancement does not. It strikes me that enhancement is no more likely to disrupt identity than is the treatment of disease, making both equal candidates to be described as benefits. Consider the case of John Nash, the subject of the book and movie, *Beautiful Mind*. Nash is a mathematical genius and a schizophrenic. The former trait belatedly earned him a Nobel prize and the latter both alienated him from family and colleagues and gave him an extensive network of beliefs about aliens on Earth. Suppose we could have modified the DNA of Nash's early embryo in one of two ways. The first is to marginally increase his mathematical ability; the second is to remove the genetic basis of his paranoid schizophrenia. The first modification enhances – it produces a person with a certain ability way beyond that considered normal for human beings. The effect of the second is therapeutic – it brings the resulting person up to a level of functioning considered normal for human beings. In spite of this, we would say that the second change is more likely to result in a numerically distinct person than the first. It seems a much more significant change.

I have argued that some uses of genetic engineering at the time of the coming into existence of an individual leave identity intact and so can be understood as conferring benefits. Misuses of the same technology can therefore be interpreted as harming. These points apply both to the use of genetic engineering to eliminate genes linked with disease, and to its use to enhance. Other changes will be too significant to leave the recipient's identity intact. They can neither benefit nor harm. Fortunately, the moral image of therapy is sufficiently flexible that we do not always need to identify a single individual who benefits. Doctors already routinely substitute well for sick people. Genetic engineers should also be allowed to do this. If we can find moral images up to the task, they may also be permitted to substitute enhanced for well people.

THE SCOPE OF THERAPY AND THE NOTION OF DISEASE

I now address another problem with our application of THERAPY to genetic technologies. This problem concerns not the individuals that gene therapists seek to benefit, but instead the conditions that they treat. It is a commonplace that the job of the doctor is to treat disease. However, the notion of disease turns out to be difficult to define, and without an adequate definition we can not be certain of what is an appropriate use of gene therapy, and what is not. This may turn out to be a case in which applying an image derived from a familiar practice, that of conventional medicine, to the unfamiliar practices of genetic engineers casts doubt on what has hitherto gone unquestioned.

Need doctors be concerned that there may be no uncontroversial definitions of the notions central to their practice? One of the lessons of analytic philosophy is that almost no concept has an uncontroversial definition.[33] For example, it is difficult to say for certain whether or not the concept 'house' encompasses igloos, substantial tree huts or habitable caves. The fact that there are no uncontested necessary and sufficient conditions for something's counting as a house does not stop builders from building them. So too, a failure to arrive at philosophical agreement about the proper definition of disease need not stop doctors from treating it. We don't need to define disease to be confident of its existence. Fukuyama scoffs that 'the only people who can argue that there is no difference in principle between disease and health are those who have never been sick: if you have a virus or fracture in your leg, you know perfectly well that something is wrong'.[34]

It would be a mistake, however, either to give up on defining disease, or to assume that the notion is just too obvious to warrant definition. The moral guideline for which we are searching must do more than cope with the most obvious cases, telling doctors to treat people with cancer, tuberculosis and Alzheimer's, but to leave alone those demonstrably in perfect health. Geneticists are now finding correlations between genetic variants and characteristics such as shortness, homosexuality, shyness and impulsiveness. They may soon be able to modify these traits. Should doing so be counted as therapy? Dismissing such questions as nothing more than bothersome philosophical irrelevancies would be like remaining content with a justice system that we believed capable of dealing correctly with the most obviously guilty and innocent, but was otherwise clueless. We need a principled way to decide which of the infinitely many ways in which a person's genome might be altered should be considered therapy.

There are two broad approaches to defining disease. Social constructivists consider diseases to be states to which society takes a negative attitude. People do not like gout or SARS and this is what makes them diseases.

Philip Kitcher notes that this account fails to provide the needed moral guidance because it seems to do little more than recapitulate and validate prejudice.[35] Had the South African apartheid regime persisted into the era of human genetic manipulation, gene therapists would have been right to approach genes that cause higher levels of melanin in the skin in the same way as they approached genes linked with cancer. This verdict explains why social constructivist definitions of disease are advanced mainly by those who reject any normative role for the concept.

Objectivist accounts avoid these difficulties by making the definition of disease independent of our attitudes. According to the most widely advocated version of this view, I suffer from disease when some part of me fails to perform its biological function.[36] Cholesterol deposits on the arteries constitute, or conduce to, disease because they impair the heart's capacity to pump blood. The heart has the function of pumping blood because this is what it evolved to do.

The biological functional account of health and disease does not meekly accede to prejudice. A biological function of melanin is to protect the skin from damage by ultraviolet light. Although racist attitudes may make life difficult for some people with high levels of melanin, they can not convert high melanin levels into a disease state. There are disease states associated with melanin. Vitiligo is a disorder in which melanocytes, the cells that make melanin, are progressively destroyed. The resulting white patches of skin are a disease state, not because of anyone's attitude to them, but because they result from the disruption of the proper function of melanocytes.

The biological functional account runs into a problem the reverse of that which derails the social constructivist account. Social constructivists make current attitudes too relevant to the definition of disease. The biological functional account errs in the opposite direction, setting goals for intervention that can seem irrelevant to modern humans. I have already described Hamer's investigation of the genetics of male homosexuality. This trait also poses problems for evolutionary biology. How could a characteristic that has such a dramatic negative effect on male fertility have been encouraged by natural selection? Some evolutionary theorists confront this problem head on, trying to show how male homosexuality might actually bring some indirect reproductive benefit. According to the 'good uncle' theory, although gay men have fewer children than straight men, they compensate by improving the reproductive prospects of nieces and nephews.[37] A man's child carries half of his genes while his nephew or niece carries a quarter. The 'good uncle' strategy makes evolutionary sense if a man does a significantly better job caring for nephews and nieces than he would do raising his own children. There are other evolutionary proposals. But suppose that none of the biological functional theories of male homosexuality turn out to be correct. This would make it, from the biological standpoint, a malfunction. Perhaps the developmental pathway that makes men sexually attracted to women is quite fragile, sufficiently so that it is sometimes disrupted. Blanchard's environmental theory described earlier in this chapter may explain the cause of this disruption – a misdirected maternal immune response. So what? Homosexuality will join the contraceptive pill as something that may oppose biological function, but in a way that is compatible with a high level of well-being.[38] Consider one case of apparent therapeutic malfunction revealed by genomics. A mutation to the CYP2A6 gene has been found to interfere with the metabolism of nicotine.[39] It is hypothesized that people with mutated versions are less likely to become smokers and therefore to suffer the lung damage, increased risk of heart disease and cancer that accompany the habit. The mutation certainly disrupts the biological functioning of part of the human body, but it seems to do so in a therapeutic way. Indeed this malfunction is sufficiently therapeutic for researchers to be looking for drugs that might imitate it. The very idea of a therapeutic malfunction would be a conceptual impossibility if therapy were simply to be defined as the restoration or protection of biological function.

BUCHANAN, BROCK, DANIELS AND WIKLER ON PROTECTING NORMAL FUNCTIONING

Buchanan, Brock, Daniels and Wikler (abbreviated to Buchanan et al.) make more subtle use the objectivist biological theory in specifying THERAPY's domain.[40] They avoid slavish commitment to the idea that doctors must fix every departure from normal biological functioning, or that doctors should be prevented from acting where there is no departure. For Buchanan et al. protecting normal biological functioning is not an end in itself; instead, it matters for its effects. Keeping people close to normal functioning preserves for them 'the ability to participate in political, social, and economic life. It sustains them as fully participating citizens, as "normal competitors" in all spheres of social life'.[41] We correct departures from normal functioning because we value 'fair equality of opportunity'.[42]

Buchanan et al. allow that there are more expansive accounts of equality of opportunity than the one that they favour. Some philosophers defend 'the equal opportunities for welfare model' of equality of opportunity.[43] They think that we should rectify every respect in which someone suffers disadvantage due to no fault or choice of their own. Others advocate the 'equal capabilities model' according to which we achieve equality of opportunity only when we have made everyone's capabilities equal.[44] Both of these comprehensive doctrines go beyond preserving normal functioning. In their discussion of the equal opportunities for welfare view, Buchanan et al. offer the example of Jane, a woman whose traditional upbringing means that she has frequent feelings of guilt about pursuing her career when she could be staying at home with her children.[45] Jane now rejects her childhood values, and complains that she did not choose to internalize them. Jane's conservative intuitions about the way she should live do not result from any breakdown in brain functioning. This makes a rule requiring that we make good on this unchosen disadvantage more demanding than one preventing or correcting departures from normal function. Consider the equal capabilities model. Some people are less capable than others because they depart in some way from normal functioning. But two people free of biological impairment may have different capabilities. Buchanan et al. argue that the biological theory of function, while being less expansive that these alternative accounts, serves as a point of convergence for them. It is 'a politically appropriate core that people who disagree about the demands of equality in other domains might nevertheless agree on'.[46] It provides guidance for doctors and gene therapists that is both philosophically uncontentious and easy to follow.

Buchanan et al. argue that genetic engineers who prevent and repair departures from normal functioning will promote the ultimate moral goal of the removal of impediments to full participation in society. However, this ultimate goal helps doctors and genetic engineers to recognize when they should ignore the dictates of the biological theory of function. Not all diseases qualify for treatment. Shortage of funds means that we will not treat impairments that have only small effects on the ability to participate in political, social and economic life. Departures from normal functioning that have no effect on participation need not be treated at all. On other occasions, we should intervene where there is no departure from normal functioning. Buchanan et al. propose that women's equality justifies the provision of abortion services by medical professionals.[47]

Presenting the protection of normal functioning as a proximate moral goal sought because of its connection with the ultimate moral goal of protecting full participation provides another point of entry for social relativity. I argue that this argumentative strategy of Buchanan et al. poses problems for their attempt to subsume genetic technologies under THERAPY.

The biological theory of function is attractive because of its independence from views about human flourishing prevalent in a community making choices about treatment. Buchanan et al. point out that the fact that masturbation was once considered a disease no more makes it one than could popular views about sea life turn a whale into a kind of fish.[48] Masturbation is an easy case – it is neither a disease nor, so long as it is not practised obsessively, is it an obstacle to full participation. However, there are more challenging cases.

Buchanan et al. allow that the extent to which a departure from normal functioning impedes full participation depends on facts about the communities in which we live. They give the example of dyslexia as a cognitive impairment that affects equality of opportunity in literate societies, but not in non-literate ones.[49] There is also some historical relativity. Many departures from normal functioning have a more significant impact on participation in political, social and economic life than they once did. Consider tooth decay. The black teeth of Queen Elizabeth the First did not stand in the way of her exercise of regal authority, but it is hard to see the voters in television-equipped contemporary liberal democracies looking beyond this particular departure from normal function when choosing who to lead them. As the citizens of liberal democracies become, on the whole, healthier, the level of functioning required for full participation tends to ratchet up. Buchanan et al. are alert to this. They predict that securing full participation will move beyond the goal of restoring normal functioning or preventing its loss. Pre-existence medical care packages may some day include genetic technologies that enhance immune function or 'improve reading or math skills, perhaps through an effect on short-term memory, attention, or some other component of cognitive processing capabilities'.[50] These enhancements will be recognized as necessary to ensure citizens' equality.

Perhaps the twentieth century and the early part of the twenty-first century is a brief period in the history of the Western world in which the goal of ensuring full participation roughly coincides with that of protecting normal functioning. Before then, protecting normal functioning was more than was required. The bodies and brains of many citizens departed from normal biological functioning in various ways and only serious disease was an obstacle to full participation, on a par with practising the wrong religion, being female or having dark skin. After the contemporary era, those who are not enhanced in a range of ways will be excluded; memories and immune systems free from significant malfunction will not suffice.

Why should this 'ratcheting up' of the prerequisites for full participation be a problem? Isn't it just a fact that as people get healthier they tend to expect more of health services both for themselves and others? My concern is with the moral guidance the image of therapy provides for enhancement technologies. Within its range THERAPY tends to support obligations rather than permissions. Expanding this range will bring a raft of new obligations, dramatically curtailing reproductive liberty. In the future, it will not be the case that parents will not be given the option to enhance their children, they will be required to do so.

THERAPY, OBLIGATION AND PROCREATIVE LIBERTY'S DIMINISHMENT

Buchanan et al. argue that the state will have the same obligation to provide gene therapy that it currently has to provide conventional medical services. However, this obligation also binds the parents whose embryo has a genetic condition that would lead to 'serious harm or disability or a serious loss of happiness or good'.[51] Not only are taxpayers required to fund universal provision of some gene therapies, parents must also provide them for their children. Buchanan et al. do not argue for a categorical obligation. It comes with the proviso that the prevention of harm not impose 'substantial burdens or costs or loss of benefits, on themselves or others'.[52] But this caveat does protect procreative freedom against the intrusions of Buchanan et al.

Consider what Buchanan et al. say in the light of some observations made by Fukuyama about the practice of medicine in liberal societies.[53] Fukuyama argues that some enhancements are already beginning to fall within medicine's range. He uses the pattern of prescription of the psychotropic drugs Prozac and Ritalin to illustrate this tendency. Prozac, manufactured by Eli Lilly, is one of a range of antidepressant medications known as selective serotonin reuptake inhibitors or SSRIs. Low levels of serotonin are associated with depression, anxiety and aggression. An SSRI achieves its therapeutic effect by blocking the brain's reabsorption of serotonin. Ritalin is used to treat attention deficit hyperactivity disorder or ADHD. The drug has an effect that is similar to, but milder than that of amphetamines. Ritalin reduces hyperactivity and improves attention span. Fukuyama endorses these drugs as treatments for clinical depression and ADHD, but he is alarmed by their inherent slipperiness. Prozac is now popped by people who want to feel better than just normally happy. Ritalin is taken by students who want concentrate harder on their exam study.

Fukuyama fears that medicine's expanding domain undermines our humanity. I will examine his argument in the next chapter, but for now I will concentrate on the worry that the expanding domain of THERAPY will radically infringe procreative liberty.

In chapter 3 I discussed the possibility of genetic manipulation that might produce some of Prozac's effects. People homozygous for the long version of the 5-HTTLPR sequence are reported to be more temperamentally upbeat than are people who have at least one copy of the short version. Do these findings provide motivation for a 5-HTTLPR therapy that works by making embryos homozygous for the long version? Normal happiness is certainly not a disease; the temperaments of people who are merely normally happy do not result from any biological dysfunction. However, this need not matter for Buchanan et al. Suppose you know that almost everyone in the society in which your child will live will be temperamentally enhanced. The widespread use of 5-HTTLPR therapy and Prozac will 'renorm' happiness. People whose happiness reaches only a level that would today be considered as normal may be shunned by those who would prefer to spend time with others as habitually upbeat as they are. This renorming may see 5-HTTLPR therapy incorporated into the package of pre-existence health care procedures.

Those who do not want to use 5-HTTLPR therapy to permanently elevate the temperaments of their future children will argue that being a little less emotionally buoyant than the norm does not greatly affect one's ability to participate in one's community. Perhaps they are right to say this. The objection now takes an epistemic form. There are objective criteria for identifying departures from normal functioning. These criteria come from the biological sciences. But in the future full participation in political, social and economic life will sometimes require superior functioning. People charged with deciding which treatments should be included in pre-existence medical packages will be faced with the task of distinguishing those enhancements that have become prerequisites for full participation from those that are merely popular. It is harder to find objective criteria for these decisions. For example, doctors may know perfectly well that the prescription of Prozac to a normally happy person corrects no temperamental malfunction, but when many of the normally happy request it, the drug may come to seem a prerequisite for just getting along, even when it is not.

Buchanan et al. may complain that the pressure for 5-HTTLPR therapy comes from society. They would see it as a pressure, much like bigotry, that should be resisted. The great virtue of the biological functional theory of disease is that it gives clear instructions to resist these pressures. However, the full participation that Buchanan et al. place such great emphasis on is, after all, full participation in a society. For example, the memory enhancements that Buchanan et al. anticipate may be soon be provided for all will only be necessary because many schoolchildren will already have enhanced memories.

Buchanan et al. do offer a way for individuals to opt out of a scheme that universalizes 5-HTTLPR therapy. Prospective parents can appeal to 'substantial burdens or costs or loss of benefits, on themselves or others' to reject treatments for conditions which would have only a small impact on someone's being a 'normal competitor in all spheres of social life'. This fact may give them an excuse for not availing themselves of what has come to be a standard element of pre-existence medical packages. However, the idea that we grant such parents an excuse seems mistaken. The parent who withholds 5-HTTLPR therapy seems quite unlike one who withholds a genetic fix for mild asthma. The obligation to treat mild asthma is perhaps easily defeasible. But we should reject the idea of any kind of obligation to provide 5-HTTLPR therapy, even if it is an easily defeasible one. By this I mean that in the ideal circumstances in which 5-HTTLPR therapy is free, painless, instantaneous and imposes no burdens on anyone else, there should be no obligation for parents-to-be to modify their embryos in this way.

In chapter 1 I described a difference between a liberal policy of enhancement and Nazi eugenics. The Nazis would oblige parents to enhance offspring according to a single eugenic template. In contrast, a state implementing a liberal policy on enhancement would not foist any unitary view of human perfection on its citizens. Rather it would furnish them with the knowledge and tools to make their own enhancement choices. It would oblige no one to enhance. The problem with THERAPY is that it supports obligations rather than permissions. Allowing its range to expand beyond the treatment or prevention of disease will almost certainly force parents to enhance their children in various ways. Advocates of liberal eugenics will need both to firmly restrict the scope of THERAPY, and to find images capable of guiding where this moral image can not. To this end, I suggest that we strictly limit THERAPY's scope to the prevention or treatment of disease. Although we might permit exceptions to a principle requiring the maintenance of normal functioning, we should reject proposals to treat conditions that involve no departure in the same fashion as those that do. Once this stand is taken, we will need moral images to help us to explore the idea that parents might be permitted but not obliged to enhance their future children. I explore two such images in chapters 5 and 6.

This liberal scheme of distribution raises questions about how enhancements will be distributed. Fairness is a virtue of the scheme that Buchanan et al. describe; procedures that the state is required to provide, it will seek to provide for all who need them. Those who defend a prerogative to enhance will need to ensure that access to the means of enhancement is fairly distributed. I will attend to this question in chapter 7.

CHAPTER 5

The Moral Image of Nature

This chapter is an act of appropriation. The moral image of nature is a favourite of opponents of biotechnology. I use it, instead, to support a limited prerogative to use enhancement technologies to select or modify the genomes of future people.

Philosophers have used the concept of nature to make a number of different moral points. The image of nature favoured by environmental ethicists indicates something distinct from and potentially at odds with human beings. Proponents of this image think that preserving the natural world often requires keeping humans out of it. The concepts of nature in play in the debate about human biotechnology are more intimately connected with us. They are best understood in historical context. There is a tradition among religious people to decry enhancement because it usurps God's role. These people say that God designed human brains and bodies, and accuse those who would improve humans of 'playing God'.[1] This overt appeal to a higher being has limited utility in societies whose citizens disagree over God(s) and divine intentions. A secular analogue of the 'playing God' argument gestures towards the evolutionary process. Human brains and bodies are nature's handiwork, the products of many millions of years of design by natural selection. Attempts to improve them usurp nature's role as designer. This argument, too, relies on a view about human origins not shared by all participants in the debate about enhancement technologies. The popularity of NATURE stems from its combination of support for the idea that humans are not the ultimate authorities on what can be done to humans, with neutrality between religious and evolutionary views about human origins. Whatever accounts for our natures, we should not presume an absolute right to change them.[2]

In this chapter I describe two ways in which conservatives have used NATURE to block enhancement technologies. Fukuyama argues that enhancement is wrong because it offends against human nature. Other conservatives, notably Bill McKibben, make no explicit mention of human nature, but they, nonetheless, argue that there is something morally right in the way nature makes us. McKibben argues that achievements that result from natural arrangements of genes have a value that those resulting from artificial arrangements lack. In response to the conservatives, I argue that the moral image of nature actually supports a restricted prerogative to enhance. This argument relies on the conditional claim that if it is morally acceptable to leave in place a given natural genetic arrangement associated with enhanced ability, then it is morally acceptable to engineer an arrangement with the same effects.

ENHANCEMENT, NATURE AND POSTHUMANITY

Some who defend enhancement technologies will have been suspicious of the last chapter's focus on THERAPY. In the brief history of moral debate about human biotechnology the idea that therapy's purpose is curing disease is a premise in many arguments against enhancement. According to these arguments, the existence of a distinction between therapy and enhancement shows that while it is all very well to correct flaws in the evolutionary or divine design, we should not allow humans to design humans.[3] This argument lacks a premise. The distinction between treatment and enhancement may show that arguments in favour of therapy do not support enhancement, but it does not show that enhancement is morally wrong. There may be some other justification.[4] Fukuyama uses NATURE to provide the missing premise.

At the end of chapter 3 I described the conservative argument that enhancement technologies will make human lives meaningless. I proposed that supermarkets and fishing rods sever activities from their customary foundations without making human lives less meaningful. If successful, Fukuyama's argument will show FOOD FINDING to be an inappropriate image for human genetic engineering. Enhancement technologies will take the meaning out of human lives precisely because they take the human out of them. Twenty-first-century supermarket shoppers and anglers are as human as Stone Age hunter-gatherers, but this is not the case for the products of enhancement technologies. Fukuyama explains that

> in the end, biotechnology will cause us in some way to lose our humanity – that is, some essential quality that has always underpinned our sense of who we are and where we are going, despite all of the evident changes that have taken place in human history. Worse yet, we might make this change without recognizing that we have lost something of great value.[5]

Herein lies the significance of the distinction between enhancement and therapy. The former destroys meaning by transforming humans into posthumans while, properly restricted, the latter need not.

Talk of posthumanity is good for book sales – Fukuyama's 2002 work, *Our Posthuman Future*, became a bestseller – but does it make for a sound argument against enhancement? Fukuyama seems to have Hollywood on his side. The subtitle of the biotech dystopia *GATTACA*, 'There is no gene for the human spirit', conveys a sense not only of what genetic engineers can not instil in their human creations, but also of what they might destroy. We need, however, to go beyond the intuitive sense that enhancing intelligence would make someone who wasn't really one of us. Fukuyama must not only show how additional NR2B genes transform human foetuses into posthuman ones, but also explain why the loss of our humanity should matter. Excessively harsh conditions are sometimes described as dehumanizing. In such cases, losing one's humanity involves losing capacities that are normally possessed by humans. By contrast, posthumanizing technologies will give us new capacities or augment existing ones. Fukuyama shares with other conservatives the view that although they may seem to be giving us what we did not have before, making us more intelligent or extending our life spans, enhancement technologies nevertheless take something more significant from us.

THE BIOLOGY OF HUMAN NATURE

Moral philosophers have long been suspicious of appeals to nature. It is the received view that facts about nature cannot, by themselves, lead to moral conclusions.[6] The logical gap between 'is' and 'ought' means that we can describe how humans typically are, or have been designed to be, without justifying any claim about how they should be. Merely pointing out that humans often lie when they have a strong personal incentive to cannot justify lying without some additional moral claim. Fukuyama needs to cross this gap if he is to show that merely remaining human is some manner of moral achievement.

Fukuyama argues vigorously against the idea of a gap between facts and values.[7] There is a voluminous philosophical literature on the fact–value gap, which I cannot explore here, but suppose for the purposes of argument, we grant Fukuyama the claim that certain facts about the way human beings typically are turn out to be moral facts in disguise. His next task is to decide *which* facts about us are moral facts. Some ways of selecting from among the complete collection of human characteristics appear to have unappealing moral implications. In a book entitled *A Natural History of Rape*, Randy Thornhill and Craig Palmer argue that natural selection has designed men to rape.[8] They claim that in the environment for which humans evolved, rape was an optimal reproductive strategy for men deprived of other options. Thornhill and Palmer's conclusions about the impact of natural selection on male psychology are controversial, and, for reasons I will not discuss, probably false.[9] However, imagine that they do turn out to be right. The disposition to rape would be revealed as a fact about human nature, more specifically about male human nature. An unselective moralization of nature might force us to endorse it.

Although Fukuyama challenges examples of evolved human nastiness on empirical grounds, I do not think he needs to.[10] Suppose we accept that human nature comprises many different and sometimes contrary tendencies. If some natural facts turn out to be moral facts, then it should be legitimate for us to use our moral intuitions to judge a given selection. The shared intuition that rape is profoundly evil shows that this is not the kind of fact about human nature that warrants moral elevation. Adopting this strategy does, however, give Fukuyama's opponents a way to criticize him. He must hope that his preferred description of human nature fits at least tolerably well with our moral intuitions. Although we would expect the identification of morality with some aspects of nature to lead us towards some surprising moral conclusions, we should reject a selection that does not fit at all with received views about the ways we should be. I argue that Fukuyama's attempt to moralize human nature fails this test.

Fukuyama's account of human nature is a fusion of two different scientific ideas. He says that human nature comprises 'the species typical characteristics shared by all human beings qua human beings.'[11] 'Species typical' is to be understood in the way that biologists do when they say 'pair bonding is typical of robins and catbirds but not of gorillas and orangutans'.[12] Fukuyama also invokes genes, saying 'human nature is the sum of the behavior and characteristics that are typical of the human species, arising from genetic rather than environmental factors'.[13] He allows that genes do not fix traits like intelligence or height. Instead, they set 'limits to the degree of variance possible'.[14] Fukuyama elaborates on this idea, saying that 'the finding that IQ is 40 to 50 percent heritable already contains within it an estimate of the impact of culture on IQ and implies that even taking culture into account, there is a significant component of IQ that is genetically determined'.[15] His point is best explained by reference to something that E. O. Wilson has called the *genetic leash*.[16] This softer version of genetic determinism specifies that although genes do not precisely fix traits, they fix limits within which traits can vary. Fukuyama says 'there are limits to the degree of variance possible, limits that are set genetically: if you deprive a population of enough calories on average, they starve to death rather than growing smaller, while past a certain point, increasing calorie intake makes them fatter, not taller'.[17]

Olympic events are often cited as illustrations of the genetic leash. Although exceptionally athletically talented humans can run a sub ten-second 100 metres, it seems unlikely that any human will ever run this distance in under the six seconds achieved by cheetahs. The leash that binds humans to their genomes simply cannot be stretched this far. This, according to Fukuyama, is what morally separates changes to a person's genes from changes to her environment. While the consequences of environmental changes could never be of sufficient magnitude to take our humanity from us, the consequences of genetic changes may be. No leash limits the efforts of genetic engineers. They can insert as many NR2B genes as their scruples allow. In doing so, they corrupt human nature by going beyond the maximum extension of the leash. Genetic engineers who want only to treat Alzheimer's and diabetes do not corrupt human nature because they respect the leash.

We should be suspicious of this argument. It so happens that the genetic leash is social conservatives' favourite bit of biological theory. For example, Richard Herrnstein and Charles Murray argued that American blacks were less intelligent than American whites, due, in large part, to genetic differences.[18] They deduced from the finding that intelligence was largely hereditary that we ought to abandon the liberal ideal of using educational programmes to close the gap in the academic achievements of the races. The hereditary nature of intelligence meant that all such attempts were bound to fail. Herrnstein and Murray's argument has been challenged on many grounds.[19] However, suppose we were to accept that their different scores in IQ tests really do show that American whites are hereditarily smarter than American blacks. Herrnstein and Murray are still not entitled their conservative conclusion. This becomes clear once we take into account what it means to say that a trait like intelligence is substantially genetic or heritable. It is tempting to think that this claim indicates how hard genes have worked to make a particular person intelligent. Suppose intelligence had turned out to be 90 per cent heritable. This statistic prompts a mental image in which genes construct almost all of an individual's intelligence, leaving diet and education to add only the finishing touches. Genes would, in effect, be keeping intelligence on a very short leash. But this is to misunderstand the claim that intelligence is 90 per cent genetic. Statements about the degree of heritability, or the extent to which a trait is genetic, say nothing directly about individuals. Instead, they address variation in populations. It is almost certain that the observed variation in human intelligence is explained by both differences in genes and differences in environmental influences, both within and without the womb. Differences in one of these factors may contribute more to this variation than do differences in the other factors. If human intelligence were to be 90 per cent genetic, then differences in genes would account for 90 per cent of the variation, with the remaining 10 per cent explained by differences in environmental inputs.

While studies of actual populations can tell us something about the relative importance of influences that have shaped them, they say nothing directly about effects that might be brought about by novel influences.[20] Yet claims about how far the genetic leash can stretch concern not only what actual influences have brought about, but also what novel influences can do. There is no logically deductive argument from the narrow range of human heights, speeds over 100 metres and performances in IQ tests in actual environments, to what might be achieved were humans to be raised in different environments. The conclusion refers to the full range of environments in which humans might be raised and therefore is importantly stronger than its premises.

Perhaps we have the basis for a good inductive argument. Human athletes have experimented with different diets and training programmes, yet no one seems even close to running 100 metres as fast as a cheetah. Does this give us reason to think that they never will? The important thing to note is that we have only sampled a small percentage of the full range of possible human environments. Aspiring sprinters have started training at a range of different ages. They have eaten a range of special diets, trained at differing intensities and implemented different race plans. If environmental engineers are to help a human break the six-second barrier they will have to find a way to explore the effects of other possible environments.

In early 2002 researchers announced that they had created an artificial human womb.[21] They did this by grafting cells from the lining of a womb onto a scaffold of biodegradable material whose shape mirrored the interior of the uterus. As the cells grew, the scaffold dissolved. Appropriate nutrients and hormones were added. When embryos left over from IVF programmes were put into the artificial wombs they attached themselves and grew, right up until the experiment's termination at six days. The researchers hope one day to be able to offer this technology to women whose wombs are damaged, or perhaps to those who just don't want to put up with nine months of pregnancy. I cannot address here the many questions raised by the experiment about the meaning of motherhood. Instead, I am interested in how artificial wombs might allow significant modification of the early environments of developing humans. Suppose we were to use these wombs to radically alter uterine environments. It seems at least possible that there is some combination of nutrients that would produce a human who could run as fast as a cheetah. If so, the barrier could be broken without any modification to the genome of the future record breaker. We would, in effect, be transforming the material of the genetic leash from relatively inelastic leather to very elastic rubber. I am not saying that this could be done, nor, still less, that it should be done. The effects of such changes would be as difficult to forecast as would be the effects of inserting two or three additional IGF-1 genes into an embryo in the hope that it might produce an Olympic weightlifting gold medallist. My point is just that advocates of the short, inflexible leash go beyond the evidence to say that environmental engineers could never significantly modify human beings.

There are more straightforward counterexamples to Fukuyama's use of the genetic leash. Although Transhumanists are certainly in favour of genetic enhancement, they also discuss means by which humans can be improved that have nothing to do with genes. Transhumanists advocate extending our intellectual and physical powers by fusing flesh with machine. Science fiction's most frightening depictions of posthumanity are of this type. Think of the Cybermen of *Dr Who* and the Borg of *Star*

Trek. Technologies that pursue this path of posthumanization are already under development. In early 2003, scientists at the University of California in Los Angeles announced that they were about to begin tests on a brain prosthesis.[22] The neuroprosthesis is designed to play the role of the hippocampus, a piece of neurophysiology whose function is to encode experiences so that they can be stored as memories in other parts of the brain. The creators of the neuroprosthesis envisage it as a treatment for brain damage resulting from stroke, epilepsy and Alzheimer's. Their vision seems similar to that of Tsien, who hopes NR2B therapy might one day help those suffering from diseases such as Alzheimer's and Parkinson's. However, like the technique for adding NR2B genes, the neuroprosthesis is a technology with at least two faces. Steve Austin, the bionic man of the 1970s TV show *The Six Million Dollar Man,* was given mechanical body parts that performed significantly better than their biological counterparts. Perhaps in the years to come some parents will equip their children with electronic hippocampuses that do a considerably better job of translating lessons into memories than do the biological hippocampuses of their schoolmates.

Doubtless Fukuyama would want to use the label 'posthuman' for a being emerging from the souped-up artificial womb or one with an electronic hippocampus that dramatically boosts memory. The key point is that both are genetically human. Persisting with the term would demonstrate that it's not really genes, or changes to genes, that matter. Perhaps the other part of Fukuyama's definition will help us to understand how these genetic humans might have been transformed into posthumans.

According to Fukuyama, human nature is defined by what is *typical* for human beings. There is a difference between being typical and being universal. Fukuyama takes a hard-headed approach to exceptions. He explains that 'here are doubtless some mutant female kangaroos born without pouches ... Facts like these do not render meaningless the assertion that pouches are somehow constitutive of "kangarooness".[23] What we somewhat inaccurately refer to as 'kangaroos without pouches' actually miss out on being proper kangaroos because they lack something essential to being a kangaroo. The same is true of 'humans' with additional IGF-1 genes, those born of souped-up artificial wombs, and those with neuroprostheses. They miss out on being proper humans.

Lists of species' typical characteristics are useful for field biologists trying to identify their quarries, but the idea that such a list sets moral limits is just the old error of translating statistical norms into moral norms. A practice's being unusual does not by itself suffice to make it morally wrong. Nor should a person's being unusual make them inhuman in any morally interesting sense. Fukuyama has missed something that Kermit the frog understands – that life can be difficult if you are green, but that there is really nothing morally wrong with being different in this way. It is not hard to think of 'humans' who are the statistical analogues of Fukuyama's pouchless kangaroos, individuals sufficiently unusual that they might not be recognized as human by a Martian field biologist who has committed to memory a short list of typical human traits. Shaquille O'Neal is 7′ 1″ tall and weighs 335 pounds. This deviation from the human – and indeed the basketballer – norm has helped him gather a host of trophies. Stephen Hawking was diagnosed with motor neurone disease in his early twenties. A distinguished career in astrophysics is not the norm for people afflicted in this way. Hawking would prefer not to be suffering from motor neurone disease, but, according to Fukuyama, he suffers harm additional to his physical limitations. From the standpoint of humanity, Hawking's intellect may be more alarming than his disease condition, simply because it may be more of a statistical anomaly than motor neurone disease. Of course, O'Neal and Hawking are not the handiwork of genetic engineers. But Fukuyama's examples are kangaroos occurring naturally, not just those on the island of Dr Moreau. If they weren't, his argument against enhancement technologies would be hopelessly circular.

Fukuyama might respond that, their abnormal characteristics notwithstanding, O'Neal and Hawking are similar enough to us in most respects to be human. This is a sensible thing to say – but it leaves Fukuyama with no objection to enhancement. Enhancers will seek to bring into existence individuals who resemble the rest of us in many respects – they will merely be brawnier or smarter. It is hard to imagine the parents of the future paying genetic engineers to provide them with rational octopuses for children, but if they did want to, a moral rule that directs that parents to look out for the welfare of their offspring will suffice to prevent them from seeking this manner of genetic modification. Appeals to posthumanity are redundant.

Perhaps Fukuyama will say that it is acceptable for chance recombinations of genetic material to produce O'Neals and Hawkings but not for us to, by arguing for the essential rightness of nature's distribution of extreme talent. Very gifted people are rare events. Genetic engineers should not be permitted to make genius commonplace. This objection is the reversal of the concern addressed in chapter 7: that liberal eugenics will polarize society, that it will enable the wealthy to use genetic enhancements to widen the gap between them and the rest of us. Genetic elitism sounds like something that Fukuyama the liberal democrat should not approve of. Insisting on the preservation of natural advantages sounds a bit like withholding remedial literacy classes on the grounds that those with a natural aptitude for language do not require them. I will return to issues concerning the social context of enhancement in chapter 7.[24]

A MORAL PARITY OF NATURAL AND ENGINEERED GENETIC ARRANGEMENTS

Fukuyama seeks to pass different moral judgements on humans genetically engineered to be intelligent or athletically gifted from those he passes on humans who possess these characteristics as the result of nature's random recombination of genetic material. Other critics of human biotechnology find a way to express this intuition that makes no use of the concept of human nature. According to Bill McKibben, those who achieve because they are enhanced are deprived of what makes achievement worthwhile:

> [A]s we move into this new world of genetic engineering, we won't simply lose races, we'll lose *racing*: we'll lose the possibility of the test, the challenge, the celebration that athletics represents. . . . Say you've reached Mile 23, and you're feeling strong. Is it because of your hard training and your character, or because the gene pack inside you is pumping out more red blood cells than your body knows what to do with? Will anyone be impressed with your dedication? More to the point, will *you* be impressed with your dedication? Will you know what part of it is you, and what part is your upgrade?[25]

The human marathon runner feels totally exhausted at Mile 23, but at least he can claim the credit for having got that far. The posthuman athlete, still feeling good, deserves no congratulations. She is simply performing up to her design specifications. Eric Juengst suggests the label 'biomedical Calvinism' for the view that those who win races because they have taken performance-enhancing drugs or had their genomes modified are denied the possibility of putting in the effort that would make their apparent achievements worthwhile.[26] If there is any credit due for the victory won by the genetically engineered athlete, it should go to the person who did the work modifying his genome. However, if an athlete's winning advantage derives from the chance recombination of his parents' DNA, then there is no other agent for the credit to default to; his parents did not choose which of their genes to pass on to him. He truly deserves his medal.

Two examples bring the image of nature fully to bear on McKibben's biomedical Calvinism. Eero Mäntyranta is a Finnish cross-country skier who won seven Olympic medals in the 1960s.[27] His feats of endurance were so remarkable that he was frequently accused of cheating, in particular of blood doping. Blood doping involves the injection red blood cells. The fact that red blood cells carry oxygen makes this procedure of particular value to endurance athletes; boosting red blood cell levels boosts oxygen reserves. Things looked bad for Mäntyranta when tests revealed that he had more red blood cells than normal. However, there was no direct evidence that this was the result of doping. Some time later, analysis of the DNA of his family members showed that he in all likelihood carried a rare genetic mutation that increased his levels of a hormone called erythropoietin or EPO. This hormone stimulates the body to produce more red cells. According to one estimate, the capacity of his red blood cells to carry oxygen was 25–50 per cent higher than normal.

It is clear that Mäntyranta's genome placed him at an advantage over many of his competitors. His rare mutation is one among many ways in which nature starts some Olympians ahead of others. But it also seems that Mäntyranta's medals were, nonetheless, significant achievements – he could not have won them without total dedication to his sport.

Perhaps Mäntyranta's dedication also resulted from an unintentional genetic cheating. Behavioural geneticists claim to have isolated genetic variants responsible for differences in what we might call will-power. The Northern Ireland footballer George Best is a famous case of someone who failed to realize his full sporting potential because of his addiction to alcohol. A number of genes have been suggested as playing a role in whether or not someone becomes an alcoholic. A particular version of the aldehyde dehydrogenase 2 gene (ALDH2) is thought to protect against alcoholism by making it more difficult for people to metabolize alcohol. Variation in the dopamine D2 receptor gene (DRD2) has been proposed as making some less susceptible to alcoholism by reducing the feelings of reward that they get when they drink. Like the rest of behavioural genetics, these claims are controversial, but a complete description of the human genome would almost certainly reveal a number of genes that influence the likelihood of alcoholism. It could be that Mäntyranta was more fortunate than Best, in that he inherited versions of these genes that made him less likely to be distracted from his training by alcohol. This fact should not prevent us from being impressed by the amount of training Mäntyranta actually did.

Although information about genetic strengths and weaknesses may be widely publicized at the Olympics of 2504, even then one will not win a gold medal simply by presenting a read-out of one's genome to race officials. The moral image of nature directs that what we say about the achievements of people whose advantages result from chance recombinations of their parents' DNA, we should also say about those who are genetically fortunate by design. Those whose genomes have been constructed by genetic engineers or selected by cloners will find winning medals and avoiding drug addiction no easier than those to whom nature has given the same performance-boosting genes. If Mäntyranta's medals are achievements, then so would be those of his clone.

It is an often-made point that parents who have paid genetic engineers to modify their children's genomes will put pressure on their children to achieve. I will address questions about what expectations it is legitimate for parents to have in respect of their genetically engineered children in this and the following chapter. For now, I note that the concern about parental expectations arises in connection with the technology of genomics alone. In a fair lottery, one does not get the winning lottery ticket by design. Nonetheless, the person who finds herself with the winning ticket still insists that she receive her prize. Consider the parent whose embryo is revealed by genomic tests to have inherited the high intelligence versions of intelligence genes. He might view himself as a winner of the genetic lottery, placing as much pressure on his child to be academically successful as the parent who had asked for these alleles to be engineered into her child's embryo.

In what follows I reverse the direction of Fukuyama's and McKibben's arguments. I appeal to the fact that exceptional people are already among us and in many cases doing very well, to support a parental prerogative to make people exceptional. This argument assumes a pragmatic optimism according to which enhancement technologies will allow genes to be removed from or added to human genomes with perfect accuracy, and without imposing additional risks on the people who result. I defend the following idea, which I label the nature principle to indicate its provenance:

If we are permitted to leave unchanged a given genetic arrangement in the genomes of our future children, we are also permitted to introduce it.

The nature principle moves from a permission not to act, to a permission to act.[28] If we are not required to change a genetic arrangement, given perfectly precise and safe tools of genetic engineering, we should be allowed to use those same tools to bring it about. Although we must seriously qualify the principle, I argue that it supports a limited parental prerogative in respect of enhancement technologies.

PLURALISM ABOUT HUMAN FLOURISHING

I have not defended obligations to genetically engineer people. Indeed, it strikes me that arguing for an obligation to modify your children's genomes should be considerably more difficult than arguing for a permission to make certain modifications. The lack of a general requirement to remove disease genes would pose problems to the nature principle; the absence of an obligation to remove disease genes will lead to the conclusion that we are entitled to introduce them. Suppose, however, that the arguments of Buchanan and his colleagues do show that we are obliged to modify the genomes of our children in certain ways. The nature principle will still stand in need of qualification. There is likely to be a threshold of harm before any obligation to genetically engineer comes into force. Alleles linked with mild asthma or slight short-sightedness may not pass this threshold. Even if there were no requirement to remove mildly harmful alleles, it would be wrong to engineer them in to someone's genome.

Deciding how to qualify the nature principle requires working out what it means for a genetic arrangement to be harmful. In chapter 4 I argued that we should be suspicious of any straightforward identification of harm with disease. We need an account of what it is for a life to go well, an account of human flourishing. This account will serve as a reference point for judgements about harm and therefore for the application of the nature principle.

There are two broad approaches to human flourishing. Monists think that there is one best way for human lives to be, and that judgements about how good a given life is depend on how close it comes to this ideal. Monism will demand that enhancement technologies be used to create humans as close as possible to the ideal state. I described two monistic views in chapter 1. The Nazis would have proposed the list of characteristics for admission to the SS as the universal template for enhancement technologies. Hedonistic utilitarianism is a less objectionable version of monism, according to which the best human life is one that contains as much pleasure and as little suffering as possible – but, like Nazism, it leaves no room for meaningful choice about enhancement.

These views underestimate the range of ways in which humans can excel. It is difficult to think of the single value that the lives of David Beckham and Socrates have come close to maximizing. These lives can be acknowledged as excellent in their own distinctive ways regardless of the suspicions of intellectual snobs about Beckham and of football fans about a man who stood around all day talking. In place of monism about the good life, I endorse the type of pluralism linked by many with liberal views about the role of the state. Isaiah Berlin and John Rawls argue that there are many good ways for persons to be, none of which is objectively superior to all the other ways.[29] Often these ends conflict with and exclude one another. Beckham's morally legitimate life plan aims at goods that Socrates' plan avoids, and vice versa.

Talk of life plans conjures up images of people beginning their lives with pen and paper in hand, scribbling down a list of goals and sub-goals. As the life is lived, ticks are placed alongside some items. Other items receive crosses or are scribbled out, to be replaced by new items. On one's death bed one inspects the heavily annotated list to decide whether or not one's life was a success. Perhaps in moments of analytical reflection, some people do write down such lists, or at least imagine them, but any suggestion that each of us has a frequently consulted list is certainly false. The idea of a life plan is an abstraction. Philosophers have used a variety of terminology to capture the notion and explain its significance. For example, Bernard Williams introduces the notion of a ground project, defined as 'a set of projects which are closely related to [one's] existence and which to a significant degree give a meaning to [one's] life...[G]round projects [provide] the motive force which propels [one] into the future, and gives [one] a reason for living.'[30] Expressed most concisely, a life plan is really just a sense of what really matters.

Parents' ranking of life plans provides a definition of enhancement for them; a gene therapy will enhance their child if it improves her chances of successfully pursuing life plans that they rank highly. But pluralism about human flourishing is not a relativism that gives a moral pass mark to absolutely any use of enhancement technologies. While there is no uniquely best way to use enhancement technologies, some uses of them are just plain wrong. There are, broadly speaking, two ways in which genetic engineers' shaping of children can cause harm.[31]

Some uses of enhancement technologies cause suffering. Lesch–Nyhan syndrome is an X chromosome-linked genetic disorder that causes, in the early months of life, self-mutilating behaviours such as lip and finger biting and repeated head banging. Severe mental retardation followed by death is the inescapable prognosis. Using enhancement technologies to have a child with Lesch–Nyhan syndrome would be straightforwardly wrong. Other cases are less obvious. Return to the example of the rare allele that caused Mäntyranta to overproduce EPO. High levels of EPO give greater endurance, but they also cause the blood to thicken, stressing the heart. Abuse of the hormone is thought to have led to the deaths of several cyclists. Those who follow Buchanan et al. in the view that the new genetic technologies bring extensive obligations with them may not think that these dangers suffice for there to be a general requirement to replace Mäntyranta's allele. However, they should preclude a permission to engineer it in.

Another way for the shaping of children to harm them is by infringing on their freedom to choose a life plan and to successfully pursue it. This idea of a freedom to choose and to pursue one's plan is a philosophically loaded one to be introducing at this point in the proceedings. In what follows, I present an account of freedom that will help us to identify this kind of harm by making clear the need to begin one's life with genuine options.

Those attracted to unifying theories may seek to collapse one of these kinds of harm into the other. They might argue that the freedom to choose one's plan is to be valued because infringements of it can often cause suffering. People deprived of genuine choice about their life plan are likely to suffer because their lifestyle is not right for them. Alternatively, advocates of freedom of choice may view suffering as bad because of its tendency to reduce the range of choice that one has about one's life. They will note that the immense pain caused by Lesch–Nyhan stands in the way of the successful pursuit of almost any life plan. Other diseases, such as diabetes and Parkinson's, are less dramatic in their effects, but still cause this kind of harm due to their likely reduction in the range of life plans that can be successfully pursued.

A cautious agnosticism about these reductionist alternatives should lead us, at least at the outset, to treat suffering and the diminishment of the freedom to choose the course one's life takes as distinct harms resulting from the misuse of enhancement technologies.

Is the term 'harm' appropriate in this context? In chapter 4 I argued that some ways of genetically modifying an embryo will leave the original individual in place. These genetic changes will either be sufficiently minor or late-acting for us to say that the resulting individual is the same as the one who would have existed had his parents not used enhancement technologies. In such cases, it is right to talk about harm. Other ways of modifying a genome will be substantial and early-acting enough to replace one individual for another. In this case, no individual can be harmed. But we should demand that enhancement technologies not be used to replace one individual with another who either suffers to a greater extent, or is less free in respect of the course his life takes.

HOW TO AVOID INFRINGING FREEDOM OF CHOICE

We have a good idea of how enhancement technologies might cause suffering. However, more needs to be said about the second kind of harm: the reduction of freedom.

The philosophical literature contains two broad approaches to freedom. The advocates of negative freedom emphasize an absence of external constraints.[32] For example, John Robertson defends procreative liberty as a negative freedom.[33] I am free to procreate so long as neither the state nor anyone else obstructs my procreative efforts. Suppose I am infertile and would avail myself of fertility services but for the fact that I am too poor to pay for them. I am no less negatively free to reproduce than are people who succeed in becoming parents by natural or artificial means. Such theories are inadequate to explain the misuses of enhancement technologies that concern us here. Those whom genetic engineers confine to a very narrow range of life plans seem to have their freedom to choose infringed even if no law restricts their choices.

If there is an account of freedom capable of shedding light on the harm that concerns us it will need to be a positive one. Theories of positive freedom specify that I am not free to do something unless I am capable of doing it. A serious disability is not an external constraint but it still reduces my positive freedom to the extent that it prevents me from doing things. The view of positive freedom I describe here comes from the capabilities approach first defended by Amartya Sen and further elaborated by Martha Nussbaum.[34] The primary practical purpose of Sen's and Nussbaum's theories is to help us to recognize the moral needs of men and women living in poverty; the capabilities approach points to needs of human beings that do not change with their cultural or material circumstances. I use the account to help us to understand needs of future people that do not vary in the face of a diversity of parents' or genetic engineers' aims.

In his recent presentation of the capabilities view, Sen begins with concept of 'functionings', which he understands as picking out 'the various things a person may value doing or being'.[35] Sen explains that the 'valued functionings may vary from elementary ones, such as being adequately nourished and being free from avoidable disease, to very complex activities or personal states, such as being able to take part in the community and having self-respect'.[36] The collection of alternative functionings available to a person determines her real freedom, her capacity to choose one way of life in preference to others. A person whose collection of alternative functionings is greater than another's is freer than that other person. Poverty and oppression reduce the real freedom of those who suffer them. Sen sets the expansion of real freedom as the primary goal of development. Hence the title of his 1999 book, *Development as Freedom*.

Advocates of negative freedom sometimes accuse defenders of positive freedom of not paying due heed to the pluralism in conceptions of the good life. Berlin thinks that the promotion of positive freedom is all too often just the promotion of a particular conception of the good life, but Sen's positive conception is perfectly compatible with pluralism about human flourishing.[37] Expanding a person's real freedom expands the range of functionings available to him. This means that those with more real freedom are more likely to be able to successfully pursue their distinctive life plans.

Some philosophers question the moral importance of real freedom and, in particular, the idea we should be striving to expand it.[38] They deny that we always benefit from having more options. My deployment of Sen's theory to identify misuses of enhancement technologies blunts the force of this objection. The appeal to real freedom in the regulation of enhancement technologies is not entirely analogous to Sen's use of the concept in his development ethic. It does not require that parents use enhancement technologies to *expand* their children's real freedom, or to have children who have *greater* real freedom than those they would otherwise have had. Instead, it demands only that they do not, in their pursuit of their eugenic visions, *reduce* their children's real freedom, or have children with *less* real freedom than those they would otherwise have had.

These points about principle leave unaddressed a host of practical concerns about the application of Sen's account to enhancement technologies. Judgements about whether someone's real freedom is diminished require us to evaluate the relative importance of functionings. Deciding whether genetic rearrangements reduce real freedom is complicated by the fact that many uses of enhancement technologies will enable the achievement of new combinations of functionings, while standing in the way of combinations that would otherwise have been available. In such cases, we need to weigh the gains against the losses. There is a *New Yorker* cartoon in which someone claims to have a disease so rare that it does not have a celebrity advocate. Few are the diseases that are so rare that support groups or even communities have not formed around them. These groups or communities offer real benefits, opportunities for functionings not fully available to those who do not have the disease. The communal benefits associated with deafness seem especially substantial. Whether or not engineering a deaf genotype reduces real freedom requires us to work out what penalties deafness imposes on the pursuit of life plans that do not specifically require the condition, weighing these against the potential advantages conferred by deaf culture. The task for advocates of deaf culture is made especially difficult by the fact that deafness compromises a wide range of life plans.[39] This reduction in real freedom should make it impermissible to genetically engineer one's child to be deaf. Suppose we are obliged to correct some harmful conditions. It is possible that the difference in real freedom is sufficiently small that it does not pass the threshold at which an obligation might come into force. If so, there would be no general requirement to replace genetic arrangements linked with deafness.

A further practical complication arises in connection with the fact that the enhancement choices we make now will not be fully realized until our children reach maturity. William Ruddick challenges choices made on our children's behalf that are based on unrealistic assumptions about the society in which their children will grow up.[40] He criticizes the assumptions of members of conservative religious communities that their children's circumstances will inevitably be identical to their parents'. Communities that have lasted centuries can easily dissolve in the time that it takes for a child to reach maturity. The problem of changing circumstances may be greater for choices involving cloning and genetic engineering. These means of enhancement are likely to be introduced at a time of rapid technological change. It will be impossible to predict which novel functionings will become possible in the societies in which these children will grow up and how the changes we make to their genomes will affect their capacity to achieve these functionings.

There are ways in which we can make the idea more practical. Those who regulate enhancement technologies should insist that parents' attempts to enhance do not rule out plans founded on conceptions of the good life radically opposed to the parents' conception. It must be possible for a person to completely reject the ideals motivating her enhancement. Furthermore, if she does reject these ideals she must have a reasonable chance of successfully pursuing her chosen plan. Consider some examples.

In chapter 1 I described Robert Graham's Repository for Germinal Choice. The best-known Repository story concerns the child Afton Blake had in 1982 with the sperm of donor Red No. 28, a science professor who performed classical music, was handsome and had haemorrhoids.[41] Afton called her son 'Doron', Greek for 'gift'. By kindergarten Doron was reading Shakespeare and grappling with algebra. At age six his IQ tested at 180. Doron was Graham's pride and joy, his eugenic vision made flesh. The interesting thing is that Doron rejected the mathematics and science destiny seemingly dictated by his genes. Instead, he studied comparative religion, with Wicca, Taoism and Buddhism as special emphases. The method of enhancing Doron's mathematical and scientific talents by selecting his sperm does not seem to have prevented his choosing a life plan opposed to these values. He managed this in spite of the widely believed but erroneous genetic determinist idea that inheriting one's genes from someone gifted in mathematics and science would make this kind of future inevitable.

Now consider another example discussed in chapter 1 – the case of Gauvin McCullough, born from the sperm of a profoundly deaf man. Sharon Duchesneau and Candace McCullough say that should Gauvin reject their eugenic ideals he will have the option of a hearing aid. Unless the technology of hearing aids improves significantly, it seems likely that Gauvin would stand at a significant disadvantage should he want to rejoin the hearing community; he would continually be having to make adjustments that would allow him to pursue life plans for which deafness is an impediment. Duchesneau's and McCullough's selection of sperm resulted in a child with less real freedom than one they might have had by other means.

ARE WE PERMITTED TO ENHANCE (OR REDUCE) INTELLIGENCE?

I have pointed to a number of practical obstacles in the way of the enhancement of intelligence. It might seem that, once we have adopted a pragmatic optimism and put issues of risk to one side, the enhancement of intelligence presents relatively few problems. However, there may be many ways in which its enhancement reduces the range of meaningful choice, forcing us to weigh the relative significance of the additions and the subtractions to the range of functionings available to a child.

In chapter 2 I described two views about the nature of intelligence that have different implications for its enhancement. According to one view, there is a single ability, general intelligence or *g*, that explains performance across a wide range of cognitive tasks. Howard Gardner defends an alternative view, according to which there are multiple intelligences.[42] These different intelligences interact with each other to solve problems presented by our social and physical environments. Gardner's roster of intelligences includes Logical-Mathematical Intelligence, Linguistic Intelligence, Spatial Intelligence, Musical Intelligence, Bodily-Kinaesthetic Intelligence, and the Intelligence that deals with our self-understanding and our understanding of others.

If there is such a thing as *g*, then we could approach the enhancement of intelligence as the boosting of a single attribute. Gardner's model requires enhancers to make choices. He suspects that some intelligences conflict. A study of the development of intelligence in children found a tendency under certain circumstances for superior artistic performance to interfere with certain spatial skills.[43] This means that the enhancement of Musical Intelligence may, in itself, reduce Bodily-Kinaesthetic Intelligence.

Plans to enhance cognitive skills may force other choices. Kay Redfield Jamison argues that there is a connection between artistic creativity and bipolar affective disorder, or manic depression.[44] She provides an impressive list of extremely creative people who were also manic depressive, including Lord Byron, Samuel Coleridge, Vincent van Gogh, Sylvia Plath, and Virginia Woolf. Jamison thinks that modern treatments for depression flatten both emotional and creative peaks. Asperger's syndrome points towards another dilemma that may confront the enhancers of cognitive abilities. Although people with Asperger's have difficulty relating to others, some compensate for this lack of social awareness with an unusual sensitivity to patterns in inanimate nature. Asperger's groups have retrospectively diagnosed a number of famous scientists, philosophers and composers with the condition. Perhaps social awkwardness is the price that one must pay for the style of mental focus characteristic of these intellectual high achievers.

Can the social awkwardness of Asperger's and its distinctive powers of focus, and creative spurts and bipolar troughs be separated? The harms may be *constitutive* of the benefits, or they may be *merely associated* with them. If the harms are merely associated with the benefits then the genetic engineers of the future may be able to pursue the benefits without producing the harms. If they are constitutive, then separating them will be impossible; the mental powers will always come at a price.

Suppose we find that the costs are constitutive of the cognitive abilities. Should parents be permitted to use genetic engineering to increase the chance that their child will have the combination of mental focus and Asperger's? It seems unlikely that boosting a child's performance in this way, thereby improving her chances of successfully pursuing certain life plans in academia, does fully compensate for the suffering resulting from the social handicap. In this chapter I have separated the question of permissions to use enhancement from the question about obligations to use them. However, imagine there is a general requirement to remove harmful genetic arrangements. If such a requirement is tenable there is likely to be a threshold of harm that genetic arrangements will have to pass before there is an obligation to remove them. Asperger's may not pass this threshold if it, on balance, reduces real freedom to only a small degree. This would mean that humanity would not be deprived of the distinctive achievements of people with Asperger's.

Many people will find it easy to see why parents should be permitted to exchange a genetic arrangement that predisposed their child to less intelligence for one that predisposed her to be more intelligent. But what about the reverse case – parents who want to swap a predisposition to be highly intelligent for a predisposition to be averagely so? Does NATURE legitimize this modification? It might.

Suppose an injury to a person with an IQ of 160 reduces her IQ to 100. This reduction in IQ causes harm: the victim will already have embarked on projects requiring the higher intelligence and her pursuit of them will be set back. However, replacing an embryo's predisposition to become someone with a high IQ for a predisposition to become someone with an average IQ is a different matter. The embryo does not yet have a life plan. A gene predisposing to intellectual disability reduces one's positive freedom, but it is not so clear that introducing a gene that predisposes to average intelligence causes this kind of harm. Although there are some goods available to the more intelligent that are not readily accessible to those of average intelligence, an average IQ may compensate for these losses. Those of average intelligence can enjoy uncomplicated pleasures denied to some with superior intelligence. They can develop parts of their characters that highly intelligent people tend to leave relatively undeveloped. Perhaps they are more likely to find intellectually compatible companions. Parents who value these benefits above high intelligence are entitled to think of the gene therapy as enhancement. They make a similar choice when they prefer an ordinary education for their child to an academically elite one.

Note that this conclusion relies on a factual claim. Exchanging a genetic arrangement that predisposes to an IQ of 160 for an arrangement that predisposes to an IQ of 100 may reduce prospects associated with some life plans – but it offers improvements in prospects associated with other plans of sufficient magnitude to compensate for the loss. It does not reduce real freedom. If this claim is mistaken, then the gene therapy reduces real freedom and so should not be permitted.

My discussion of a moral parity between engineered and natural genetic arrangements leaves significant issues unresolved. One concerns the social context of enhancement. Consider the following application of the principle defended in this chapter. In chapter 4 I described Hamer's claim to have evidence of an X chromosome male sexual-orientation gene with homosexual and heterosexual variants. If genetic tests were to reveal the heterosexual variant in the genome of a future person, it ought to be permissible to leave it in place. The same goes for the homosexual variant. This should make it permissible to for parents-to-be to exchange homosexual genetic arrangements for heterosexual ones. James Watson has gone on record advocating a parental prerogative to modify genes that influence sexual orientation. He says: '[i]f you could find the gene which determines sexuality and a woman decides she doesn't want a homosexual child, well, let her.'[45] Watson neglects to mention that the same reasoning that would legitimize using genetic engineering to make a child who would have been gay, straight, will also permit someone to have a gay child in place of a straight one. There are morally legitimate conceptions of the good life that can justify either procedure as enhancement. Neither considered in isolation from views about them reduce real freedom. However, any suggestion that this point places homosexuality and heterosexuality on an equal footing ignores the social context of enhancement. Homophobia exists even in modern liberal societies that set themselves against prejudice. A prerogative to use enhancement technologies to modify a child's likely sexual orientation would end up colluding with prejudice, worsening its effects. This would be the case even if the pluralist approach to the good life allows others to defend the substitution of 'gay' genes for 'straight' genes as enhancement. I postpone discussion of this, and other issues connected with the social context of enhancement, until chapter 7.

CHAPTER 6

The Moral Image of Nurture

The moral image of nature helps us to respond consistently to the benefits and harms brought by natural and artificial genetic arrangements. This chapter illuminates a different axis of consistency about enhancement. Enhancement technologies improve people by selecting or modifying their genomes. The moral image of nurture is informed by improvements that parents can achieve by selecting or modifying their children's environments. Parents are free to improve their children's intelligence and physical prowess by selecting their schooling or diet. NURTURE supports a freedom to achieve the same ends by genetic engineering.

A MORAL AND DEVELOPMENTAL PARITY OF GENES AND ENVIRONMENT

John Harris presents the following scenario in his 1998 book, *Clones, Genes, and Immortality*:

> [S]uppose a school were to set out deliberately to improve the mental and physical capacities of its students, suppose its stated aims were to ensure that the pupils left the school not only more intelligent and more physically fit than when they arrived, but more intelligent and more physically fit than they would be at any other school.[1]

Harris thinks that although we might be sceptical, wondering what sacrifices children were expected to make to achieve these high levels of intellectual and physical prowess, we would welcome this educational breakthrough. He continues:

> Now we can entertain conjecture of a different sort of breakthrough with the same or comparable consequences and suppose the new biotechnological procedures could engineer into the human embryo characteristics which would make highly probable the expression of adult phenotypes like build, height, and even intelligence and could even reduce susceptibility to disease.[2]

According to Harris, welcoming the breakthrough in educational methods entails welcoming biotechnologies with similar consequences. John Robertson, the advocate of procreative liberty, follows a similar line of reasoning:

> A case could be made for prenatal enhancement as part of parental discretion in rearing offspring. If special tutors and camps, training programs, even the administration of growth hormone to add a few inches in height are within parental rearing discretion, why should genetic interventions to enhance normal offspring traits be any less legitimate?[3]

NURTURE cannot serve as a moral image for genetic modification if genes and upbringing make fundamentally different contributions to human development. Genetic determinists find such differences. They say that an organism's significant characteristics result from its genes alone. An organism may require food in order to grow and lessons to trigger the genetic programmes that will equip it to navigate its world, but differences in environmental influences make comparatively little difference to how it grows or how it navigates its world. However, the evidence supports a different, interactionist model of development. An organism's environment is as significant an influence on it as its genes.

Genetic determinists view the ethics of changing someone's genes very differently from the way they view the ethics of changing someone's environment. The interactionist conception gives the lie to this moral dichotomy. NURTURE's utility does not, however, rely on the assumption that genes and environment make identical contributions to the traits that we may seek to modify. Instead, it specifies that when changes to genes and changes to diet or schooling have the same effects, we should evaluate them similarly; we can give different moral verdicts only when we find a difference in effects. It will turn out that some human traits are more easily modifiable by genetic engineering, while other traits are more readily changed by environmental means. There is no reason to think that morally promising changes will be either exclusively genetic or exclusively environmental. The same goes for morally frightening changes. We should not expect the distinction between the morally acceptable and questionable to discriminate between environmental and genetic changes. The moral image of nurture suggests the following idea, which I call the nurture principle for its connection with NURTURE:

> If we are permitted to produce certain traits by modifying our children's environments, then we are also permitted to produce them by modifying their genomes.

I have already described a number of ways in which enhancement technologies might boost intelligence. Some of the statistical tools that behavioural geneticists use to isolate and measure the influence of genes on intelligence also illuminate previously invisible environmental influences on intelligence. A study published in the *Journal of the American Medical Association* investigated the effects of breastfeeding on adult intelligence.[4] The study focused on two samples of Danes born between October 1959 and December 1961. The physicians of the subjects' mothers had recorded data on the length of time the subjects were breastfed, and whether they were exclusively breastfed during this time. The subjects were given IQ tests. Even when variation in socio-economic background, the mothers' smoking habits, and some other possible influences on adult intelligence were accounted for the study found a 'robust association between the duration of breastfeeding and adult intelligence.'[5] The IQs of those who had been breastfed for between seven and nine months were, were on average, six points higher than the average of those breastfed for one month or less. A statistical correlation is not a causal explanation, but Mortensen and colleagues float a possible explanation. Docosahexaenoic acid (DHA) is a polyunsaturated fatty acid present in human milk, but absent both from cow's milk and from the infant formula that the test subjects were fed. It is an important element of the membranes of cells in the central nervous system, hypothesized to play a role in the transmission of signals within and between neurons. Different exposure to DHA might, therefore, account for cognitive differences between those who were breastfed over a relatively long period and those who were breastfed little or not at all.

The six IQ point advantage that Mortensen et al. put down to breast-feeding should be compared with the four IQ points that Plomin originally attributed to variation in IGF2R.[6] As with male homosexuality, hypotheses about environmental and genetic effects are not mutually exclusive. Genes and dietary influences may be independent influences, or they may work together. Perhaps there are variations in genes that influence how a baby's brain responds to DHA.

Makers of baby formulas now market their products on the basis of added fatty acids, and there is evidence that these formulas have closed the cognitive gap that might have existed between breast- and bottle-fed babies.[7] It is possible that there are combinations of fatty acids that can be added to formula that will, on average, lead to babies whose intelligence is higher than those raised on human milk. If the NURTURE principle is true, we should apply the same kinds of moral tests to proposals to feed babies formulas with elevated fatty acid levels that we would to proposals to boost intelligence by genetic engineering.

Many people think that genetic engineers have potentially greater powers to modify intelligence than those experimenting with infant formula, or other environmental influences. In the last chapter I challenged Fukuyama's contention that while changes to genes have the potential to significantly boost intelligence, the genetic leash limits what nutritionists and educationalists can achieve. However, the moral image of nurture can be instructive even if the powers of genetic engineers are greater than those of environmental engineers. The impossibility of achieving a twenty IQ point boost in intelligence by modifying the level of fatty acids in baby formula does not prevent us from having moral intuitions about an imaginary formula that had this effect. The unrealistic nature of this case may, of course, make us less certain of our judgements. It is this less confident endorsement that we should transfer from the hypothetical environmental enhancement to a genetic enhancement that has the same effect.

The moral parallel between gene and environment enables an additional response to the claim that genetically enhanced people do not really deserve their achievements. We are impressed if someone achieves beyond our expectations. In the age of the genome those expectations will be set, in part, by our awareness of a person's genetic strengths and weaknesses. Although Eero Mäntyranta's seven Olympic medals were marvellous achievements, they would have been even greater achievements had they been won by someone with normal levels of EPO. However, in the age of the genome our expectations will continue to be influenced by our understanding that some people have had educational advantages that others lack. Consider the early twentieth-century Indian mathematical genius, Srinivasa Ramanujan. In spite of very little formal training in mathematics, Ramanujan made a number of advances in number theory. His methods of solving mathematical problems were quite unlike recognized techniques. Ramanujan is impressive in absolute terms, but he is even more impressive when his starting point is taken into account. He achieved so much with next to no formal training.

The beneficiaries of genetic engineering to boost intelligence, like the beneficiaries of the best educations, ought to be capable of more than others, but this does not mean that they live lives without character-building struggle; it does not make their achievements meaningless.

MANUFACTURING HUMANS

Consider the following objection to human genetic engineering made by Leon Kass:

> [T]he price to be paid for producing optimum or even genetically sound babies will be the transfer of procreation from the home to the laboratory. Increasing control over the product can only be purchased by the increasing depersonalization of the entire process and its coincident transformation into manufacture. Such an arrangement will be profoundly dehumanizing...[8]

Kass is concerned that the new genetic technologies will lead to an era in which humans are manufactured. MANUFACTURE is a powerful image, congruent with the moral thinking of Kantians, who emphasize that persons should never be treated as mere things. Those who mount this challenge to enhancement technologies see a big difference between 'having' children and 'making' them. Couples who 'have' children are delighted if they turn out to be academically talented, but accept that they may not. Couples who ask genetic engineers to 'make' children for them will view academic failure as evidence of faulty design. Rather than just loving their children regardless, they will be contacting their lawyers.

The plea for consistency about genetic and environmental influences seems to allow swift rebuttal of MANUFACTURE. The image appears to assume a genetic determinist view of human development. It is because genes determine personalities that we can manufacture personalities by choosing genes. Once we accept that environments also make personalities, we should be prepared to pass the same judgement on 'manufacture by education' as we do on 'manufacture by genetic engineering'. If some forms of education are innocent of the charge of manufacture, then likewise so are some forms of genetic engineering.

Jürgen Habermas has recently challenged the liberal claim that since parents are permitted to improve their children by providing them with after-school maths tuition, they should also be allowed to improve them by providing them with genes predisposing them to be gifted at mathematics.[9] Habermas identifies what he thinks is a difference between environmental and genetic improvements. Unlike the latter, environmental enhancements can be questioned or challenged by the person who receives them. One has the option of rebelling, perhaps unsuccessfully, against after-school maths lessons. No similar option exists in respect of genetic engineering. One is simply born with one's genome engineered to include a parental 'fifth column'.[10] Habermas describes the likely experiences of a genetically enhanced adolescent:

> To the extent that his body is revealed to the adolescent who was eugenically manipulated as something which is also made, the participant perspective of the actual experience of living one's own life collides with the reifying perspective of a producer...The parents' choice of a genetic program for their child is associated with intentions which later take on the form of expectations addressed to the child, without, however providing the addressee with an opportunity to take a *revisionist* stand. The programming intentions...have the peculiar status of a one-sided and unchallengeable expectation.[11]

Habermas presents this analysis as marking a moral difference between treatment of disease and enhancement. Although there is no possibility for 'a revisionist stand' when we fix an embryonic gene that raises the risk of early-onset Alzheimer's, we are entitled to presume consent.[12] The genetic engineer who adopts the role of doctor does not impose values on the embryo.

Habermas's sharp distinction between environmental and genetic influences does not match the reality of human development, however. There are many environmental improvements that do not grant any realistic right of reply. David Wasserman points towards social influences that seem as uncontestable as genetic influences.

Why should Habermas believe that it is any more hopeless to be at odds with the 'genetically fixed' than the 'environmentally fixed' intentions of a third person? To the extent that parents shape the character and abilities of their already-born children, they do so largely at a time when those children are too young to contest their influence in any coherent or effectual way... [13]

A one-year-old's tantrum may reflect a preference for sleep over lessons, but it is surely too generous to interpret it as the rejection of a father's plan to turn her into a maths whiz.

There is also some scope for challenging genetic enhancements. Wasserman argues that Habermas's claim about the irresistibility of genetic interventions relies on a genetic determinist view of development. [14] If modifying your child's genome does not force characteristics on her then your eugenic plans can be challenged. According to Wasserman, Habermas's objection is best understood as hinging not on the irresistibility of genetic interventions, but instead on their unilateral nature. Even if it does not fix her traits, the decision to genetically modify the embryo that will become your child is unilateral. The child has no say in how her genome is altered.

I think we can recognize genetic enhancement as less unilateral if we take into account how genes influence traits. It is true that someone cannot, as an adolescent, change the fact that his parents have engineered his genome – but he does have some control over the *influences* of the genes that he has received. Many genetic influences on complex traits such as intelligence take place after a person's birth, and they require a specific environment to have the effects that geneticists associate with them. The adolescent has a say in whether the influence of the inserted gene gets matched with the environment without which it cannot have its intended effect. The child's act of refusing to go to school does not change genes, but it does prevent them from having the effects on his intellect that they would otherwise have had. As with educational influences, this rebellion may be unsuccessful. However, genetic enhancers of intelligence cannot exclude it entirely.

We already have one example of someone resisting the motives of a parent communicated by way of her selection of his genes. When Doron Blake rejected a mathematics and sciences future, he, in effect, chose not to co-operate with his mother's eugenic desires. There is also the more familiar example of disease genes. Someone who has inherited a gene that confers a higher than normal risk of heart disease has the option of 'collaborating' with the gene. She can smoke and eat plenty of fatty food, thereby helping the gene to have the effect by which we identify it. However, she also has the option of non-collaboration: she can live healthily and prevent a genetic influence from becoming a genetic effect.

Those who advocate genetic testing for serious illnesses hope to make this strategy of non-collaboration widely available. Testing would enable anyone with a higher than average risk of a disease to avoid the habits that might turn that risk into actual disease. However, evidence published in the *British Medical Journal* suggests that people tend not to respond to genetic information in this therapeutic way.[15] Researchers found that people told that they had an elevated risk of cancer were no more successful at quitting smoking than others. A tacit but stubborn genetic determinism seemed to lead them to ignore their doctors' explanations of the significance of the test results, making them fatalistic about their propensity for disease. In thinking this way, they make the same mistake as Habermas.

Gregory Stock describes how a child might be empowered by genetic engineers to exercise more direct control over the genes his parents have given him.[16] This option would involve the child's doing more than just resisting a gene's influence, but eliminating it. A gene is associated with a sequence of DNA known as a promoter that serves as an on/off switch for it. The promoter is set up to respond to a specific chemical signal that indicates whether the body requires more of the protein that the gene produces. Humans have no direct control over the promoters of the genes that nature has given us, but genetic engineers might give us control over the promoters of genes that they place in our genomes. The promoter of an introduced gene could be designed to respond only when in the presence of a chemical not normally found in the human diet. A genetically engineered person could decide whether to consume the chemical and thereby enjoy the gene's benefits.

These techniques may grant the people of the future a power over their genomes that no one today possesses. The mere possibility of a free choice does not mean that real genetically engineered people will have genuine choice in respect of the improvements their parents have purchased for them. The child knows that her parents have paid a large sum of money for the added gene. Will she be able to resist the pressure to make use of this genetic gift? Such questions reach out towards the broader social context of enhancement, the focus of chapter 7. However, we have reason to think that some will be able to exercise this option. Doron Blake, for example, refused to put his 'maths and science' genes into an environment in which they could turn him into a leading mathematician or scientist. It is not hard to imagine his refusing to drink the potion required to activate the genes that would have further locked him into this kind of future.

Habermas mounts a further objection that does not rely on the irresistibility or unilateral nature of genetic enhancements. This objection concedes, and indeed assumes, that parents need the child's assistance to implement their plans. The problem lies in the question of how parents contribute to their children's characteristics. Habermas finds the way in which engineered genetic influences work insidious. A parent who uses education to influence her child works from the outside, but someone who uses genetic means 'makes himself the *co-author of the life of another*, he intrudes – from the interior, one could say – into the other's consciousness of her own autonomy.'[17] This interior intrusion is bad because '[t]he programmed person, being no longer certain about the contingency of the natural roots of her life history, may feel the lack of a mental precondition for coping with the moral expectation to take...the *sole* responsibility for her own life.'[18] Suppose you muster the resolve to resist the influences of the genes your parents purchased for you. You must question the source of that resolve. Should it be traced back to their selection of your genes; is the delusion that you are resisting their influences just another part of your genetic engineers' plan for you?

It would be a mistake, however, to place too much moral weight on Habermas's distinction between interior and exterior intrusions. In chapter 4 I argued that we have a choice between descriptions of the influences on development that subordinate genes to the environment and descriptions that subordinate the environment to genes. Exercise can make an elite sportsperson, but only with the assistance of the right genes. Alternatively, an optimal combination of genes can only make an elite athlete with the help of the right training programmes. An analogous point applies to *changes to* influences. We can view any change as a change to a genetic influence – or, to use Habermas's terminology, a kind of interior intrusion – but we can also view any change as a change to an environmental influence – an exterior intrusion.

Interior intrusions can be placed on a spectrum that indicates their timing. The earliest intrusion will modify a genetic influence by changing letters of DNA. Swapping one version of the IGF2R gene for another would be one way to do this. Other changes to genetic influences come slightly later. Changes to a woman's diet during pregnancy would normally be viewed as changing an environmental influence on her child. But we can also think of it as a relatively early change to a genetic influence, an interior intrusion, because it interferes with the causal chain leading from the contents of a person's cellular nucleus to the construction of his brain and body. Researchers from Duke University have shown how dietary changes during pregnancy can change how genes work.[19] Although these dietary changes don't modify genes directly, they modify their expression. A process known as methylation involves the attachment to genes of a chemical known as a methyl group. Different patterns of methylation explain how an allele, or version of a gene, can have a different impact on one person's development from the effect it has on another's. The researchers speculate that improvements to a woman's diet during pregnancy may result in better patterns of methylation, and therefore better gene expression. The point of impact of other changes will be still further down the chain of causation leading from the contents of a person's nucleus to her attributes. For example, a weight-training programme taken up in adulthood changes the trajectory of the causal chain leading from genes to the building and maintenance of muscles at a later point than either the addition of an IGF-1 gene or the improvement of a pregnant woman's diet.

This is all to say that we can view almost any intervention as being in some sense interior, a change to the way in which genes make a person. Exactly the same manoeuvre is available to those prefer to view changes to developmental influences as emanating from outside. When a genetic engineer adds DNA to an embryo, she introduces into the inside of an organism something that originates from outside of it. This manner of exterior intrusion takes place earlier than the exterior intrusions of an instructor teaching Latin vocabulary.

Interior intrusions seem subversive, but we should be aware that each interior description of an intrusion has a counterpart that represents it as a less subversive exterior one. Habermas would have us choose between blanket endorsement or rejection of enhancement. In what follows, I present an analysis that enables us to separate the changes to children's genomes that unduly influence them from those that do not.

ENHANCEMENT AND BAD PARENTING

In chapter 5 I argued that the absence of a general requirement to prevent genetic harms meant that we had to limit the scope of the nature principle. Parents could not use that fact that they are not required to remove a harmful gene from their child's genome as justification for introducing such a gene. It is a virtue of the moral image of nurture that it explains some of these harms. In what follows, I use NURTURE to identify morally problematic ways to manipulate our children's genomes by first examining abuses on the environmental side. I argue that we should ban genetic modifications similar to morally impermissible ways to raise children.

In 1997 Sufiah Yusof won a place at Oxford University at the exceptionally precocious age of 13. Was Sufiah a rare prodigy? Not according to her father Farooq, who denied that Sufiah was especially gifted. In an interview published in the *Guardian*, he claimed that her precocity was the result of a rigorous home schooling method that interspersed intensive lessons with prayers, and stretching and breathing exercises.[20] Television and pop music were banned. The Yusof house was kept permanently cold 'to aid concentration'. Farooq Yusof said that his goal was 'to prove that you can accelerate children's learning process. This century is about knowledge-based information and we have shown that one can nurture and accelerate learning programmes'. Initially things went well at Oxford. On 22 June 2000, however, Sufiah was supposed to have boarded a train for home after her exams. Instead, she disappeared. When finally located, Sufiah swore she would never return home. In an e-mail to her father she explained, 'I've finally had enough of 15 years of physical and emotional abuse.' Sufiah described her home as a 'living hell'.

Sufiah Yusof was the victim of an extreme case of a form of environmental manufacture known as 'hothousing'. Many hothoused children are home-schooled in educationally enriched environments designed to give them an edge over their contemporaries attending conventional schools. Educational psychologists identify several dangers in hothousing.[21] The increased focus on formal learning can leave children socially underdeveloped. Some commentators are suspicious of the apparently impressive educational results achieved by hothousing. These critics allege that it produces only superficial learning. Children need to actively organize facts, rather than just storing them. They need to be able to apply them to situations that they encounter. Children presented with large amounts of information they are not ready to properly assimilate are forced to rely on rote learning. As a consequence, they can lag behind their conventionally schooled contemporaries in the acquisition of learning skills, long persisting with strategies that emphasize memorization.

One way to explain the wrongness of overly ambitious educational programmes such as that of Farooq Yusof is in terms of their impact on children's autonomy. Joel Feinberg captures the idea of a child's autonomy by appeal to a 'right to an open future'.[22] He explains that any ideas that parents have about their children's future 'must retreat before the claims of children that they be permitted to reach maturity with as many open options, opportunities, and advantages as possible'.[23]

The trigger for Feinberg's discussion is an appeal by the Pennsylvania Old Order Amish religious community against a law requiring that they send their children to state schools. The Old Order Amish live in ways that are reminiscent more of eighteenth-century rural Europe than of heavily urbanized twenty-first-century America. They are biblical literalists. They live apart from others, rejecting any practice or device that they judge to be a threat to their community. This suspicion of technology has left them without cars, television and electricity. The Old Order Amish educational system transmits the crafts and virtues deemed necessary for their pre-industrial, religiously conservative lifestyle. Children are taught to read just well enough for lifetime study of the Bible, and provided with only enough arithmetic to balance their budget books and to conduct basic transactions. In fitting children to their community, the Amish hope to ensure its continuation, and it was on these grounds that they challenged the law requiring the state schooling of their children.

Feinberg rejects their claim. He argues that action taken in defence of a distinctive way of life must not violate children's rights to reach maturity equipped to make their own choices about the lives they will lead:

> An education that renders a child fit only for one way of life forecloses irrevocably his other options. He may become a pious Amish farmer, but it will be difficult to the point of practical impossibility for him to become an engineer, a physician, a research scientist, a lawyer, or a business executive. The chances are good that inherited propensities will be stymied in a large number of cases, and in nearly all cases, critical life-decisions will have been made irreversibly for a person well before he reaches the age of full discretion when he should be expected, in a free society, to make them himself.[24]

According to Feinberg, the Old Order Amish violate their children's right to an open future by closing off many of the ways of life pursued in the contemporary United States.

If we translate Feinberg's idea that we should be maximizing our children's future options into the language of real freedom, we arrive at a restriction importantly stronger than the one described in chapter 5. Protecting the child's right to an open future is equivalent to an obligation to maximize real freedom. William Ruddick finds this principle too self-effacing on the part of parents. He argues that 'it requires them to make some unrealistic assumptions, especially about their own capacities for parental self-denial'.[25] Ruddick continues: 'If their children are to "reach maturity with as many open options, opportunities, and advantages as possible," they may have to give up or at least reduce the importance of their own ideals for their children's lives.'[26] Other philosophers of the family also argue that parents' values should be granted some role in determining the direction their children's lives will take.[27]

It is difficult to identify criteria for a principle that would direct us to the exact proper balance between parents' interests in promoting their ideals and children's need for self-determination. We should probably be suspicious of too precise an answer. A first point to make is that the example of the Amish does not support Feinberg's intuition that our children be brought up so as to have as many options as possible. Feinberg complains that the denial of state schooling to Amish children infringes their eventual autonomy by leaving them with significantly fewer alternatives than they would have had. Suppose the Amish were to concede that their children lack options available to state-schooled children, but countered that an Amish upbringing provides options that are not available to state-schooled children. Suppose they were also to claim that the options opened up were as substantial as those that are closed off. This second claim is unlikely to be true of the United States of the 1960s and 1970s, the time of the Amish challenges to the law requiring them have their children state educated. However, it might have been true at a time when the United States was a patchwork of agrarian communities built around a variety of different spiritual and philosophical beliefs. In this America, the Amish might have argued that an ability to more readily join these communities compensated for the loss of other kinds of options.

If the options provided by parents pursuing experimental educational strategies turn out to be as substantial as those lost through the lack of a state schooling, then they would be justified in saying that they do not infringe the children's eventual autonomy. Translating this idea into the terminology of chapter 5 would lead to a recommendation that we do not reduce real freedom. This convergence in recommendations may seem contrived, but it reflects the fact that both NATURE and NURTURE direct us towards the same moral concerns about enhancement.

The weighing of the relevance to autonomy of the options closed off by a particular upbringing against the relevance of those opened up will be no trivial task. The idea of counting options so as to ensure that those who want to educate their children in strange ways add at least as many options as they take away seems an absurdity. In chapter 5 I suggested a test to assess whether a particular use of enhancement technologies reduces real freedom. We will deem an enhancement to have reduced real freedom if it makes unlikely a successful life founded on values that oppose those of the enhancers. A similar test enables us to assess the significance to autonomy of the options opened up and closed off to the child. It is a condition for the implementation of an educational programme that makes a child better able to lead the kind of life that parents want for him that it also leave open the possibility of a lifestyle diametrically opposed to his parents' values. It is not enough for an Amish parent to point to the various roles within his society, explaining that he would acquiesce to the son's decision not to become a minister. If his child has no realistic prospect of pursuing a lifestyle radically opposed to Amish values then the upbringing is likely to infringe autonomy.

THE LIMITED POWERS OF GENETIC ENGINEERS

Consider the following apparent disanalogy between upbringing and genetic engineering. Feinberg explains that parents' choices about how to raise their child can be guided by certain facts about them. He says:

> Right from the beginning the newborn infant has a kind of rudimentary character consisting of temperamental proclivities and a genetically fixed potential for the acquisition of various talents and skills. The standard sort of loving upbringing and a human social environment in the earliest years will be like water added to dehydrated food, filling it out and actualizing its stored in tendencies.[28]

Feinberg's presentation has hints of genetic determinism. However, regardless of whether the tendency to acquire talents and skills is fixed by genes or is the result of the interaction of genes and environment, it is nonetheless present. It is a genuine element of the child's nascent character. Farooq Yusof's crime was that he was indifferent to any signs that his daughter might have made choices about the life she wanted to lead. Suppose, however, that he had had access to the tools of genetic engineering. He would have been able to remove the last vestige of resistance to his plan – he could not only have accelerated Sufiah's learning but could have made her want the lifestyle for which this knowledge was necessary.

In what follows, I question the claim that enhancement technologies will ever give parents this kind of control over their children's futures. The points I make hold true even against the backdrop of a pragmatic optimism about enhancement technologies.

For a parent to be able to choose the life plan of her child there must be a *reliable* connection between a course of action available to her and a particular lifestyle her child might choose. If there is no such reliable connection then nothing she does should be construed as choosing her child's plan. Although genomic information may give parents the power to influence the probability that a given life plan will be chosen, it is unlikely that the probability could ever be raised to the point of reliability.

In chapter 4 I described Hamer's evidence for a gene that had influenced the sexual orientation of a group of gay brothers. Suppose the sexual-orientation gene is isolated and sequenced, and we then discover how to substitute one version for the other in a human embryo. It would be wrong to view this as selecting an aspect of the life plan of the person that the embryo will develop into. Hamer acknowledges that many gay men lack the gay version of the sexual-orientation gene and that many heterosexual men have the homosexual version. This will not change in the era of genetic engineering. Although choosing the version of the gene at Xq28 may raise the child's probability of being straight or gay, selecting a straight or gay life plan requires more than raising its probability.

Any society that gives people choices about their lives is bound to make unreliable the link between any particular combination of genes and a particular life plan. This does not reflect any deficit in genomic knowledge. Rather, it reflects facts about how people arrive at their life plans. A wide variety of environmental factors combine with any genetic predispositions to provide us with our life plans. Apparently, tiny variations in a person's environment can have far-reaching consequences for the life plan that is pursued. Exposure to five minutes of a television medical drama may inspire someone to be a doctor, or to seek acting lessons. An early encounter with a rugby ball may lead someone to decide on a career as a sportsperson; alternatively, it may inspire a life-long aversion to sport. This point about the environmental sensitivity of life plans applies doubly in modern liberal societies in which people encounter a diverse range of often contrary influences. The heterogeneous collection of factors that come between a change to a person's genome and the formation of her life plan makes it misguidedly optimistic for a genetic engineer to conceive of himself as engineering a specific life plan into the person he helps to create.

The difference between selecting a life plan and raising its probability is a significant one. Were prospective parents to be able to choose their child's life plan then they could justify equipping her with the specific set of capabilities required for that plan. If they can only raise the probability that a life plan will be chosen, they must make provision for the eventuality of their child's rejecting their choice. This is to say: they must respect their child's autonomy, ensuring that he comes into existence able lead a lifestyle founded on values opposed to those of his parents. Herein lies autonomy's significance for genetic engineers. The inability to select a life plan means that we must be cautious in our attempts to enhance capacities. Parents who pursue ambitious educational strategies risk ignoring choices that their children have already made about their futures. Those who enhance by means of genetic engineering must admit their ignorance of the kind of life their child will lead. Deprived of this information, they should ensure that their use of enhancement technologies equips their child for any choices that he might make.

ARE ENHANCEMENTS PROBLEMATIC BECAUSE THEY ARE POSITIONALLY VALUABLE?

The moral image of nurture helps us to understand a popular objection against genetic enhancement. According to this objection, we should not allow enhancement because attributes like increased intelligence, stronger muscles and more charming personalities are positional goods. Positional goods are sought because they give a competitive advantage over others. Buchanan et al. imagine the effects of a policy permitting parents to genetically engineer additional height into their children.[29]

To the extent that extra height is desirable only because of the competitive advantage it brings with it, widespread use of the intervention is self-defeating. Perhaps some very short people for whom there is true inconvenience in living in a world geared for taller people would gain temporary relief, but if the variance in height remains unchallenged except that most people are six inches taller, then markets will end up discriminating against the shortest (and tallest) again. Competitive advantage of additional height in (some) sports or in social acceptance would not change from what it was before the intervention. The intervention is thus self-defeating for those whose reasons are strictly competitive.[30]

Buchanan and his colleagues think that the attempt to enhance height may be self-defeating. The universal availability of height enhancement will thwart the aim of increasing the height of one's child relative to others. There are also substantial social costs. We would need to redesign cars, toilets and dwellings to accommodate the new population of giants.

The proper assessment of the hypothesis that enhancements are positional goods demands terminology to express the alternative view. We can contrast positional value with what I call *independent value*.[31] While an attribute's positional value varies according to the degree to which others possess it, its independent value does not. Both intelligence and height combine positional and independent value. High intelligence certainly has great positional value; scholarships and medical school positions tend to go only to the brightest. But it also has substantial independent value – the understanding of the world that intelligence brings is not undermined by everyone else's having the same or better understanding. Even height, the attribute presented by Buchanan et al. as a paradigm of positional value, has some independent value. Tall people can reach objects out of reach of short people. The fact that one can reach an apple growing on a tree does not change because others can reach it more easily.

Because high intelligence possesses great independent value, those who enhance it need not fear that others will entirely gainsay their efforts. Consider this claim in the light of the moral image of nurture. Parents who use environmental means to boost the intelligence of their young children know that pre-school lessons or DHA-enriched foods are also available to other parents. Some might see their provision of the lessons and special diet as defensive measures: they must be provided because other parents will provide them for their children. Perhaps some who save to send their children to university have the same pessimistic attitude, but even they should concede the independent value of intelligence and a university education.

The fact that most goods combine independent and positional value is no news to advocates of the free market. They present competition as the most efficient means of generating independent value. Manufacturers of computers want products that sell better than those made by other businesses. The pursuit of positional value leads them to make machines that perform the independently valuable tasks of connecting to the internet, playing DVD movies and recording music. So it could be with enhancements. The profits of the companies selling enhancements will depend on their satisfying the competitive needs of prospective parents. The market in technologies that enhance intelligence will result in the expansion of children's understanding of their world.[32]

REGULATING THE PURSUIT OF POSITIONAL VALUE

It would be wrong to uncritically endorse a picture in which the pursuit of enhancements for their positional value promotes their independent value, however. Some of the free market's most vigorous advocates think that it should be expanded to almost any facet of human experience. More moderate advocates concede that market forces should be excluded from some parts of human lives. The family is high on the list of things warranting protection. In this chapter, I have justified the use of enhancement technologies by comparing them with the means of making people that parents already have at their disposal. However, a consequence of this argument may be the subjection of families to yet another destructive influence. Many of the choices parents make about how to educate their children are motivated by the recognition that failing to procure advantages that other parents procure will condemn their children to last place in the race for status and material benefits. We should not be rushing to give the market yet another point of entry into families. In what follows, I explore some ways in which the intensity of the competition in enhancement might be limited, thereby minimizing its destructiveness.

We might limit the competition's intensity by requiring parents to choose their children's attributes for their independent rather than positional value. However, such a law could prevent the socially ruinous consequences of the universal pursuit of positional value only if it is possible to enforce. The problem is that prospective parents could easily circumvent a law directing that their use of enhancement technologies not be motivated by the quest for positional value. They would point out that any attribute combines both positional and independent value. When filling in their application forms they would place emphasis on the independent value of the enhancement they are seeking. Prospective parents will point to the pluralistic moral underpinnings of liberal eugenics to defend a choice that may seem eccentric to those charged with vetting the applications.

The restrictions on enhancement recommended in this and the preceding chapter will rule out some positional enhancements. Although extreme height may be an advantage on the basketball court, genetic engineers would need to undertake a massive overhaul of the human body plan to reduce this trait's impact on real freedom and on autonomy. But what of the competitive pursuit of enhancements that do not reduce real freedom or autonomy? I propose that we limit the kinds of competitions that prospective parents can participate in.

Economists describe some competitions as 'winner-takes-all'. In such competitions, those who come first are well rewarded while those finish behind them get nothing. For convenience's sake I will broaden the definition of winner-takes-all competitions to include ones in which those who finish at or towards the top, are amply rewarded, but those who do less well get either nothing or very little. It is a characteristic of winner-takes-all competitions that those who get nothing or very little may have done only slightly less well in absolute terms than those who finish at or near the top. Olympic events are obvious examples of winner-takes-all competitions. Those who finish first are very well rewarded – they get the gold medals, the media recognition and the sponsorship deals. Second- and third-place achievers are rewarded, but much less amply. On the occasions that those who finish fourth are even noticed, they are swiftly forgotten. This is so even if, in terms of the amount lifted, distance thrown or finishing time, the fourth-place achiever performed almost as well as the person who finished first.

Other competitions are not winner-takes-all. They give the greatest rewards to those who do the best, but also give good rewards to those who finish behind them. For example, academics judged to be the best are rewarded in ways that their colleagues who perform less well are not. These rewards are sufficient to inspire many to seek them. However, academics whose performance does not match that of the elite are still well rewarded for their endeavours.

Winner-takes-all competitions can have ruinous consequences for those who participate in them. There has been much discussion about East German athletes who took life-shortening performance-enhancing drugs presented to them as vitamins. It would be interesting to know what they would have done had they been aware of the tablets' and injections' likely impacts on both their performance and their health. In a 1995 survey, Olympic-level US athletes were asked whether they would take a drug that would grant them a five-year winning streak terminated by their deaths.[33] Over half said that they would. I wonder how many would have answered in this way had they thought that the rewards for five years of merely excellent performance, though less than those of the winning streak, were still substantial.

We cannot ban the pursuit of enhancements on the basis of their positional value, but we can prevent parents from seeking enhancements that prepare their children exclusively or principally for winner-takes-all competitions. An impartial judge may be in no position to dispute a parent's assertion that she is seeking an enhancement primarily for its independent value. An attribute's independent value is relative to the values of the parents choosing it, and the parents can always claim the values that would legitimize the attribute that they want for their child. However, the judge can decide whether the dominant effect of the attribute that a parent is seeking is to prepare his child for a winner-takes-all competition. This is because whether or not an attribute equips one principally for a winner-takes-all competition depends on facts about the society in which the choice is being made, not on the particular values of the parents.

A ban on prospective parents' engaging in winner-takes-all competition with other parents would prevent the use of enhancement technologies to produce extreme athletic ability. The extreme height useful in top-level basketball is not so valuable off the court. Those who want to use enhancement technologies to boost the IQs of their children do prepare them for some winner-takes-all competitions, but they can also point to many competitions that do not reward only the winners. The brightest may get the best jobs, but those who are slightly less intelligent also get good jobs.

The preceding argument should not be read as a plea for social reform. I am not advocating a ban of winner-takes-all competitions. There should continue to be Olympic games in the era of enhancement, and athletes should be permitted to dedicate their lives to the pursuit of gold medals. Rather my suggestion is directed at the regulation of enhancement technologies. I am arguing for a ban on the uses of enhancement technologies whose main effect is to equip children to participate in winner-takes-all competitions. While it is fine for someone to choose to compete for gold medals, that choice should not be made by others, whether by genetic engineering or by drug regimes.

I have explored two reasons for opposing the use of enhancement technologies to pursue positional value. First, such uses will in many cases intrude on the child's autonomy, giving her less real freedom to seek the kind of life that she wants. We now have a second reason, one that applies to certain enhancements that do not infringe autonomy. Some uses of enhancement technologies involve prospective parents in winner-takes-all competitions with other parents. Engaging in these competitions is likely to be self-defeating, preventing enhancement from having its intended effects.

In this chapter I have begun to investigate the wider social context of enhancement. This investigation continues in the next chapter.

CHAPTER 7

Our Postliberal Future?

The freedom of citizens to design other citizens goes considerably beyond the familiar freedoms of speech, movement and worship. It really is a radical extension of the liberal doctrine. Up until now, I have been concerned about whether enhancement technologies will harm the people they bring into existence. We must now broaden our focus to consider the potential for harms to the communities that will contain enhanced people. This chapter explores two ways in which the freedom to enhance may undermine the very liberal social arrangements that give rise to and support it.

The best way to introduce concerns about the biotechnology's impact on liberal social arrangements is by way of Fukuyama's reflections on both of these topics. His 1992 book, *The End of History and the Last Man*, established him as a leading defender of liberal democracy. In it, Fukuyama declared that history, considered as a progression of political arrangements, was over. Soon, and evermore, all human societies would be liberal democratic ones. Fukuyama spent much of the 1990s rebutting arguments for the staying power of various illiberal social arrangements. With the 2002 publication of *Our Posthuman Future*, he turns his attention towards biotechnology, a threat that he finds more potent than communism or religious fundamentalism. According to Fukuyama, biotechnology has the power to restart history by replacing humans with posthumans. Posthumans may have imposed upon them, or perhaps even choose, political arrangements very different from liberal democratic ones.

Fukuyama paraphrases a famous line of Thomas Jefferson, author of the American Declaration of Independence, to introduce biotechnology's threat. According to Jefferson, liberal democracy finds its foundation in the empirical equality of human beings: 'The general spread of the light of science has already laid open to every view the palpable truth that the mass of mankind has not been born with saddles on their backs, nor a favored few booted and spurred, ready to ride them legitimately.'[1] Fukuyama fears that biotechnology will turn this palpable truth into a falsehood:

> The political equality enshrined in the Declaration of Independence rests on the empirical fact of natural human equality. We vary greatly as individuals and by culture, but we share a common humanity that allows every human being to potentially communicate with and enter into a moral relationship with every other human being on the planet. The ultimate question raised by biotechnology is, What will happen to political rights once we are able to, in effect, breed some people with saddles on their backs, and others with boots and spurs?[2]

What remains of this allegation after the discussion of the past hundred pages? In chapter 5 I used the moral image of nature to contest the view that enhancement technologies will deprive our descendants of their humanity. Liberals can counter the most obvious and direct ways in which biotechnology will divide us into the booted and the saddled. Authoritarian eugenicists might find it expedient to manufacture a class of people to perform menial roles – much like the deltas and epsilons of *Brave New World*. However, the liberal view I have described takes away from social planners responsibility for choices about what kinds of human beings there will be and gives it to parents, who are unlikely to want children subservient by design. Those few who did would be told that intentionally bringing children into existence 'with saddles on their backs' considerably reduces their real freedom and infringes their autonomy.

In this chapter I describe threats to liberal democracy more subtle and indirect than those imagined by Huxley and Fukuyama. My discussion is, of necessity, more speculative than that of earlier chapters. Pragmatic optimists idealize about how enhancement technologies will work, but they are not entitled to assume people will always respond in the best ways to them and to their human products. We will need to make educated guesses about how our rationally and morally imperfect descendants will react to the widespread availability and use of genomics, genetic engineering and cloning. The speculative nature of the discussion means that I will be more cautious in my conclusions than I have been in earlier chapters.

Rather than just dismissing threats to liberal social arrangements, I will describe the measures that must be taken if they are to be met.

TWO BIOTECHNOLOGICAL TENDENCIES: POLARIZATION AND HOMOGENIZATION

Successful liberal democracies balance celebrating the differences between citizens and forging a common bond between them. Two biotechnological tendencies, explored extensively in novelists' and screenplay writers' forecasts, threaten this balance between diversity and solidarity.

The tendency of *polarization* may make us and our descendants too different from one another for there to be any possibility of a social bond. Consider the prediction of Princeton geneticist Lee Silver.[3] His world of 2350 is inhabited by people divided into a number of different genetic classes. At the bottom of the heap are the Naturals – people whose parents, grandparents and great-grandparents have either had no access to gene therapies, or have chosen not to use them. Lording over them are various classes of the GenRich, enhanced along different dimensions of human performance. There are GenRich athletes, who are separated into various subtypes, including the GenRich football player, and sub-subtypes, among which is the GenRich running back. Other GenRich types are the scientist, the businessperson and the artist, each with their corresponding subtypes and sub-subtypes. The manufacture of classes of GenRich will be limited only by genomics' progress in finding genetic variations that correspond with differences in physical and intellectual abilities. Silver imagines changes of such magnitude that the Naturals and GenRich will be on the verge of becoming separate species of humanity, a fracturing of our biological unity not seen since the demise of Neanderthals some 30,000 years ago. It is hard to see much of a basis for a social common bond in Silver's world of 2350. Anthropologists used to think that *Homo sapiens* systematically annihilated *Homo neanderthalensis*. They now favour a theory according to which Neanderthals were continually outhunted, outforaged and excluded from the choicest shelters. Will the fate of our unenhanced descendants be the same as that of the Neanderthals – extinction by exclusion?

The biotechnological tendency of *homogenization* inspires the opposite fear. It may make citizens so similar that liberal protections of diversity will become redundant. Critics of genetically modified foods warn that genetic engineers will send into overdrive the global spread of agricultural monocultures.[4] Market forces direct farmers to plant the crops that are the easiest to cultivate, that ripen the quickest and produce the highest yields. The era preceding agricultural biotechnology has already seen a dramatic reduction in the diversity of farmed crops. For example, between the years 1903 and 1983 there was a 93 per cent narrowing in the range of varieties of corn cultivated in the United States.[5] Biotechnologists empowered to genetically modify corn may accelerate convergence on a single economically optimal variety. Opponents of enhancement technologies foresee human monocultures. They think that any differences between GenRich types and subtypes will be a faint echo of the diversity found in contemporary liberal democracies.

Although polarization and homogenization are contrary tendencies, they might be simultaneous consequences of a prerogative to enhance. The societies of 2350 may, at one and the same time, be polarized and homogenized. While the film *GATTACA* depicts a society divided – there is a class of genetically enhanced people supported by a class of unenhanced Invalids – it also presents a reverse trend. Enhanced people are all super-intelligent and super-athletic over-achievers, products of a single eugenic mould. The divisions feared by those who emphasize polarization result from unequal access to enhancement technologies. Those concerned about homogenization worry that parents who do have access to enhancement technologies will select from among a very restricted range of human designs.

Some with strong commitments to liberty may doubt that polarization is really a concern. Those who prize social solidarity may even find the prospect of homogenization appealing. I have argued that the addition of the word 'liberal' to 'eugenics' transforms an evil doctrine into a morally acceptable one. It should be no surprise, then, that I am convinced of the worth of liberal arrangements and take threats to them seriously. This chapter addresses the question of whether societies that are in part polarized and in part homogenized are the inevitable consequences of free access to enhancement technologies. It would be convenient if I could show that these concerns rely on misconceptions of biotechnology. But I do not think this. Rather than assuring readers that the prerogative to enhance will not polarize or homogenize, instead I limit myself to showing what we must do, and what conditions must obtain, if enhancement technologies are not to undermine liberal social arrangements.

DISTRIBUTING ACCESS TO ENHANCEMENT TECHNOLOGIES

Silver's story about the world of 2350 involves two kinds of polarization: *intrinsic* polarization and polarization *resulting from differential access.* The relationship between different classes of GenRich exemplifies the first kind of polarization. The relationship between the GenRich and the Naturals provides an example of the second.

We can trace intrinsic polarization back to the different values of those who make use of enhancement technologies. It can occur when people who happen to prefer a certain way of life make their children different from others in ways that enable their children to better pursue this way of life. Prospective parents whose vision of the good life encompasses surfing will make different enhancement choices from those whose choices encompass quantum physics. Silver envisages choices that are very intrinsically polarizing indeed: a few hundred years of the use and refinement of enhancement technologies seem to have resulted in people very different from one another.

The limitations on individual enhancement choices proposed in chapters 5 and 6 should minimize intrinsic polarization. A parent's realization of her particular values in her child must leave room for the child to make meaningful choices about the course of his life. The labels 'GenRich running back' and 'GenRich physicist' reflect choices that have reduced real freedom and infringed autonomy and would be inappropriate for someone enhanced in a way that left open genuine choice about the course his life will take.

The threat I am concerned about here is of polarization resulting from differential access to enhancement technologies. In his book *Anarchy, State, and Utopia*, Robert Nozick imagined a 'supermarket' that would make a wide variety of genetic technologies available to those with the money for them.[6] This would be fine if genetic technologies were as cheap as most supermarket items, but enhancement technologies are likely, at least initially, to be expensive. Consider the price tags associated with the relatively limited options available today. Infertile couples are now offering financial inducements of up to US $100,000 for the eggs of women with demonstrated Ivy League educations, attractiveness, elite scholastic aptitude scores, specific ethnicities, and backgrounds free of 'major family medical issues'.[7] CLONAID has made a series of unverified announcements that they have cloned humans. It will cost you US $200,000 to enrol in their cloning programme. If your goal is enhancement, you may have to add whatever price Sachin Tendulkar or Jodie Foster would charge for the use of their genomes. We should expect the cost of the first therapies that enable the manipulation of human intelligence genes to be even more expensive.

Suppose the great cost of enhancement means that only the rich will have any real freedom to enhance their children. Inequalities resulting from genetic enhancement layered on existing educational and dietary inequalities will turn the gap between the rich and the poor into a gulf between their children. There need be no state directive to create Huxleyan epsilons. While wealthy parents procure every possible improvement, nature will provide the menial class through the reproductive efforts of the poor.

In chapter 1, I stressed that enhancement technologies present us with problems that seem quite unlike those we have confronted before. However, the challenge I have just described seems quite familiar. Isn't it just the issue, long pondered by philosophers, of what counts as a just distribution of the goods required for a good life? Political philosophers have proposed a number of accounts of how houses, doctors' visits and retirement moneys should be distributed and of how best to achieve what they deem a just distribution. Why shouldn't we see enhancements as just more goods to feed into a society's distributive apparatus? John Rawls's distributive scheme currently enjoys the most widespread philosophical support.[8] Rawls proposes a 'difference principle', which allows deviation from equal distribution of goods such as liberty and opportunity only when an unequal distribution helps everybody, most especially the worst off. Were we to entrust enhancements to Rawls we would grant the rich better access only if the worse off were to be benefited by this pattern of access. We would be confident about the fairness of this way of allocating enhancements to the extent that we were confident about Rawls's theory of justice.

However, the problem of differential access is not so easily dealt with. Suppose we can agree on a theory of distributive justice. If enhancements are like other goods, we should understand that the apparatus of distributive justice will almost certainly fail to allocate them in ways that political philosophers think is just. Silver feigns sympathy for those who will not receive the access to enhancement technologies that is their moral due. He says: 'Many people think that it is inherently unfair for some people to have access to technologies that can provide advantages while others, less well-off, are forced to depend on chance alone. I would agree. It is inherently unfair.'[9] But Silver responds to this moral squeamishness in robust libertarian terms: 'American society adheres to the principle that personal liberty and personal fortune are the primary determinants of what people are allowed and able to do. Anyone who accepts the right of affluent parents to provide their children with an expensive private school education cannot use "unfairness" as a reason for rejecting the use of reprogenetic technologies.'[10]

Treating enhancements as goods that we may or may not succeed in distributing fairly ignores a respect in which they differ from other goods that we complacently allow markets to misallocate. We need to distinguish goods that grant some people better lives than others from those that make people different from others. Enhancement technologies are certainly not alone in making us different from one another. The method of moral images has allowed us to compare novel genetic technologies with more familiar means of enhancement. Fukuyama is wrong to think that there is something called human nature vulnerable to genetic engineers but impervious to environmental change. Nevertheless, we should appreciate that genetic enhancements do not have to be fundamentally different from environmental improvements for them to create new problems. We face a problem of degree rather than of kind. Superior educations and health services already make a rich child different from a poor one, but they do not make people so different that they cannot consider each other fellow citizens. The combination of existing and novel means of enhancement may make people so different that any sense of solidarity is lost.

REDUCING THE BURDEN OF UNIVERSAL ACCESS

We could meet this threat by insisting on universal access to enhancement technologies. This would involve the state's making available to the poor any enhancement that rich people are permitted to purchase. Forcing the wealthy to subsidize such a scheme would seem to be one way to apply Rawlsian justice to enhancement technologies and it appears an effective response to the allegation of polarization. But surely the point is that this option would be impossibly expensive? States that fail to provide universal health care will almost certainly lack the will to force the wealthy to pay for universal access to enhancement technologies.

Perhaps the burden of universal access will not be as heavy as it initially seems. Some people may pursue relatively cheap enhancement options. It is important to remember that we are distributing *access to* rather than *the use of* the technologies. Universal access to enhancement technologies is not the same as universal use of them. Some people prefer organic food because they believe it to be free of dangerous additives, but others prefer it simply because it is more natural. We should expect there to be parents who will appeal to nature to justify their exclusion of technology from the conception and gestation of their children. In an age in which many parents use genetic engineering and PGD to enhance, these parents would, in effect, be enhancing by not interfering in any of these ways.

Kass's criticism of reproductive cloning echoes fears that the process may destroy or fail to replicate the human soul. This claim goes beyond the scientific evidence. But even if we suppose that an immaterial soul is a significant part of a human being, it is hard to see how the difference between an embryo that is the direct result of the meeting of sperm and egg and one produced by somatic cell nuclear transfer could be the difference between having a soul and not having one.[11] This dispute notwithstanding, in the age of enhancement there will almost certainly remain people who believe in souls and other spiritual entities. The naturally conceived children of GATTACA are sometimes referred to as Invalids, a term that makes it difficult to see any sense in which they might be enhanced. However, other times in the movie they are referred to as 'God births'. So long as the societies of the future contain individuals with religious or spiritual beliefs, there will always be prospective parents who view children conceived the natural way as better than those who are not. One could imagine that God births may have a competitive advantage over genetically engineered humans in certain lines of work; Ethan Hawke's character in GATTACA conceals his status as a God birth from his employers at the space programme. Perhaps in the future, genetically engineered humans will find themselves concealing the facts about their origins to gain entry into the Catholic priesthood or a management position in an organic foods co-operative. Vigorous advocacy of the 'natural way' by those with strong religious or spiritual commitments is unlikely to convince everyone. However, it should make everyone aware that there is a viable conception of human excellence that disdains genetic modification. We should treat a situation in which the 'natural' path of enhancement is pursued as often by the rich as by the poor as evidence that we are close to universal access.

Facts about the development of enhancement technologies may also make the goal of universal access more achievable. Although enhancement technologies are likely at first to be expensive they may soon become cheaper. Those who study the social impacts of technology distinguish two processes in their development – *innovation* and *diffusion*. The process of innovation involves the invention of new technologies and expansion of the power of existing ones. The diffusion of technologies occurs as they become cheaper over time, and therefore more widely available. The innovation of enhancement technologies tends towards greater polarization, but the process of diffusion points in the opposite direction, promoting their spread.

Genomics is an enhancement technology on the verge of diffusion. The first complete record of a human genome cost billions of dollars. In mid-2003 it was estimated that it would cost some US $50 million for an individual to get a complete record of her genome. The push is now on for what has come to be called the '$1,000 genome'. Some scientific commentators predicted that technologies that could produce a complete record of one's DNA, to be sold for US $1,000, might be ten to fifteen years away.[12] Perhaps a few years later the price of genomic information will drop sufficiently for it to be within reach of people outside of the affluent 'first world'. We cannot say how the processes of innovation and diffusion will play out in the future development of other enhancement technologies. It is possible that biotechnological breakthroughs will suddenly make a wide range of enhancements available to the rich and that these enhancements will become more moderately priced only much later. This pattern of development would be polarizing. However, it is also possible that new enhancement techniques will be discovered only gradually, with sufficient time between these advances for them to become widely available. This pattern would make universal access easier to achieve.

A further technological tendency may make enhancement technologies less polarizing. Conservatives tend to present a genetic underclass as something original to enhancement technologies. But contemporary liberal societies already have genetic underclasses – many people who suffer from serious genetic diseases struggle for access to services from public health systems increasingly starved of funding. Although people who have genetic diseases may seem the least likely to be able to afford enhancement technologies, they may nonetheless receive them. Nick Bostrom speculates that 'it may well turn out to be technologically much easier to cure gross genetic defects than to enhance an already healthy constitution. We currently know much more about many specific inheritable diseases, some of which are due to single gene defects, than we do about the genetic basis of talents and desirable qualities such as intelligence and longevity, which in all likelihood are coded in complex constellations of large numbers of genes.'[13] Bostrom infers from this pattern that the 'trajectory of human genetic enhancement may be one in which the first thing to happen is that the lot of the genetically worst-off is radically improved, through the elimination of diseases such as Tay Sachs, Down's Syndrome, early-onset Alzheimer's disease, and eventually lesser advantages are... done away with'.[14] Perhaps rich people with genetic illnesses will receive treatment ahead of similarly afflicted poor people. If so, this will make definitive judgements about the equality of societies with genetic technologies difficult. According to some measures, a society in which serious genetic disorders are found only in the poor would be less equal than one in which the wealth of one's parents does not affect the probability that one has such a disease. However, the former society might be viewed as more equal simply because a greater percentage of its citizens are not barred from full participation by genetic disease.

BIOTECHNOLOGY'S THREAT TO CITIZENSHIP

If the child of a poor person is as likely to be enhanced as the child of a rich person then there need be no exaggeration of existing social divisions. However, the previous points notwithstanding, it seems improbable that the state will be able to make any enhancement that rich parents could purchase available to all. To insist on universal access would be, in effect, to ban all but the most rudimentary enhancement technologies. Many liberals will find it unacceptable that we should ban something that cannot be made universally available. Suppose we cannot provide places at Oxford or Harvard for all who demonstrate sufficient academic ability to benefit from attending these institutions. Surely that does not mean that we should abolish them? The idea that we cannot make it a condition for anyone's receiving a good that it be available to all has force even in the case of goods that shape our natures.

Fukuyama thinks that biotechnology threatens moral relationships. I now use the idea of a moral relationship to establish the extent to which we can safely fall short of providing universal access to enhancement technologies. The analysis I present places great emphasis on the maintenance of the kinds of moral relationships that obtain between fellow citizens. Any standard less demanding than universal access must preserve the possibility of such relationships between those with the fullest access and those with the worst.

What is involved in the moral relationship between citizens? A first essential element is the acknowledgment of moral worth. One cannot have any kind of moral relationship with another if one does not recognize that the other is morally considerable. Hollywood screenplay writers anticipate problems in this area. In movie depictions, enhanced people are often oblivious to the moral worth of unenhanced people, indeed almost unaware of their very existence. It is easy to imagine uses of enhancement technologies that would vindicate the Hollywood prediction. Some very competitive people view morality as little more than an obstacle in the way of success. They might want to engineer into their children a disregard for others' moral worth. The discovery of genetic arrangements linked with the lack of empathy characteristic of psychopaths might promote this particular eugenic end.

The moral image of NURTURE can help us to respond to such a use of enhancement technologies. R. Paul Churchill argues that parents have an obligation to educate their children to be moral altruists.[15] He claims that the aim of raising healthy, happy and autonomous human beings does not conflict with, indeed is often promoted by, the goal of raising altruists. It does seem unlikely that parents would benefit their children by making them psychopaths. Those completely devoid of empathy may flourish in the short term, but they are usually exposed in the end. Perhaps geneticists will find genes that can be modified so as to reduce but not entirely eliminate the capacity to empathize. It seems to me that even slight moral impairment is likely to handicap many life plans. A person who is incapable of acknowledging the full moral worth of others is likely to find forming meaningful relationships with them more difficult. However, even if enhancement by way of moral impairment did not harm its recipients, it should be banned. This should be apparent once we take into account the plights of those whose spouses, neighbours and colleagues are morally impaired.

Of course, enhanced people may ignore unenhanced people not because they have been designed specifically to be amoral – they may ignore them simply because they are different from them. The transhumanist Mark Walker hopes that we will soon create beings who exceed humans in intelligence 'by the same margin as humans exceed that of chimpanzees'.[16]

Perhaps these beings will have the same lack of interest in and concern for humans as humans currently have for chimpanzees.

Perhaps enhanced people will be less prone to the moral alienation that normally accompanies distance. Many of our moral blind spots result from our inability to apply rules consistently. A television image of someone in the final stages of AIDS inspires sympathy, and for the moments that the advertisement is showing, we feel moved to act. However, few of us end up doing anything. It is not that we cease to be concerned about human suffering. Rather we cease to combine in our minds the knowledge that there are many millions of poor people suffering from AIDS with our understanding of the difference we can make. It is possible that intellectually enhanced GenRich people will make this kind of mistake less frequently than we do. Their greater powers of reasoning may make them less susceptible to inconsistencies in moral judgement, less likely to understand one minute that there is a great deal of suffering in the world and forget it the next. If so, the members of an intellectually enhanced genetic elite may compensate for their distance from the unenhanced with a better understanding of the consequences of their actions on other moral beings.

It is possible that enhanced people will avoid these moral burdens by endorsing moral systems that privilege properties possessed by them alone. In this way, they could both ignore us and avoid the charge of inconsistency. Doing so would require a conception of morality completely unlike ours. Nick Bostrom speculates that enhanced people may 'discover values that will strike us as being of a far higher order than those we can realize as un-enhanced biological human beings'.[17] However, for this new moral understanding to exclude us, the GenRich would have not only to add values but to subtract them. For example, they would need to reject the moral value of sentience. It seems to me that a requirement that we not use enhancement technologies to produce people whom we would consider immoral will prevent this eventuality, at least early in the era of enhancement.

THE IMPORTANCE OF RECIPROCITY

There is no reason to think that enhanced people will ignore the moral worth of unenhanced people. The problem is that full moral relationships involve more than just acknowledging the moral value of others. They require *reciprocity*. Moral and political philosophers have defended a variety of views about reciprocity's significance. According to some, it is at the heart of morality. Moral rules emerge from the needs of rational beings to co-operate with one another to generate goods and protect against threats. Other philosophers accord reciprocity an instrumental role. Co-operation is necessary to generate moral goods that have no direct connection with our powers of reciprocity. Whether reciprocity is intrinsic to morality, or merely instrumental to many moral goods, it is clearly of utmost importance.

Compare the moral relationship one has with a fellow citizen with the relationship one has with one's pet. Both cases involve the recognition of the moral worth of the other, but only in the latter relationship is there true reciprocity. Citizenship is a collective enterprise founded on the shared understanding of co-operation's great importance. We count a few marginal persons, such as the extremely young, elderly or sick, as citizens because we know that this relatively minor extension preserves the motivating ideal. An entire class of unenhanced Naturals might not be so easily subsumed under a general rule of reciprocity.

We are more likely to acknowledge and to live up to our responsibilities in reciprocal relationships than we are in one-sided ones. Our partners in reciprocal relationships both have things to offer us and may pose credible threats to us. Partners in one-sided relationships are harder to derive benefits from and easier to ignore. Perhaps the enhanced reasoning powers of the GenRich will not permit them to ignore the needs of those from whom they do not benefit, but they will grant them something short of full recognition. They will not treat them as full partners in the creation of social goods.

It is possible that the refined moral senses of the enhanced will lead them to set aside a protected role for unenhanced people. There may even be calls for systematic affirmative action on behalf of Naturals. GenRich advocates of the Naturals may employ versions of the moral arguments for affirmative action used today on behalf of members of ethnic minorities. However, there is some reason to think that these arguments will work less well in post-enhancement societies than they do today. Behind contemporary appeals for affirmative action is the idea that we are made worse off if we cannot profit from the talents of all who live in our communities. This understanding may not bolster affirmative action on behalf of a class of people whom the GenRich correctly judge have little to offer. Maybe the protected moral role for unenhanced people would be like the protected role that some now want to set aside for the great apes. This recognition of moral worth would fall short of the full recognition required for the maintenance of liberal social arrangements.

I call the following condition on enhancement 'Jeffersonian' because it preserves the empirical equality necessary for liberal democracy:

> We can grant access to enhancement technologies only if the relationships between those who have the best access and those who have the worst remain reciprocal.

The Jeffersonian condition assumes that there is a threshold of difference beyond which reciprocal moral relations are either impossible or very unlikely. I offer no precise account of where this threshold is, but the relationship between Valids and Invalids in *GATTACA* does not seem to have reached the critical point. Although the Invalids form a janitorial class, their restriction to menial work seems to result more from mistaken views about their capabilities than from any systematic deficits on their part. Ethan Hawke's character may have to cheat to gain entry to the space programme, but he still seems up to the intellectual, emotional and physical demands of the role of astronaut.

We should not conflate making a lesser contribution to a collective enterprise with failing to make a meaningful contribution to it. Critics of enhancement tend to place great emphasis on winner-takes-all competitions. The enhanced investor has long taken his profits before his unenhanced competitor has realized that there was money to be made. Many human enterprises, however, are collaborative at the same time as they are competitive, and unenhanced people will still be able to make meaningful contributions to these. Nobel prizes go to those who cross the finishing line of scientific discovery first, but those who do not make the big breakthroughs still contribute much of value, and are acknowledged by the laureates as having done so.

It is not hard to extrapolate beyond the period depicted in *GATTACA* to imagine a time when unenhanced people really do have little more to offer than janitorial services. At this point, the relationship between the two genetic classes would no longer be reciprocal. The Invalids will have little to contribute, other than by offering their backs up for saddles. A Jeffersonian restriction on enhancement enables liberals to identify this situation as wrong.

THE THREAT OF HOMOGENIZATION

We can minimize the harm of polarization by preventing enhancement technologies from softening the glue of reciprocity that forms individuals into communities. The harm of homogenization results not from how access to these technologies is distributed, but instead from how people will use them. Liberal societies have laws protecting the many ways of life that correspond with the plural values of its citizens. Perhaps the politicians of the future will point to widespread agreement about the good life to justify repeal of these laws.

How likely is this to happen? In *Star Wars: Attack of the Clones* enhancement technologies are used with the explicit aim of homogenization. The biotechnology of cloning by somatic cell nuclear transfer creates the Stormtroopers, the army of identical, obedient soldiers who will later confront Luke Skywalker and Princess Leia. While it is easy to see what interest a dictator might have in homogenization, it seems an unlikely outcome of a liberal scheme. After all, the distinguishing mark of the new liberal eugenics is state neutrality about the good life. There will be no directive to evolve people towards a single optimal type. Rather, access to information about the full range of genetic therapies will allow the values of prospective parents to inform their eugenic plans. Differing ideas about the good life will surely disrupt any centrally directed pattern of enhancement.

However, some differences are clearer in principle than they are in practice. Handing choice over to parents may not stand in the way of the monopolizing tendencies of some ideas of the good. For example, some early twentieth-century advocates of eugenics agreed with Hitler that the proper goal of eugenics was the improvement of human stock, and that this would involve stymieing the reproductive efforts of the unfit and encouraging those of the fit. But they disagreed with Hitler about the means necessary to achieve this eugenic end. They did not see a conflict between centrally determined views of the good and what they took to be 'informed choice' about improvements.[18] Once made aware of the impact of their choices on the gene pool, women would end up choosing sexual partners with the appropriate mix of moral, intellectual and physical virtues. Restrictive laws would, therefore, not be required to ensure that the fit replaced the unfit.

Before I go into detail on threats to diversity, we need to establish clearly why diversity matters to liberal democracies. There are two ways in which one can understand the value of the diversity and its connection with the interests of individuals. We might think of diversity as a purely *instrumental* good, something to be sought because it promotes the interests of individuals. Or we may count diversity an *intrinsic* good, something to be valued regardless of its relationship with the interests of individuals.

Conceiving of diversity as only instrumentally valuable makes it vulnerable to enhancement technologies. It is the manifest diversity in conceptions of the good life that supplies much of the motivation for the liberal doctrine. As enhancement technologies eliminate or reduce differences between people, they eliminate or reduce the need for laws protecting citizens' rights to make unpopular choices about the good life.

Liberals find it difficult to defend diversity as an intrinsic good. One of the central themes of contemporary liberalism is a rejection of the idea that individual liberties should be sacrificed in order to maintain a given social pattern. Forcing everyone to worship at the same church, learn the same history and speak the same language promotes a solidarity absent from societies in which there are a variety of religions, people take pride in different histories, and speak different languages. Liberals allow that individual choices have the propensity to disrupt social patterns, but they deny that the pursuit of the social good of solidarity should override individual freedoms. The same arguments that liberals deploy against those who trample individual freedoms in the name of solidarity can be directed against those who would cancel procreative freedoms to preserve diversity.

In what follows, I argue that the instrumental value of diversity supports a ban of some uses of enhancement technologies. Protection of this instrumental value will also protect society against the tendency of homogenization. This defence of diversity will be limited in scope and this means that it will not lead to a ban of all homogenizing choices of individuals. Among the things that make us different from one another are our distinctive disease susceptibilities, chronic illnesses and handicaps. It would be wrong to refuse to treat a childhood illness in the hope that leaving it untreated will generate a distinctive personality type. It seems equally wrong to appeal to diversity to justify a ban of the use of genetic technologies to treat or prevent serious diseases.

PREJUDICE AND ENHANCEMENT

The morally noxious homogenizing influence that I will focus on is prejudice. A programme of liberal enhancement would prevent a state from using the reproductive acts of its citizens to implement its bigoted ideology. But no society is entirely free of prejudice. Despite efforts to protect them, people suffer because of their genders, racial backgrounds, religious commitments and sexual orientations. Often this prejudice is subconscious but, conscious or not, it can still influence enhancement choices. Enhancement technologies will turn reproduction into another means of expressing prejudice. They will grant racism and homophobia an unprecedented efficacy. While today these attitudes make many people miserable, in the future genetic technologies may enable them to shape successive generations. The progressive elimination of psychological and physical characteristics that, for whatever reason, attract prejudice will dramatically reduce diversity.

We have already examined Hamer's claim that there is at least one sexual-orientation gene with homosexual and heterosexual variants. Parents may one day be able to swap one version for another. They will be informed that the procedure cannot guarantee them the kind of son they want – the rejection of genetic determinism means that we should expect there to be both gay men with straight genes and straight men with gay genes. But they may be willing to pay to boost the chance of having a heterosexual son. Many racists wrongly believe that the colour of one's skin indicates the possession of particular intellectual, moral and physical virtues. Racism has the great advantage, from the perspective of the genetic engineer, of focusing on superficial characteristics of human beings. There are thought to be between three and six major genes that influence skin colour, principally by way of the pigment melanin. Variants of these genes work together to produce shades of skin ranging from very dark skin, with high levels of melanin, to very light skin, with low levels. Genetic engineers could help prospective parents to choose the skin colours of their children by altering these genes.

It might seem that racism is an unlikely motive for using enhancement technologies. Parents would, after all, be modifying the melanin genes that they themselves have bequeathed to their children. But the moral image of the singer Michael Jackson warns against overconfidence in this area. Indeed, it is possible to imagine reasons for changing the genes that influence skin colour. Perhaps some people who consider themselves white will want to purge from their genomes any hint of the wrong kind of ancestry. In other cases, would-be enhancers will not be modifying the skin colour genes that they have bequeathed. Leon Kass worries that the advent of reproductive cloning will create an immoral market in Michael Jordan's genome.[19] The combination of genetic engineering and cloning may enable people to become the parents of a white Mike.

Racism may become relevant to decisions about the welfare of future persons in another, more insidious, way. It does not have to be a motive of parents-to-be for it to influence their enhancement choices. Although prospective parents may recognize that the claims of homophobes or racists are false, they should nevertheless acknowledge that these claims make up part of the social environment in which their children will live. Consider this fact in the light of my appeals in chapter 5 and chapter 6 that we ought neither to reduce our children's real freedom, nor to infringe their autonomy. Racism and homophobia are threats to real freedom and autonomy. A person may think about the transmission of his dark variants of the melanin-producing genes in the same way as he does about passing on his asthma-risk genes. This prospective parent is unlikely to be fooled into thinking that being black or having asthma reduces one's moral worth. He may feel that his conception of himself has been formed by these characteristics, and hence be reluctant, or even find it impossible, to imagine his life as a white non-asthmatic. However, he may at the same time understand that the path of the person he is about to bring into existence will be easier if he is white and non-asthmatic.

One could doubt the efficacy of the avoidance of bigotry by altering the characteristics on which bigots fix. The most rigorous Nazi racists were interested not only in those who bore what they thought were the outer marks of Jewishness, but in those who could be given away only by their genealogies. Racists might separate those whose light skin results from genetic engineering from 'natural' whites. Homophobes may consider those whose heterosexuality results from cheating by genetic engineering as morally inferior to 'natural' heterosexuals. But pragmatic optimism demands that we concede that it is within the power of genetic engineers to eliminate all traces of a stigmatized characteristic. This enables us to focus on the ethics of doing so.

The problem is that concern for prospective welfare may result in genocide by stealth. Those who administer enhancement technologies in liberal societies will not say: 'We insist that you replace the homosexual with the heterosexual variants of any sexual-orientation genes in the embryo of your future child, because we hate homosexuals.' But they might say: 'You might consider therapy to replace the homosexual with the heterosexual variants. Due to a regrettable fact about the society in which your child will live, this therapy is likely to lead to a higher quality of life.' This appeal to prospective welfare might achieve the same end as the earlier command without an explicit endorsement of homophobia.

KITCHER AND BUCHANAN ET AL. ON RESISTING MORALLY DEFECTIVE ENVIRONMENTS

Philip Kitcher thinks that a society that sets out to protect the diverse life plans of its citizens can minimize the effects of prejudice to the extent of making them irrelevant to reproductive choices:

> When certain allelic combinations occur, the parents know that neurodegeneration will set in during infancy, that their child can be supported for a few years with elaborate care, that there will be no opportunity for the development of a self. By contrast, in affluent societies, although discrimination against women persists, its impact is not so severe as to make it impossible for those who have two X chromosomes to live happy and fulfilling lives. Nor *should* similar opportunities be out of reach for homosexuals, the congenitally obese, or the left-handed.[20]

Kitcher's point is relevant to an early stage in the development of enhancement technologies. Some women are already deciding whether to carry their foetuses to full term on the basis of genetic information. This information is currently limited to a small range of genetic and chromosomal disorders. However, there is no technological obstacle in the way of providing them with information about any genes that might slightly boost or reduce the chance that their child will be gay. Kitcher is surely right: that appeals to prospective welfare cannot mandate the abortion of gay foetuses, in the way that they might of foetuses found to have a genetic make-up predisposing to Lesch–Nyhan, for example. The prejudice endured by homosexuals only rarely makes their lives not worth living.

However, the enhancement technologies of the future will give prospective parents a wider range of choice than just between aborting and not aborting. Prospective parents will be empowered to modify their children's genomes. Even if replacing a gay gene with its heterosexual analogue does not make the difference between a life not worth having and one worth having, it can nonetheless improve prospects. This difference in prospects is likely to fall short of justifying an obligation to correct all genomes to the economically optimal white, heterosexual varieties, but the absence of an obligation leaves room for a permission for parents to boost the prospects of their future children by removing more minor obstacles to their flourishing. Consider a parent's attitude to her child's diabetes. It would be negligent for a parent to take no interest in whether her child, newly diagnosed with diabetes, takes any insulin at all, but once an adequate standard of treatment is achieved, the parent has a choice. Perhaps it is permissible for a parent to allow that the hormone be injected, but only once a day, thereby ensuring moderate regulation of his blood sugar. But it must also be permissible for a parent to go beyond this standard and encourage her son to inject insulin before every meal, thereby keeping his levels of blood glucose as close as possible to normal without running an unacceptable risk of hypoglycaemia, or very low levels of blood sugar. The second kind of parent might take an analogous attitude to genes that slightly raise the chance that her son will be gay. She will feel justified in replacing genetic variants that have only a relatively small impact on prospective welfare.

Buchanan et al. find a difference in the way in which being gay or black reduces someone's one's future opportunities, and the way in which being deaf does. Unlike the latter, the former two characteristics harm prospects only in a morally defective social environment:

> There is . . . a fundamental difference between the limitations on opportunity that result from being deaf and those that result from being gay or African-American. The limitations a gay or black person suffers are injustices in a quite uncontroversial sense: They are forms of discrimination. While deaf people and others with disabilities certainly do continue to experience discrimination, they would continue to suffer limited opportunities even if there were no discrimination against them.[21]

Helping a person to escape prejudice by changing his genome misdiagnoses the problem. Being black or gay is not a disability. It is a mistake to seek biotechnological solutions to problems that have nothing at all to do with genes. The fault is in the attitudes of racist people, not in the genomes of the people they hate. We should change the attitudes, not the genomes. We would block the homogenizing combination of enhancement technologies and prejudice by banning choices that collude with unjust environments.

I think that the conclusion that Buchanan et al. draw is correct. But the path to the conclusion that we should change attitudes not genomes is not as easy as it might at first seem.

A PARALLEL BETWEEN GM HUMANS AND GM FOOD

The issue we have been investigating can be usefully compared with one of the most intensely contested contemporary debates concerning agricultural biotechnology – that involving the genetic modification of food. Some 134 million children suffer from some degree of vitamin A deficiency. This deficiency leads annually to five million cases of permanent eye damage and 500,000 cases of blindness.[22] However, there is a GM solution. Golden rice has beta-carotene-producing genes taken from daffodils. This beta-carotene is converted by our bodies into vitamin A. Eager to improve their public images, biotech companies advertise a willingness to make golden rice freely available to farmers in poor countries. Golden rice has many opponents, however.[23] Some argue that far from helping prevent blindness, golden rice may make the problem worse. Vandana Shiva points out that deriving one's quota of vitamin A from golden rice requires that one consume 2.272 kilograms of it every day.[24] Defenders of golden rice respond that they do not envisage it as the sole source of vitamin A, but as a supplement for the many people whose diets already contain vitamin A and beta-carotene but in quantities that leave them deficient.[25]

The line of objection I want to focus on is a different one. Pragmatic optimists about golden rice assume for the sake of argument that it does deliver vitamin A in a way that can prevent blindness without causing other problems to those who consume it, or that any other dietary deficiencies can be remedied by introducing appropriate transgenes. This is not in any way to concede that golden rice will achieve these ends, but instead to bring into focus a different kind of objection against it.

I am interested in the widely put argument that the inventors and promoters of golden rice have misdiagnosed the problem of Third World malnutrition. The diets of poor people are inadequate not because we cannot grow enough good food; there is ample productive land. But this productive capacity is put to unjust ends. For example, traditional crops are uprooted so that coffee can be grown for people in the developed world. Poor people deserve the same remedy for blindness as affluent people who are not vitamin A deficient because they eat dairy products and vegetables, rich in vitamin A and beta-carotene. We should be providing this food, or, better still, helping them to grow it for themselves, not foisting Franken-rice on them. Food is more than just a receptacle of calories, vitamins and minerals. Shiva emphasizes its cultural dimension. She contrasts the monotony of the 2.272 kilograms of golden rice that would provide one's recommended daily allowance of vitamin A with vitamin A- and beta-carotene-rich foods that make up the traditional diets of people in India, one of the countries high on the list of the advocates of golden rice. Shiva offers the Hindi names of these foods, including milk (*doodh*), pumpkin (*kaddu*) and coriander leaves (*dhania*), to make the point that getting vitamin A from these sources is not only a matter of having a varied diet, but also a matter of culture.[26]

Midgley generalizes the point to encompass biotechnology as a whole:

> [T]he luminous fascination of bioengineering is making us look for biochemical solutions to complex problems that are not biochemical at all but social and political. For instance, much of the demand for liver transplants is due to alcohol. But it is a lot harder to think about what to do about alcohol than it is to call for research on transplants. Similarly, infertility is largely caused by late marriage and sexually transmitted diseases. But changing the customs that surround these things calls for quite different and much less straightforward kinds of thinking. Again, food shortages throughout the world are caused by faulty systems of distribution rather than by low crop yields, and – in the opinion of most experienced aid agencies – the promotion of patented transgenic crops in poor countries is calculated to increase the faults in those distribution systems, not cure them.[27]

Midgley thinks that GM solutions narrow our vision, obscuring the real causes of malnutrition, liver disease and infertility.

It strikes me that this line of response to biotechnology misses the point. It embodies a mistake in moral reasoning that I shall call the ought-implies-is fallacy. This fallacy is the reversal of the is-implies-ought fallacy, the widely recognized error in moral thinking that arises when one assumes that because something is natural it must be good. Suppose that humans are designed by natural selection to be selfish. This does not mean that it is morally mandatory for them to remain this way, regardless of what Fukuyama tells us. The ought-implies-is fallacy is the error of saying that because something ought to be a certain way we are entitled in moral reasoning to assume that it is that way. Suppose a friend comes to visit. On the evening of his arrival, he proposes to go jogging through an area of town that you know to be dangerous. Should you tell him? Certainly, it ought to be the case that every part of town is safe at all times for anyone not engaged in an immoral purpose; furthermore, frequent warnings that people should not go to the dangerous area have made it even more dangerous. Your warning would, in some small way, reinforce this trend. But I suspect that few would let this perception of the moral facts stop them from advising a friend to find somewhere else to run.

Suppose we concede that the biotech solutions of making spent land productive, and putting vitamin A in rice are not morally optimal. This concession allows that there are morally preferable ways of responding to the problems of vitamin-deficient diets and hunger. However, those investigating the GM option should ask not whether these morally optimal options can be achieved, but *will* they. Only those who are confident that the injustices in food production distribution are about to be corrected can be excused from considering GM solutions. It is one thing to say that vitamin-deficient people in the developing world should be denied golden rice because there is a preferable non-GM alternative *and then* to supply that alternative. It is quite another thing to rule out golden rice because there is a morally cleaner alternative that is not then supplied.

One issue concerns which moral agents or collections of moral agents have the power to make which decisions. Although the same government agencies that determine GM policy may have some ability to bring about the redistribution option, it is clear that much must happen to get rich people to accept less wastefully produced food. Perhaps the fairer distribution of non-GM food is, all things considered, easier to achieve than the GM solution. This does not stop it from being the case that agricultural biotech companies have it within their power to implement the GM option but not the redistribution option.

Opponents of GM food might have a further reason for resisting what they claim to be a morally suboptimal option. Feeding the starving with GM food may make us less likely to later provide them with better food. GM food is, in effect, a moral Band-Aid, something that will allow us to go on ignoring the real problem. The idea that people in the developed world need a steady supply of television images of starving people to prompt them into eliminating the many injustices in the global system of producing and distributing food seems a chilling one. It is better, surely, that developing-world advocates continue to argue their case without underlining their moral conclusions with preventable deaths.

Let us return to human genetic engineering. One of the examples I have been discussing involves substituting light variants of melanin-producing genes for dark ones to avoid the ill effects of racism. Consider how a different morally defective environment supplies a reason for a reverse therapy, one that would replace light with dark variants of these genes. Ozone depletion is a consequence of the overuse of CFCs. The thinned ozone layer lets in higher levels of UVB light that, among other effects, damages the skin of humans, boosting the cancer rate. Melanin provides some protection against UVB. Perhaps genetic engineers will one day be asked to make skins less susceptible to cancer by replacing low melanin with high melanin variants. Like the other problems we have been considering, this one does not have its origin in the colour of people's skins, but instead in a corrupted environment. Making skins darker colludes with the attitudes responsible for this corruption; it encourages the continued use of ozone-depleting technologies.[28] But real though these dangers are, they do not make any less real the harm that high levels of UVB inflict on the light-skinned. The moral image of sunblocks is a useful one for light-to-dark skin gene therapy. Sunblocks misdiagnose the moral problem in the same way as genetic engineers who replace low with high melanin genetic variants. Even if they do not get to the root of the problem, and indeed make us slightly more likely to ignore the real issues, the protection of light skin from UVB justifies their use.

By analogous reasoning, the fact that dark-skinned people suffer only because they live in a social environment shaped to some extent by morally wrong racist attitudes does not make any less real their suffering. If light-to-dark skin gene therapy is justified to avoid the ill effects of UVB then why should not dark-to-light skin therapy be justified to avoid the ill effects of racism? Both ozone depletion and racism are ugly realities, but they are realities nonetheless. Of course, it would certainly be preferable to eliminate racism, but prejudice, racial or otherwise, is an entrenched feature of most societies – it cannot be changed overnight. Optimists may think that education can reduce prejudice, but they would not deny there is still much to do. Parents have little control over whether their child will be born into a society in which there are many racists – but they can use enhancement technologies to prevent the child from being harmed by this morally defective environment.

THE ETHICS OF SHIFTING BIGOTRY'S BURDEN

The logic of the above reasoning can be summarized as follows. The mere recognition that a certain harm has its origins in a morally defective environment does not alter its reality. If parents are allowed to use enhancement technologies to spare their children the harms imposed by mild asthma then they should also be allowed to spare them the same amount of harm inflicted by racists and homophobes.

However, there is a difference between using genetic engineering to escape the harmful effects of ozone depletion, on the one hand, and using it to escape the harmful effects of prejudice, on the other. In the former case, collusion with injustice may remove part of the motivation for addressing the real problem, but it does not prevent us from doing something about it. The technologies that would make a future person's skin darker are not themselves ozone-depleting. We can darken people's skins while still fighting to reduce emissions harmful to the ozone layer. This two-pronged approach to the problem should be motivated by the recognition that the thinning of the ozone layer not only harms humans, it also harms the environment. Some philosophers think that the environment is valuable in itself. Even those who deny that nature has intrinsic value think that humans derive a wide range of goods from it. Ozone depletion threatens these goods.

Now consider parents who replace dark with light skin alleles in the genomes of their future child. The value of a procedure that transforms a black foetus into a white one depends to some extent on the continuing existence of people to serve as targets for the prejudice that is avoided. Prospective parents may succeed in sparing their child the burden of prejudice, but, in doing so, they increase the burden on children who continue to be born with the dark variants. Whether they intend it to or not, their complicity with prejudice will be seen as endorsing the idea that moral value really is determined by one's skin colour. The complicity is likely to make racism more efficacious, encouraging the very idea of prejudice. The same points apply to genetic engineering to change sexual orientation. The perhaps accidental endorsement of homophobia will make it worse for the gay people who remain in our society. It is hard to imagine a successful fight against prejudice in the very society in which there is a widely exercised freedom on the part of parents to remove from their children the characteristics that would make them objects of prejudice.

Suppose, improbably, that therapy to alter sexual-orientation genes and skin colour genes were not only to be made universally available, but also that every prospective parent used them to make their children invisible to bigotry, and furthermore that they are universally successful. There would be no more black or gay people left to hate – but the arbitrariness of bigotry allows the same motives that underlie the prejudice whose targets we have eliminated to fix on other targets. They would default to other morally irrelevant attributes of people. Those who would have been homophobes could find some part of the broad spectrum of heterosexual behaviour to focus on with equivalent vehemence. The hatred of racists would be replaced with loathings fixed on other easily recognizable distinguishing characteristics of people, such as their religious beliefs or sporting affiliations. Thus, in order to put an end to prejudice, the processes of homogenization would need to proceed to the point of making us all indistinguishable from one another.

It is because of this close connection between the moral badness of racism and the action of removing dark skin alleles that we should not allow parents to choose this modification for their children. We imagine a widely exercised prerogative to use genetic engineering to spare one's future child the harmful effects of UVB being combined with a successful struggle against the agents damaging the ozone layer. Neither the gene therapy nor sunblocks prevent us from recognizing and acting against the wrongness of the circumstances that necessitate them. This is not case when we deflect bigotry by genetically modifying skin colour or sexual orientation.

In earlier chapters I have been more forthright in my defence of liberal eugenics than I have in this one. The caution of this chapter reflects a recognition that the social harms of polarization and homogenization result from influences external to enhancement technologies themselves. Will the rich gain a near monopoly on enhancement? Will enhancement technologies grant prejudice a new terrifying efficacy? If we, collectively and individually, make the wrong choices, then we will be faced with the harms to which these questions point. But the right choices can help a society implementing liberal eugenics to avoid them.

CHAPTER 8

Enhanced Humans When?

An appropriately constrained prerogative to enhance need not harm the people that it allows to come into existence. Nor need it bring to an end the liberal social arrangements that give rise to and support it.

Significant though these conclusions are, they fall short of establishing the right to use any particular enhancement technology. The pragmatic optimism defended in chapter 2 encourages us to consider enhancement in isolation from technological matters of fact. We have arrived at the conclusion that there is no objection against the principle of using genomics, cloning and genetic engineering to enhance human beings. But this conclusion can only be a starting point for an investigation that dispenses with any pragmatic optimism, so as to address enhancement technologies as they really are, not as they might ideally be. We cannot grant access to any enhancement technology in advance of this.

At the level of principle, familiar means of enhancement, such as education, stand at no moral advantage over the unfamiliar means of genetic engineering. However, investigation of the practicalities of human enhancement reveals a significant moral advantage of the familiar over the unfamiliar. There is no difference in principle between improving your child's intelligence by giving her building blocks and by providing her embryo with an extra NR2B gene. But while generations of parents have sought, without any obvious ill effects, to enhance their children's intelligence by giving them building blocks, the modification of genes that influence human intelligence is something that has never before been attempted. Those who want to genetically enhance intelligence must interfere with the enormously complex, incompletely understood developmental process that transforms a single-cell embryo in a many-billion-cell human brain and body. NR2B therapy brings risks that are entirely unknown in enhancement by the provision of building blocks or after-school maths lessons.

THE PRECAUTIONARY PRINCIPLE
AND ENHANCEMENT TECHNOLOGIES

Questions about how to balance intended benefits and potential harms have come to the fore in the debate about agricultural biotechnology. Defenders of genetically modified crops describe many ways in which they might benefit us. In chapter 7 we explored the claim that golden rice could be a cure for forms of blindness prevalent in the Third World. Inserting a gene from the *Bacillus thuringiensis* bacterium into corn might reduce the need for environmentally ruinous insecticides. Genetic engineers want to add antifreeze genes to crops so that they can be grown in cold climates. Opponents counter these advertised benefits with an even longer list of potential dangers. A process known as horizontal transfer may enable genes that protect crops against insects to migrate to other plants, creating 'super-weeds'. These genetically improved weeds may escape their ecological niches, ravaging natural ecosystems. Perhaps a soaring cancer rate will alert us to threats to human health only decades after genetically modified crops have replaced natural varieties everywhere. The opponents of genetically modified crops can point to many historical examples of seemingly insignificant modifications of nature leading to disaster. The few malnourished rats that struggled on to New Zealand soil from European ships not only survived, but thrived, devastating ground-nesting bird species. The use in refrigerators and car air conditioners of a seemingly safe, stable coolant has helped strip the planet of its protective ozone layer.

Defenders of new technologies counter that we now understand nature sufficiently well to avoid these particular mistakes; we have learned about some of the potential dangers posed by exotic species and industrial chemicals. However, biotechnologists want to change nature at a more fundamental level than people who release rats or manufacture white ware. Those fearful of the new kinds of mistakes that genetic engineers might make propose that biotechnologists submit to what has come to be called the Precautionary Principle. A widely quoted version of the principle, the Wingspread Statement, specifies that

[w]here an activity raises threats of harm to the environment or human health, precautionary measures should be taken even if some cause and effect relationships are not fully established scientifically. In this context the proponent of an activity, rather than the public bears the burden of proof. The process of applying the Precautionary Principle must be open, informed and democratic, and must include potentially affected parties. It must also involve an examination of the full range of alternatives, including no action.[1]

The idea that one should try to avoid 'threats of harm to the environment or human health' does not sound particularly controversial, but the Precautionary Principle has become a powerful moral weapon against technological innovation. Two elements of the principle make the road for the advocates of new technologies especially arduous.

One obstacle in the way of novel technologies lies in the idea that the process of applying the principle must be 'open, informed and democratic'. Those who want to democratize the process of evaluating new technologies claim that a diverse range of voices must be heard on whether or not a given technology should be adopted. This seems consistent with my plea in chapter 2 that we make technologies affecting human beings morally transparent. Those who make genetically modified food should not complain that the science behind their products is too complicated to explain to the people who will grow it or eat it. In chapter 2 I explained that one does not need to understand every last scientific detail to gain a sense of the human impacts of a new technology. However, I noted also that the obligation of the advocates of new technologies to produce morally transparent descriptions is matched by an obligation on the part of their opponents. They must give these morally transparent descriptions due consideration. People who persist in thinking of human clones as mindless automata are unlikely to have worthwhile views about the ethics of reproductive cloning. Yet, this reciprocal obligation is undemocratic. In democracies the votes of those who are primarily influenced by candidates' television make-up jobs count for as much as those whose choices are determined by candidates' policies. Democratizing the process of evaluating new technologies seems likely to give too much weight to the revulsion valorized by Kass. It would grant an uninformed majority a veto over technologies that they neither like the sound of, nor want to find out more about.

The second, more apparent obstacle to technological innovation comes from the Precautionary Principle's placement of the burden of proof. The principle demands proof that a new activity causes no harm. Those who oppose the activity do not have to show anything. They have only to suggest the possibility that the accidental transfer of pest-resistant genes from a crop to a weed species will devastate natural ecosystems. Once this possibility is on the table, biotechnologists must prove that they will not make superweeds. However, they must do more than this. Their opponents are under no obligation to have imaginations sufficiently capacious for all of the ways in which technological innovation might lead to disaster. Who could have conceived of the possibility that feeding the carcasses of sheep afflicted with scrapie to cattle would infect humans with a form of Creutzfeldt–Jakob disease? Those who propound the Precautionary Principle want assurance that biotechnologies will not lead to a host of disasters as yet unimagined.

With the Precautionary Principle in hand, conservatives can give up arguing against the *idea* of enhancement and focus instead on the *means* by which people would be enhanced.[2] They would demand that their advocates conclusively rule out an impossibly long list of catastrophic possibilities. Fukuyama, Kass and McKibben are free to imagine almost any threat to human dignity or civilization. They even get a helping hand from Gregory Stock, the determined defender of the new genetic technologies. He suggests potential disasters ranging from the transformation of our descendents into 'biological time bombs' with bodies that 'will fail at some point, like flawed mutants in a horror movie' through the loss of genetic diversity, leaving us vulnerable to 'plaguelike diseases', to the loss of 'spiritual mooring' imagined by conservatives.[3] Defenders of enhancement must counter not only these challenges, but assure us that they can rebut all nightmare scenarios, both conceivable and inconceivable.

The best-known applications of the Precautionary Principle are to technologies that affect non-human nature, but the process of human development shares two properties with natural ecosystems that make the principle especially relevant to enhancement technologies. First, in both cases we are dealing with very complex systems about which we have only a rudimentary understanding. It is one thing to know how some of an ecosystem's species feed and breed, but quite another to understand how all of them interact to maintain its diversity, stability and integrity. Although we know something about how a few genes influence human development, we are a long way off understanding how more than 30,000 of them interact with one another and an array of environmental influences to make a human person. Second, although we may be able to dream up many ways in which human bodies and ecosystems could work better, we should at least concede that they work well. Changes to imperfectly understood complex systems produce effects that, relative to our knowledge, are random. Random changes to complex well-functioning systems are much more likely to make them work worse than better. For example, skilled technicians can repair the small fault in your computer because they understand well not only the immediate consequences of their interventions, but also the wider ones. Your well-intentioned but ill-informed interventions, on the other hand, are more likely to turn the small problem into a big one than to fix it.

Proponents of technology complain that the Precautionary Principle sets an unrealistic and immorally high standard. The online magazine *Spiked* solicited the views of forty scientists and technologists, publishing their answers in the form of 'an A–Z of historic achievements that would have been thwarted by the Precautionary Principle'.[4] The list includes the aeroplane, all drugs with side-effects, the contraceptive pill, fire, open-heart surgery, the polio vaccine, the telephone, the wheel and x-rays. For example, John Adams, professor of geography at University College London, explains that fire is 'very dangerous – plus all other forms of energy, such as electricity and microwaves. Energy misdirected can cause harm, and the Precautionary Principle requires that if it can be misdirected, you must assume that it will'.

Advocates of enhancement may pursue a similar strategy. I have argued that enhancement technologies, like the discoveries and inventions on *Spiked*'s list, offer significant benefits. Human genetic engineering, cloning and genomics allow prospective parents to realize their procreative visions while benefiting the people they bring into existence. If the contraceptive pill, the telephone and open-heart surgery were worth taking risks for then so should enhancement technologies be. Panos Zavos compares himself and other cloning pioneers with the first astronauts.[5] Humans could not have walked on the Moon unless astronauts had been prepared to take risks with essentially untested technologies. The risks that the first cloners take may help us towards a human cloning protocol as safe as IVF.

The opponents of technological innovation draw up a list of disasters that past meddlers could not have predicted. They feel entitled to dream up even more horrifying disasters for technologies that will alter us and nature in more profound ways than any technology in history. Proponents of technological innovation make up their own list of cures and conveniences without which human life as we know it would not exist. They argue that zealous application of the Precautionary Principle would have prevented their discovery and feel entitled to suppose that more powerful technologies will produce correspondingly better cures and conveniences.

Should we be tempted by the intended benefits of enhancement technologies or deterred by potential disasters? The magnitude of the good of securing individuals' procreative freedom seems negligible when placed alongside the possibility that enhancement technologies might lead to humanity's extinction. This extinction would not be of the kind envisaged by Fukuyama, resulting from humans choosing to replace themselves with posthumans. Instead, it would be the consequence of their catastrophically failing to do so. The difference between having a child with enhanced intelligence and having one with normal intelligence seems small when compared with the difference between the human species' survival and its extinction. If the introduction of a new genetic technology leads to human extinction then it imposes a near infinite penalty, wiping out the goods that would have been generated by an indefinite number of future human generations now prevented from existing.

But appearances mislead. Enhancement technologies actually do present potential benefits of a magnitude comparable with the nearly infinite potential penalties imagined by opponents. Suppose that each person who uses an enhancement technology derives only a small benefit from it. A technology developed now can benefit not only the generation that first comes into contact with it, but also each successive generation. It can also allow the development of other beneficial technologies. We can generate the near infinite potential good by multiplying these perhaps small goods by the indefinite number of generations of people who will have access to them.

THE REAL PROBLEM WITH DEVELOPING ENHANCEMENT TECHNOLOGIES

This debate over the magnitude of the potential benefits and harms produced by enhancement technologies overlooks the key moral issue. The question I now address concerns neither the reality nor the magnitude of potential benefits and harms, but instead their distribution.

The experimental lives that must be created for us to realize the great promise of enhancement technologies are central to the discussion that follows.

Let us return to Zavos's comparison of the first human clones with the first astronauts. There may be similarities in the magnitude of the benefits brought by the first humans in space and the first human clone baby, but there is certainly a difference in the way that these benefits are procured. The first astronauts consented to their role in advancing science. Taking risks upon oneself in science's name differs from enforcing sacrifices on others. In chapter 2 I described some of the physical problems that may afflict the first human clones. We can add to these the harm of stigmatization inflicted by communities who will not accept them. A parent who decides to have a child by somatic cell nuclear transfer does accept some of the burden of stigmatization, but she bears it in a much less intimate fashion than does her child. A tearful announcement at a press conference that Raël had tricked her will put distance between her and the anathematized idea that human cloning is morally acceptable. The clone has no easy path of recantation. She cannot separate herself from her various physical problems and her living embodiment of what is widely perceived to be an offence against God or nature.

Kantian bioethicists emphasize the wrongness of treating someone exclusively as a means. We saw in chapter 3 that the Kantian intuition carries over awkwardly to decisions to bring people into existence. The idea that it is wrong to bring someone into existence purely as a means sounds right only until one appreciates that it would make almost any procreative choice immoral. The fact that a boy has been conceived to carry his father's name into the next generation is unlikely to deprive him of a life filled with good things. This is because the father's instrumental motive is likely to run in the same direction as the child's need for a worthwhile existence. It is not that we cannot think of cases in which the two motives point in opposite directions – the son's declaration that he is gay may thwart the father's desire that he have grandsons to bear his name – but for the most part one looks out for the interests of those one considers one's heirs.

The kind of instrumentality involved in the creation of the first generation of enhanced humans differs from that involved in having a baby to save a marriage or to ensure survival of the family name. These first generations would effectively be human experiments. Here is what Stuart

Newman thinks about the experimental human lives necessary for the development of safe enhancement technologies:

> The only way we could ever do this with people is through experimentation [on people] – only by putting in the genes and seeing what happens. And that's impermissible. No matter what happens on the other side, there's an ethically impossible passage through which you must go – the generations of humans that would be experiments.[6]

In contrast with the instrumentality of the father who wants a son to carry his name, the experimenter's instrumentality often runs counter to the welfare of the human beings she creates. The suffering of the first human products of enhancement technologies will be no mere by-product of the process by which we will perfect them. Rather, the precise manner of the suffering and the means of the premature deaths of the first generations of human test subjects will provide valuable data. They, like innocents killed by terrorist bombs, are part of the means by which the end of enhancement will be achieved. This makes creation as the means of developing a new enhancement technology a more profound abuse than the commonplace instrumentality involved in having children.

We must be careful not to overplay the moral significance of the kind of instrumentality implicated in experimenting; there should be no absolute prohibition of the creation of experimental human lives. Louise Brown, the first IVF baby, was essentially a human experiment. As defenders of the new reproductive technologies frequently point out, she is living a very satisfactory life. What separates her case from the cases of the first human clones and of humans with enhanced intelligence is the degree of risk involved in bringing her into existence. Experimenters were able to approach the first IVF baby in a gradual way. Patrick Steptoe and Robert Edwards, the doctors who helped make Louise, could draw encouragement from a record of success with mammals whose reproductive systems and early development were extremely similar to those of humans. They could be confident that the experimental human being that they created would be almost as likely as any child to have a life filled with valuable experiences. Louise's parents and the IVF experimenters may have had different motives for bringing her into existence; the focus of the former was more on the baby that emerged from the process, while the latter were more concerned about the process itself. However, given what was understood about IVF, the experimental motive was not inconsistent with Louise's right to be brought into existence with a reasonable chance of a life worth living.

The involvement of technology in her origins may only have made Louise's conception more risky than conventional conception. I think that we are justified in using reproductive technologies that impose slightly greater risks of a life not worth having than those associated with conventional conception. If parents are permitted to take their children on holiday car journeys down busy motorways or to move them from safer to more dangerous neighbourhoods, then they ought to be able to use reproductive technologies that are slightly riskier than the natural method. This tolerance of risk means that recent evidence that certain artificial means of reproduction are more dangerous than the conventional method does not support an automatic ban of them.[7] There is likely to be a point at which additional risk would make an artificial means of reproduction immoral. It is difficult to say with any precision what this degree of risk would be. One complication stems from an historical and cultural relativity in the perception of risk. Settlers preparing to cross the Atlantic in a wooden sailing ship would have laughed at the risks that nowadays deter people from travelling the same distance in an aeroplane. People living in Europe of the first millennium would have been happy to take up a habit only as dangerous as smoking.

The fact that we cannot say with any certainty how far the threshold of morally acceptable risk extends should not prevent us from recognizing ways of bringing people into existence that are clearly beyond it. Those experimenting with human reproductive cloning impose much greater risks on their creations than practitioners of IVF ever have. CLONAID is unlikely to be able to offer its experimental humans the same guarantee of a reasonable chance of a life worth living that Steptoe and Edwards offered Louise Brown. Scientists' successes with mammals strongly suggest that humans can be cloned. But we have also seen that transferring the technology from one mammal species to another requires quite a few tries to get it right. Each new mammal species has posed new challenges. It is unlikely that there could be a safe human cloning protocol without many failures. Cloners have the longest experience with sheep and mice. Even with the many improvements in the technology, they are still creating sheep and mice that suffer more than their conventionally conceived conspecifics.

What is the case for human cloning is also true of human genetic modification. Consider the insertion of additional NR2B genes into human embryos. There is no gradual way to approach the creation of the first humans whose powers of memory and learning have been enhanced in this fashion. In chapter 2 I discussed Min Zhou's suggestion that Doogie mice remember painful events well only because they feel pain so intensely. Suppose that Tsien were to win his debate with Zhou and to decisively demonstrate that an extra copy of NR2B does not make a mouse whose experiences are less pleasant than those of normal mice. Genetic engineers now want to use NR2B therapy on humans. First, they need to show that the addition of NR2B genes boosts the learning and memory powers of pigs, monkeys and chimpanzees without inflicting any detectable ill effect on them. The word 'detectable' is important in this context. While moral philosophers care greatly about the subjective states of the beings that we bring into existence, scientists tend either to deny the existence of such states or to disavow any ambition to study them. This scientific blind spot should make us cautious of assurances that the increased mental powers of Doogie pigs and Doogie chimpanzees have come at no cost to them. Consider now the challenge confronting those who would enhance memory by adding NR2B genes to a human embryo. Researchers might draw confidence from the 98.5 per cent similarity between chimpanzee and human genomes. But the 1.5 per cent difference between the two species' genomes should give them pause. Although the genetic differences may be small when placed alongside the genetic similarities, they still translate into a difference of 45 million bases or letters of DNA.[8] Moreover, given that some of the most significant differences between human and chimpanzee are in intelligence, it is reasonable to expect that many of the genetic differences will be in genes that affect learning and memory. Researchers may promise to terminate extra-NR2B embryos developing in an obviously abnormal way, but demonstrating that NR2B therapy enhances human intelligence without imposing some major penalty will require that some embryos be allowed to develop to personhood. Only in this way can we assess the impact of the therapy on human cognitive functioning.

Buchanan and his colleagues argue that considerations of risk separate experimentation whose end is the treatment of a disease from experimentation whose end is enhancement.[9] The experimental treatment of SCID described in chapter 4 may have left some of the test subjects with leukaemia, but this may even be an improvement over an existence with no effective immune system. The cost/benefit analysis is different for enhancement. While those who are experimenting with treatments for serious diseases may only succeed in substituting one kind of misery for another, those experimenting on human enhancement are likely to substitute a miserable life for a happy one.

A CLASH OF MORAL GESTALTS

The problem we face is a familiar one to moral philosophers. The first dilemma encountered by students in introductory ethics courses typically tests their commitment to the utilitarian idea that welfare should be maximized and to the Kantian idea that individual dignity must be respected. It concerns a case in which a huge benefit can be secured or harm prevented only by sacrificing an innocent. H. J. McCloskey's famous version of this problem involves a sheriff in a racist town in the Southern United States.[10] There has been a rape and the townsfolk are convinced that the culprit must be black. Unless someone is visibly brought to justice soon there will be a riot that will result in many deaths and cause lasting enmity between the town's blacks and whites. Framing and hanging a black man whom the sheriff knows to be innocent is the only way to pacify the gathering mob and save at least ten other innocent lives.

Bernard Williams complains that it is not so much that utilitarianism dictates that in cases like McCloskey's we should sacrifice the few to save the many, but that this conclusion is supposed to be *obvious*.[11] Were the sheriff to be a utilitarian he would have no more difficulty in deciding what ought to be done than in working out that ten is a larger number than one. I think Williams is right to be concerned about this aspect of utilitarianism. But I think we should be similarly alarmed by those who find the Kantian solution obvious – that it is utterly straightforward that many innocents should die in place of one.

This dilemma is unlikely to be solved by any advance in moral science. Cases like that of the Southern sheriff will almost certainly remain perplexing. In my experience, when students are presented with this case they experience a series of moral gestalt shifts. Perceiving the story's moral qualities is a bit like perceiving an ambiguous image like the Necker Cube. One can see two different three-dimensional objects in the Necker Cube, depending on how one looks at it. The story about the Southern sheriff is morally ambiguous. McCloskey wants us to focus on the innocent man in the sheriff's cell. When his plight is made vivid, it seems completely obvious that he must not be hanged for a crime he did not commit. We see the Kantian gestalt. However, focusing on the perhaps ten equally innocent people about to be violently killed by the racist mob draws some people to the utilitarian gestalt. McCloskey's telling of the story makes it difficult to empathize with the innocents the mob will kill. We don't know which homes the rioters will succeed in breaking into, which people they will lynch, but the suffering of those who are attacked is no less real than that of the man in the gaol cell. Imagine, however, an investigative journalist telling the stories of the ten some time after the event. This would help us to perceive the utilitarian gestalt that would have authorized the sacrifice of one to save ten.

Those who have an interest in the history of medicine should recognize the moral dilemma pointed to by McCloskey's story. Earlier in this chapter I mentioned *Spiked* magazine's list of beneficial technologies that the Precautionary Principle might have denied us. Some of the items on the *Spiked* list pose dilemmas similar to that confronted by the Southern sheriff. Consider the discovery of smallpox vaccination. No one should doubt that this brought enormous benefits. But think about how these benefits were procured. An English country doctor, Edward Jenner, noticed that milkmaids infected with the non-life-threatening disease cowpox seemed to be protected against smallpox. To test his theory he injected pus from the cowpox blisters into a young boy, James Phipps, who was then exposed to smallpox, which, fortunately both for him and for medical science, he survived. Reflection on what would have happened to his young experimental subject had his hunch been incorrect should make the wrongness of Jenner's actions apparent. At the time of his experiment, smallpox killed approximately a third of those it infected and disfigured survivors.[12]

Another technology on the *Spiked* list is organ transplantation. Those who performed the first human-to-human organ transplants knew little about the workings of the immune system that made it inevitable that their efforts would fail. However, a modicum of epistemic modesty ought to have helped them to see that the first patients, although essential for the development of the technology, were unlikely to receive any benefit. The benefits would be received by successive generations of patients. We can say in defence of the experimentation that the organ recipients were very sick indeed, with no chance of life beyond the tiny one offered by the replacement organ. But it is wrong to think that they had nothing to lose, just because they were dying anyway. What researchers may have deprived them of was a dignified end to their lives – an end appropriate to any spiritual values their experimental subjects might have had. Some people who are told that they are dying will willingly submit to almost any medical procedure that raises their chances of survival. Medical ethicists are suspicious of claims that we can make free choices under such circumstances.[13] Sometimes an experimental treatment may raise a patient's chances of survival sufficiently for it to be worthwhile for her. On other occasions, however, the actual increase in survival chances is so slight that it should not justify forgoing a dignified death, any more than should a very slight heightening of the risk of violent death justify never crossing a road. Again, when thinking about the history of organ transplantation we have the choice of two gestalts. The utilitarian gestalt directs our attention towards the many lives now saved by transplant operations. The Kantian gestalt directs us to hopes falsely raised in the early stages of the technology's development.

Contributors to the *Spiked* list oversimplify if they think the main difficulty presented by new technologies concerns the reality of the benefits associated with them. Perhaps these benefits do outweigh the harms caused by their development. However, many of the medical advances of history subjected people to risks from which they were unlikely to benefit. Part of the reason we think differently about the smallpox case than we do about the story of the Southern sheriff is that James Phipps survived, whereas we presume the innocent man in the gaol cell will die. The fact of his survival does not obscure the fact that he was subjected to a real risk of death. Jenner's hunch turned out to be good, but in science there have been many hunches that did not correspond with the facts. Another reason is that we are more likely to focus on the utilitarian gestalt in the former than we are in the latter. For us the story of smallpox is about the horribleness of its symptoms and effects and the huge number of people who were killed by it. We feel fortunate to be living at a time free of the disease. Each visit to the movies presents us with people who might have been disfigured or killed but for Jenner's discovery. The Kantian gestalt is easier to overlook simply because of the fact that James Phipps lived centuries ago; we know relatively little about him. Were we to have been living at the time of Jenner the Kantian gestalt would be more obvious. Phipps and his family would be our contemporaries and the beneficiaries of inoculation would be less salient. In McCloskey's story, the ten or more people saved from the mob by the blaming of the innocent man are hard to empathize with because we don't know who they are. Jenner's contemporaries would be in similar doubt about the identities of those to be saved from smallpox by his experiment.[14] The same is true of human-to-human transplantations. There are many people among us who are alive only because of transplanted tissue. It is easy to overlook the first experimental subjects. These facts about our relationships to the affected parties lead us to prefer the utilitarian gestalt to the Kantian one.

We find exactly the same choice of gestalts when we investigate the benefits and risks associated with development of enhancement technologies. The Kantian gestalt will be more salient to us because we will feel more intimately connected with the experimental lives that human cloners and genetic engineers will create. Even if we do not see the members of the first generation of human clones on television, we will hear rumours of their suffering. Future generations of people who have benefited from the use of safe enhancement technologies will be less obvious targets for our empathy.

In what follows I present a conditional argument. Privileging the Kantian gestalt makes it impermissible to develop enhancement technologies because they benefit some only by imposing immoral penalties on others. I propose that even if we view experimentation in human enhancement in this way, we will still be in a position to convert our pragmatic optimist support for the principle of enhancement into an endorsement of actual technologies.

THE BIOTECHNOLOGICAL CATCH-22

Suppose we do view experimentation on enhancing humans in Kantian terms. Doing so would vindicate Stuart Newman's claim about the 'ethically impossible passage' to enhancement technologies.

Many of the scientists who write about enhancement technologies express impatience about this kind of ethical qualm. They avoid genetic determinist misunderstandings of the results of enhancement technologies only to fall prey to a technological determinism about morality. Technological determinists insist that moral pronouncements have little or no influence on which technologies will be developed and who will use them. Stock formulates a version of this argument that compares the restraint that liberal democracies can achieve with the absence of moral controls in other technologically ambitious societies. He contrasts Western moral sensibilities with the Chinese 'resources, . . . predisposition, and . . . self-reliance to independently pursue the new technologies'. When it comes to biotechnology, '[t]he fleetest, not the most cautious, will set the pace'.[15] These comments capture well one strand of the American debate over therapeutic or research cloning. Defenders of human stem cell research pointed to rumoured Chinese cloning breakthroughs to warn policymakers that the United States might be surrendering the lead in what could become a multi-billion dollar industry.[16] When, in February 2004, Korean scientists announced that they had made clone blastocysts, the defenders of the US competitive edge in biotechnology had a different Asian bogeyman.[17] But the message was the same: Chinese and Korean biotechnologists race ahead because they are not encumbered by the bothersome moral restrictions that handicap their Western counterparts.

Asian biotechnologists operate outside of the legislative range of Western governments. But these governments are also unlikely to be able to check the ambitions of many of their own citizens. Wealthy Westerners expect to be able to use their money to purchase what they want. Most people share policymakers' reluctance about human reproductive cloning. This, however, has not prevented some with more money than moral sense from accepting the offers of CLONAID, Severino Antinori and Panos Zavos to clone them. The biotechnological determinist claims that because we cannot prevent biotechnology's advance we should either endorse it or, at least, give up on condemning it.

There is something very wrong about this technological determinism, and something right about it.

Let's start with what is wrong with the view. Technological determinism does not render morality redundant. There will almost certainly never be a human society in which there is no murder – but this is no reason not to pass moral judgements on murderers. There is something deficient in the character of a person who is not at all appalled by the intentional sacrifice of an innocent life. Moreover, when we make these moral judgements we are doing more than just striking a pose. Although people guided by the conviction that murder is wrong cannot prevent all murders, they can prevent some, and an understanding of the wrongness of murder should lead us to recognize each prevented murder as a good thing. Likewise, those who understand the wrongness of creating experimental human beings that have too low a chance of any quality of life may be unable to stop all such acts. But they can take pride in each attempted abuse of human dignity that is prevented.

There is, however, something to claims about the inevitability of human cloning and genetic modification. Technological determinists are wrong about whether we should bother to moralize about enhancement technologies, but right that this moralizing will fail to stop their development. Moral prohibitions are efficacious if they prevent *at least some* of the violations of human worth that those experimenting with enhancement technologies would perpetrate. However, preventing the development of the technologies requires more than that prohibitions of human experimentation be efficacious. We must prevent *all* or *almost all* of these human experiments.

Some people will be prepared to use experimental technologies to realize their procreative desires regardless of the law or widespread moral condemnation. CLONAID and Antinori and Zavos have taught us this lesson. In the years to come, groups equally unconcerned about the welfare of the human beings they bring into existence may offer NR2B therapy for a sum similar to the US $200,000 currently charged by CLONAID for enrolment in their cloning programme. Some people will present themselves, with money and embryos in hand. Kass is right that some scientists may be deterred by laws against cloning because they will not be 'able to stand up proudly to claim the credit for their technological bravado and success'.[18] However, others will be motivated by what they see as the intrinsic worth of the research, and the example of the dissident scientist Galileo. They will be happy to go underground where they can continue their work free of regulation. These scientists will be confident of the eventual triumph of their side of the moral argument, confident of their posthumous fame.

Those who seek to prevent immoral use of untested enhancement technologies confront a biotechnological catch-22. The banning of a technology for which there is a strong desire and that does not require large-scale state-maintained infrastructure will not stop research. Indeed a ban may accelerate it. By operating underground the CLONAID researchers can freely flout the ethical guidelines binding researchers at publicly funded institutions whose work is supervised by ethics committees. CLONAID says that they have provided people with clone babies. Even if these babies are fantasies whose purpose is the raising of funds, it does seem likely that CLONAID has experimented on human embryos. How many embryos have they experimented on? How did they procure the human oocytes required for the creation of the embryos? Were the donors told what would happen to their eggs? We have no answers to these questions. While CLONAID takes what it needs from research whose conformity with ethical norms has enabled it to be published in the top scientific journals, its researchers can tell their publicly funded counterparts whatever they want about their own work.

Here is the dilemma. Banning research for which there is a strong desire, and which can be pursued without large-scale, state-maintained infrastructure, is unlikely to stop it altogether. It will be driven underground where it can continue, possibly at an accelerated rate due to the absence of ethical controls. Acquiescing to the research that involves the creation of clone embryos for reproductive purposes would allow some moral supervision of it; most of those who want to be cloned would choose an organization whose procedures have been scientifically and ethically vetted over a secretive UFO cult. However, those who view experimentation on human enhancement from a Kantian perspective will not see this pragmatic reasoning as justifying it.

ONCE WE HAVE TRAVERSED THE ETHICALLY IMPOSSIBLE PASSAGE...

I submit that underground experimentation is likely to help us to traverse the ethically impossible passage to safe enhancement technologies whether we like it or not. Traversing this passage changes our moral situation.

The question about what use we should make of knowledge procured by immoral means is brought into starkest relief by the activities of scientists tried at the end of the Second World War for medical war crimes. Although 'medical war crime' seems something of an oxymoron, there is no better term for the experiments conducted by Nazi researchers on concentration camp inmates. Much of what was done to concentration camp inmates had no scientific value; it was motivated by a misguided racial ideology masquerading as science. The real dilemmas arise in connection with data that may have some scientific value. For example, the Nazis conducted extensive research into hypothermia. The means by which the data were produced, the immersion of inmates for long periods in vats of freezing water, were grossly immoral. The Nazi researchers killed some eighty to a hundred people on the way to what appears to be the correct conclusion that rapid, intensive warming in hot water gives the best chance of survival after rescue from very cold seas.[19] Some people think that we should not make use of information procured in such an immoral fashion. Rejecting the Nazi data does seem the most forthright way of condemning what they did. But deaths may be a predictable consequence of acting as if we do not know that rapid warming in hot water is a better way to treat people suffering from hypothermia than the other alternatives tested by the Nazis. Even so, it is not hard to understand the ambivalence people feel about the use of data produced by such sadistic means.

The Nazi hypothermia experiments are an extreme example of the abuse of human dignity for a scientific end, but, as we have seen, there are many other cases in which abuses of human beings have made advances in medical science possible. The fact that we now routinely transplant organs and vaccinate against infectious disease does not necessarily vindicate the experimental paths leading to the mature technologies. But we should not deny ourselves the benefits that we now derive from vaccinations and organ transplants. There is an aspect of the Nazi experiments that we do not find in the smallpox or the transplantation experiments. This difference is not in the magnitude of the good being pursued, but rather in the attitude to those experimented on. Having disregarded their subjects' welfare to justify experimenting on them in the first place, Jenner and the first transplanters of organs would have hoped for the best for them. The Nazis' attitude to the inmates 'fortunate' to be revived from hypothermia was very different from this.

I propose that Jenner and the organ transplant pioneers, rather than the Nazi doctors, are the moral counterparts of pioneers in human enhancement. Even if they stand ready to learn from the failures, these experimenters will want the best for the clones and genetically modified humans they create.

It is impossible to guess the exact means by which we will eventually enhance human abilities. Perhaps none of the technological paths discussed in this book will lead anywhere. However, it is a reasonable bet that the biotechnologists of some future century will develop techniques capable of safely enhancing human attributes. Once this point is reached we will be able to implement a liberal eugenics, granting prospective parents a limited prerogative to use enhancement technologies to choose their children's characteristics.

Notes

1 Genius Sperm, Eugenics and Enhancement Technologies

1 See David Plotz (2001), 'The "genius babies" and how they grew', *Slate*, slate.msn.com/id/10331/.
2 Galton quoted in Paul (1995: 3).
3 Galton (1973). For informative histories of eugenics see Kevles (1995) and Paul (1995).
4 Stephen Saetz (1985) 'Eugenics and the Third Reich', *Eugenics Bulletin*, www.eugenics.net/papers/3rdreich.html.
5 Stock (2002), Harris (1998a) and Silver (1997) are examples of writers who advocate a liberal approach to human enhancement while separating what they are advocating from eugenics. Kitcher (1996) is a liberal who is more friendly to the label.
6 See Kelves (1995) and Paul (1995).
7 See Paul (1995).
8 For the most influential recent defence of liberal pluralism, see Rawls (1971).
9 See Robertson (1994).
10 Quoted in Beckwith and Alper (2002: 316).
11 See Report of the American Association for the Advancement of Science (2003): www.aaas.org/news/releases/2001/human.shtml.
12 See Lewontin (1972).
13 See for example Elliott (2003). My use of the term 'enhancement technology' is narrower than Elliott's. He applies the term to a wide range of ways in which people seek to better themselves – Prozac, cosmetic surgery, etc. I limit the term to ways in which people might be brought into existence.

14 See www.clonaid.com.

15 Haldane (1963: 352–3). Brock (1998b) discusses this possibility.

16 Haldane (1963: 353).

17 See Carina et al. (2002) for non-technical explanation of the meaning and import of this announcement.

18 For the press release announcing this event go to www.ornl.gov/TechResources/Human_Genome/project/50yr/press4_2003.htm.

19 Tang et al. (1999).

20 See the discussion of this case by President Bush's Council on Bioethics at www.bioethics.gov/background/strong_muscles.html.

21 'Scientists create a genetically engineered "smart mouse"', CNN, 1 September 1999, www.cnn.com/HEALTH/9909/01/brainy.mice/.

22 David Teather, 'Lesbian couple have deaf baby by choice', The Guardian, Monday, 8 April 2002.

23 BBC News, 'Couple "choose" to have deaf baby', news.bbc.co.uk/1/hi/health/1916462.stm.

24 Ibid.

25 Habermas (2003: 76).

26 For an example of a liberal who argues along these lines, see Harris (1998b). Harris reasons that it would be wrong to impose tests on people who need assistance in reproducing that those who need no assistance avoid.

27 This is the definition presented in the Transhumanist FAQ at www.transhumanism.org/resources/faq.html.

28 Mark Walker, 'Prolegomena to any future philosophy', at www.jetpress.org/volume10/prolegomena.html.

29 See Ridley (2003: 36–7).

30 Silver (1997: 237).

31 Ibid., p. 238.

32 Bostrom (2003: 494–5).

33 Visit www.transhumanism.org/resources/faq.html to see if the hackers have returned.

34 For the distinction between a better human life and a whole one see the October 2003 report of President Bush's Council on Bioethics at www.bioethics.gov/reports/beyondtherapy/index.html.

35 Fukuyama (2002) and McKibben (2003).

36 Kass (1971).

37 Kass (1997).

38 Kass (2002a: 5).

2 A Pragmatic Optimism about Enhancement Technologies

1   Gray (2002: 14).
2   Quoted in McKibben (2003: 181).
3   Story on BBC News, 'Dolly scientists play down US clone', 25 November 2001, available at news.bbc.co.uk/1/hi/sci/tech/1676037.stm.
4   Kyla Dunn, 'Cloning Trevor', *Atlantic Monthly* 289(6): 31–52, June 2002.
5   Pinker (2003).
6   Ibid.
7   See Philip Cohen, 'Introducing a spit personality...', *New Scientist* 165(2222), 22 January, p. 5.
8   Nicholas Wade, 'Human cloning marches on, without US help', *New York Times*, 15 February 2004.
9   See, for example, Philip Cohen and David Concar, 'The awful truth', *New Scientist*, 170(2291), 19 May 2001, p. 14.
10 See Andy Coghlan, 'The unclonables', *New Scientist*, 171(2305), 25 August 2001, p. 16.
11 See Ridley (2000) for an excellent discussion of genetic copying error.
12 See Elliot Sober's postscript in Buchanan et al. (2000) for helpful discussion of genetic causation.
13 For an engaging account of the science of twins, see Wright (1997).
14 Alison Motluk, 'Family brains', *New Scientist*, 172(2316), 10 November 2001, p. 12.
15 For a user-friendly overview of the search for genes that influence intelligence, see Ridley (2003: 88–95).
16 For an account of this view see Anderson (1992).
17 Gardner (1983, 1993).
18 For criticism of some of the assumptions behind IQ tests, see Gould (1996).
19 See Tanzi and Parson (2000).
20 Chorney et al. (1998).
21 Ridley (1999: 87).
22 Hill et al. (2002).
23 For a collection of articles that, for the most part, defend behavioural genetics, see Benjamin et al. (2002).
24 Wei et al. (2001).
25 Quoted in Deborah Stull, *The Scientist* 15(7): 21, 2 April 2001, www.the-scientist.com/yr2001/apr/research1_010402.html.
26 See Singer (1993).
27 O'Neill (2002: 70–2).

28 Solter and McGrath (1984).
29 Ibid., p. 1319.
30 See the essays in McGee (2000).
31 Kitcher (2000: 140).
32 See Swinburne's essay in Shoemaker and Swinburne (1984).
33 See Unger (1990) for defence of a physical continuity theory.
34 Parfit (1984) is a prominent defence of this view.
35 The term 'brain-state-transfer device' comes from Sydney Shoemaker's contribution in Shoemaker and Swinburne (1984).
36 Kyla Dunn, 'Cloning Trevor', *Atlantic Monthly*, 289(6): 31–52, June 2002.

3 Making Moral Images of Biotechnology

1 See Heyd (1994) for the argument that conventional moral theories fail to guide us in our choices about potential persons.
2 Lesch et al. (2002).
3 Singer (1993) defends preference utilitarianism and uses it to resolve a range of moral issues.
4 Kuhse and Singer (1995: vi).
5 For a defence of a person-affecting approach to genetic engineering, see Heyd (1994).
6 The idea that we have no obligations in respect of merely potential persons is defended in Heyd (1994).
7 For a recent exposition of the Kantian approach to bioethical problems, see O'Neill (2002).
8 Heyd (1994: 52–3).
9 See for example Marquis (1989) and Tooley (1972).
10 Singer (1993).
11 Goodman (1972).
12 Midgley (2000).
13 Ibid., p. 13.
14 See Alexandra Goho, 'Embryonic hope', *New Scientist* 179(2402), 5 July 2003, p. 19.
15 Nicholas Wade, 'Word war breaks out in research on stem cells', *New York Times*, 21 December 2002.
16 Krauthammer (2002: 21).
17 See Kass (2002b: 52); Wade, 'Word war breaks out in research on stem cells'.
18 President's Report (2002: 52).
19 Ibid., p. 43.
20 Ibid., p. 63.

21 Krauthammer (2002).
22 President's Report (2002: 50–1).
23 This is how Noonan (1994) explains the foetus's potential.
24 For details of this story see Wilmut et al. (2000: chap. 6).
25 See Philip Cohen, 'This little piggy had none', *New Scientist* 173(2325), 12 January 2002, p. 7.
26 Atwood (2003: 56).
27 Kass (1997: 20).
28 Ibid.
29 See for example Kass (1971).
30 Shaoni Bhattacharya, 'Brave new treatments', *New Scientist* 179(2403), 12 July 2003 p. 18.
31 Pence (2002: 105–6).
32 See Winston (2002: 228).
33 Kass (2002a: 12).
34 Ibid., p. 155.
35 Bostrom (2003: 494–5).

4 The Moral Image of Therapy

1 Paul (1995).
2 Quote from the *Genetics and Society* website at www.genetics-and-society. org/newsletter/archive/13.html.
3 Quoted in Kass (2002a: 7).
4 Quoted in Wade (2001: 18).
5 Quoted in Carina et al. (2002: 49).
6 David Brown, 'French research offers promise of gene therapy cure', *Washington Post*, 18 April 2002.
7 Andy Coghlan, 'Double trouble for gene therapy', *New Scientist*, 177, 26 January 2003, p. 12.
8 See Sheryl Gay Stolberg, 'The biotech death of Jesse Gelsinger', *New York Times: Sunday Magazine*, 28 November 1999.
9 See ibid.
10 Buchanan et al. (2000).
11 Ibid., pp. 82–4.
12 See Hall (2003) for a fascinating account of attempts to commercialize life-extension biotechnologies.
13 Kripke (1972).
14 Ibid., pp. 112–13.
15 For an exchange on gene therapy and identity in the journal *Bioethics*, see Zohar (1991), Elliot (1993), Persson (1995) and Elliot (1997).

16 Kass (2002a: 110).

17 Compare this case with the discussion in Parfit (1984: 357–61) of a 14-year-old girl who faces the choice of having a child now or waiting to have one when she is more mature. Although she expects the child she would have now to have a worse life than the one she would have later, she has reason to believe that both children will have lives worth living. Parfit argues that it is wrong to bring into existence the worse-off child. This claim supports the contention that the doctor who asks the heavily drinking woman to conceive later does not stray outside of the therapeutic domain – he uses his medical expertise to achieve a moral good. I do not require the truth of the stronger claim (Parfit 1984: 366–71) that there is no difference between knowingly bringing an embryo into existence in a handicapped state, and not preventing an embryo from suffering an injury that would handicap it in the same way.

18 Philosophers have advanced a number of principles to explain the wrong that is done in cases in which no one is harmed. For example, James Woodward (1986) argues that one's rights may be infringed even in cases in which one is not harmed. Buchanan et al. (2000: 249) advance a principle that directs that we should not create suffering, even when its creation does not harm someone.

19 McMahan (1998) and Wasserman (2001a) provide excellent overviews of this debate.

20 Olson (1997).

21 Some philosophers have argued for the stronger view. See for example Persson (1995). Kripke (1972: 113) seems to come close to endorsing a sufficiency thesis.

22 See Pinker (2002).

23 See Ridley (2003) for a very user-friendly description of the interactionist view of development.

24 Dawkins (1989).

25 Hamer et al. (1993).

26 Hamer and Copeland (1994: 147).

27 Rice et al. (1999).

28 Hamer (2002: 270).

29 For an account of this research see Alison Motluk, 'Big Brother effect', *New Scientist* 177(2388), 29 March 2003, pp. 44–7. See also Ridley (2003: 160–1).

30 Hamer and Copeland (1994: 146).

31 For an illuminating popular account of discoveries of the genetic bases of Alzheimer's, see Tanzi and Parson (2000).

32 McMahan (1998) makes similar points in connection with events that pre-date someone's existence.

33 See Fodor (1983).

34 Fukuyama (2002: 209).

35 Kitcher (1996: chap. 9).
36 See for example Buchanan et al. (2000).
37 See Hamer and Copeland (1994: chap. 11).
38 Kitcher (1996: 212–17).
39 See Sellers et al. (2000).
40 See Buchanan et al. (2000: chaps 3–4).
41 Buchanan et al. (2000: 122).
42 Ibid., p. 123.
43 Ibid., pp. 137–41.
44 Ibid., pp. 130–7.
45 Ibid., p. 139.
46 Ibid., p. 149.
47 Ibid., p. 120.
48 Ibid., p. 122.
49 Ibid., p. 123.
50 Ibid., p. 152.
51 Ibid., p. 226.
52 Ibid.
53 Fukuyama (2002: chap. 3). Elliott (2003) is a fascinating investigation of some of these issues.

5   The Moral Image of Nature

1 See for example Graham (2002: chap. 4).
2 This invocation of nature should be distinguished from arguments that reach a prudential conclusion. The prudential argument moves from the claim that whoever or whatever designed human brains and bodies, they currently work well, to the conclusion that it is too risky to attempt to improve them. My pragmatic optimist strategy allows us to put this argument to one side. We will instead be concerned with reasons not to interfere with divine or evolutionary design regardless of the risks. I will, however, address the prudential argument in chapter 8.
3 Juengst (1998) explores a variety of ways to defend the moral significance of the distinction between treatment and enhancement.
4 Parens (1998: 10–11) makes this point. He argues that failing to defend enhancement as medicine does not show that it cannot be defended in some other way.
5 Fukuyama (2002: 101).
6 Hume (1973) is the originator of this argument.
7 Fukuyama (2002: chap. 7).
8 Thornhill and Palmer (2000).

9   See the critical essays in Travis (2003).
10 Fukuyama (2002: 140–3).
11 Ibid., p. 101.
12 Ibid., p. 130.
13 Ibid.
14 Ibid., p. 132.
15 Ibid., p. 138.
16 Wilson (1978).
17 Fukuyama (2002: 132).
18 Herrnstein and Murray (1994).
19 See for example the essays in Devlin et al. (1997).
20 For this argument see Kaplan (2000). See also Sober (2000).
21 Robin McKie, 'Men redundant? Now we don't need women either', *The Observer*, 10 February 2002.
22 Duncan Graham-Rowe, 'The world's first brain prosthesis', *New Scientist*, 177(2386), 15 March 2003, pp. 4–5.
23 Fukuyama (2002: 134–5).
24 See also Wachbroit (2003) for discussion of Fukuyama.
25 McKibben (2003: 6).
26 Juengst (1998: 38).
27 '"Gene cheat" athletes could escape detection', BBC news website, 13 January 2000, news.bbc.co.uk/1/hi/health/601031.stm.
28 The nature principle differs from another plea for consistency about the consequences of actions and inactions. The widely discussed consequentialist argument that if we are required not to kill then we are also required to save lives involves obligations. The nature principle concerns permissions.
29 Berlin (1990) and Rawls (1971).
30 Williams (1981: 12–13).
31 Kitcher (1996) proposes a three-dimensional account of prospective well-being: 'The first [dimension] focuses on whether the person has developed any sense of what is significant and how the conception of what matters was formed. The second assesses the extent to which those desires that are central to the person's life plan are satisfied: Did the person achieve those things that mattered most? Finally, the third is concerned with the character of the person's experience, the balance of pleasure and pain' (Kitcher 1996: 289). The analysis I present addresses the first two of Kitcher's dimensions of well-being together.
32 Berlin (1990).
33 Robertson (1994).
34 See Sen (1999) and Nussbaum (1999) for recent presentations.
35 Sen (1999: 75).
36 Ibid.

37 See Berlin (1990).
38 For example, Gerald Dworkin (1988) rejects the assumption that one always benefits from having more options.
39 See Buchanan et al. (2000: 281–4) for a persuasive presentation of this line.
40 Ruddick (1999: 247).
41 See David Plotz (2001), 'The "genius babies" and how they grew', *Slate*, slate.msn.com/id/10331/.
42 Gardner (1983).
43 Gardner (1993: 96).
44 Jamison (1996).
45 Interview with Watson in London, *Sunday Telegraph*, 16 February 1997.

6   The Moral Image of Nurture

1   Harris (1998a: 171).
2   Ibid., p. 172.
3   Robertson (1994: 167).
4   Mortensen et al. (2002: 2365–71).
5   Ibid., p. 2370.
6   Chorney et al. (1998: 164).
7   Greg Retsinas, 'The marketing of a superbaby formula', *New York Times*, New York, 1 June 2003.
8   Kass (2002a: 131).
9   Habermas (2003).
10 Wasserman (2003: 105) characterizes Habermas's point in this way.
11 Habermas (2003: 50–1).
12 Ibid., pp. 51–2.
13 Wasserman (2003: 105).
14 Ibid., p. 106.
15 See Marteau and Lerman (2001) and Claire Ainsworth, 'Life-saving tests make people think they will die', *New Scientist* 170(2289), 5 May 2001, p. 16.
16 Stock (2002: chap. 4).
17 Habermas (2003: 81).
18 Ibid., pp. 81–2.
19 Sandra Blakeslee, 'A pregnant mother's diet may turn the genes around', *New York Times*, 7 October 2003.
20 Simon Hattenstone and Emma Brockes, 'I'm not Crybaby Soo-Fi any more', *Guardian*, 7 July 2000.
21 See Elkind (1988).
22 Feinberg (1980).
23 Ibid., p. 130.

24   Ibid., pp. 132–3.
25   Ruddick (1999: 246).
26   Ibid., p. 246.
27   See for example Murray (1996) and Archard (2003).
28   Feinberg (1980: 149).
29   For this objection see Buchanan et al. (2000: 182–7).
30   Ibid., p. 185.
31   Brock (1998a) makes this point about the competitive and non-competitive benefits conferred by enhancement. He uses the term 'intrinsic value' for what I refer to as independent value.
32   In chapter 5 I argued that genetic changes replacing a predisposition to have superior intelligence for a predisposition to have average intelligence might have the same impact on real freedom as changing a predisposition to have average intelligence for one to have superior intelligence. This judgement depends on the range of functionings available to people of average intelligence, on the one hand, and to people of superior intelligence, on the other. Does what I have just said about the independent value of high intelligence count against this? I don't think so. Whether or not some attribute brings a positional advantage is not relative to one's values. Rather it depends on facts about the society in which one lives. However, the degree of independent value an attribute possesses can be relative to a person's conception of the good life. Some parents will place lesser value on the understanding of the world that high intelligence can bring. They will find greater independent value in functionings more easily accessible by those of average intelligence.
33   See Tim Blair, 'Just say go', *Time*, 27 July 1998, www.time.com/time/magazine/1998/int/980727/sport.just_say_go.the_la5.html.

7   Our Postliberal Future?

1   Jefferson (1944: 729–30).
2   Fukuyama (2002: 9–10).
3   Silver (1997: 4–7).
4   See for example Crouch (2001).
5   Winston (2002: 27).
6   Nozick (1974: 315).
7   See for example Dan Wachtell, 'Couple advertises for elite egg donor, sparks controversy', *Daily Princetonian*, 3 March 1999, available at www.dailyprincetonian.com/Content/1999/03/03/news/wachtell.html.
8   Rawls (1971).
9   Silver (1997: 9).
10   Ibid.

11 See Pence (1998: chap. 9) for arguments that cloning is not sufficiently different from conventional reproduction to justify the differences that some religious people claim to find.
12 www.cnn.com/2003/HEALTH/09/08/genome.price.ap/.
13 Bostrom (2003: 503).
14 Ibid., pp. 503–4.
15 Churchill (1999).
16 Mark Walker, 'Prolegomena to any future philosophy', at www.jetpress.org/volume10/prolegomena.html.
17 Bostrom (2003: 495).
18 See Paul (1995: 36–9).
19 Kass (1997).
20 Kitcher (1996: 217–18).
21 Buchanan et al. (2000: 283–4).
22 Statistics in Winston (2002: 216).
23 See 'Feed the World', *New Scientist* editorial, 15 June 2002, p. 3; Midgley (2000: 13); Shiva (2002); and the Greenpeace Statement (2002).
24 Shiva (2002: 59).
25 See for example Potrykus (2002) and Conway (2002).
26 Shiva (2002: 60).
27 Midgley (2000: 15).
28 Harris (1998a: 226) expresses this concern. See the discussion of Little (1998) about the complicity of cosmetic surgery with oppressive norms of appearance.

8 Enhanced Humans When?

1 The Wingspread Statement as it appears on the Greenpeace Website at www.greenpeace.org.au/toxics/pdf/wingspread.pdf.
2 This strategy is pursued by President Bush's Council on Bioethics in its October 2003 report. See www.bioethics.gov/reports/beyondtherapy/index. html.
3 Stock (2002: 140).
4 Sandy Scarr, 'Science, risk and the price of precaution', *Spiked*, www.spiked-online.com/articles/00000006DD7A.htm.
5 For Zavos's comparison of cloners and astronauts visit the website of the Zavos Organization at www.zavos.org/library/library_arhpspeech.htm.
6 Stuart Newman quoted in McKibben (2003: 42).
7 Shaoni Bhattacharya, 'Brave new treatments', *New Scientist*, 179(2403), 12 July 2003, p. 18.

8 Ridley (2003: 24–6).
9 Buchanan et al. (2000: 192).
10 McCloskey (1957).
11 Smart and Williams (1973: 99).
12 See Horton (2002: essay 6) for discussion of Jenner.
13 See Holm (2002) for a discussion of issues arising in connection with consent procured under such circumstances.
14 Unger (1996) and Singer (1993: chap. 8) discuss ways in which our proximity to those who suffer influences how we think about them morally. Because they are arguing from a consequentialist perspective they propose that we control for this defect in our moral vision. I present this phenomenon as reflecting a situation's Kantian gestalt.
15 Stock (2002: 159).
16 See for example, Charles Mann, 'The first cloning superpower: inside China's race to become the clone capital of the world', *Wired Magazine*, issue 11, 1 January 2003, pp. 114–43.
17 See for example Nicholas Wade, 'Human cloning marches on, without US help', *New York Times*, 15 February 2004.
18 Kass (1997: 25).
19 See www.pbs.org/wgbh/nova/holocaust/experiside.html.

Further Reading

This book has answered the question of whether liberal eugenics is morally justified in the affirmative. However, I leave it open to the reader to use the method of moral images to arrive at a different conclusion. Below are some sources that may be useful in taking this different approach to the morality of enhancing humans.

THE HISTORY AND SCIENCE OF HUMAN ENHANCEMENT

David Plotz's account of Robert K. Graham and his Repository for Germinal Choice is well worth a look. It can be found on the Slate website at http://slate.msn.com/id/100331/. Kevles (1995) and Paul (1995) are informative histories of eugenics. Both trace the movement's history from Galton's founding of it, through its twentieth-century excesses, to the threatened revival prompted by advances in genetics. Black (2003) is a recent work focusing on the American eugenics movement. It makes a strong case that the Nazis were deeply influenced by American eugenic ideas.

The rapidity of the advance of the technologies that might be used to enhance humans means that any book is soon out of date. Progress has certainly been made since Silver (1997). However, that book remains, nonetheless, a very interesting survey of the wild permutations of human genetic material that might one day be achieved. Stock (2002) is a more recent presentation of technological possibilities. Readers of both of these books should be aware that their presentations come packaged with libertarian conclusions about the morality of human enhancement. Stock's book was published in the same year as Fukuyama (2002) and this prompted journalists to pit the enhancement liberal and conservative against one another.

Wilmut et al. (2000) is a 'from the horse's mouth' account (or better still, a 'from the horses' mouths' account) of the invention of mammalian somatic cell nuclear transfer. Ian Wilmut and Keith Campbell give very accessible accounts of the parts they played in making Dolly. Kolata (1998) describes the science behind Dolly in a way that conveys the excitement of the events leading up to and immediately following her creation. The Dolly breakthrough gave rise to a lively debate about the morality of human reproductive cloning. For good discussions of the ethics of human reproductive cloning, see the articles in McGee (2000) and Nussbaum and Sunstein (1998). For vigorous advocacy of human reproductive cloning see Pence (1998).

Ridley (2003) and Pinker (2002) are very readable defences of heredity's importance. Ridley illustrates very well how genes and environment interact to make human traits. The articles in Benjamin et al. (2002) cover many of the contemporary avenues of research in behavioural genetics. Although almost all of the contributors are working behavioural geneticists, the collection does include a sceptical piece by Evan Balaban. Kaplan (2000) offers more systematic scepticism about behavioural genetics. I used Hamer et al. (1993) as my primary illustration of gene–environment interaction. Readers interested in a different example of this interaction should look at Caspi et al. (2002). This study of violent behaviour focuses on a gene that comes in two versions. One version appears to make it significantly more likely that an abusive upbringing will translate into violent behaviour later. The other version seems to protect against this consequence of abusive upbringings. This paper is available on the internet at http://www.med.umich.edu/hg/EDUCATION/COURSES/HG803/Burmeister/CaspiMaoAmaltreatment.pdf. Wasserman (2001b) contains a series of papers that investigate the philosophical implications of research into the genetics of violence.

The most up-to-date information about enhancement technologies cannot be found in books. Major advances in the technologies receive good coverage in quality newspapers. The science section of the *New York Times* is particularly good. Its internet edition can be found at http://www.nytimes.com/pages/science/index.html. Popular science magazines such as *New Scientist* and *Scientific American* are other valuable sources of information about breaking developments. The *New Scientist* website has an excellent page that gathers together the magazine's reports on and discussions of cloning. The address of this page is http://www.newscientist.com/hottopics/cloning/. Readers who are sufficiently game will be able to use the information provided in these sources to read the original journal announcements.

THE MORALITY OF HUMAN ENHANCEMENT

The literature on the moral viability of human enhancement is philosophically and ideologically diverse. The most enthusiastic supporters of human enhancement are the transhumanists. The best place to find out about transhumanism is by visiting the Frequently Asked Questions page on their website at http://www.transhumanism.org/resources/FAQv2.pdf. Last time I checked, the site was free from sabotage by internet penis enlargers. Bostrom (2003) defends transhumanism against several philosophical objections.

Kitcher (1996), Harris (1998a), Buchanan et al. (2000) and Robertson (1994) all consider enhancement in the context of liberal views about our entitlements and responsibilities. This does not stop them from drawing quite different conclusions about enhancement. For recent expressions of the conservative view, so important in the formulation of public policy about human biotechnology, see Fukuyama (2002), Kass (2002a) and McKibben (2003). Kass and Fukuyama exercise their influence on US government policy through their membership of President Bush's Council on Bioethics. The Council publishes discussions of various moral issues in biotechnology. These can be found at http://bioethics.gov/topics/beyond_index.html. Although Council members are not unanimous on all of the issues they consider, the conservative line can easily be discerned in its reflections. Parens (1998) contains a useful series of articles that focus mainly on the potential pitfalls of human enhancement.

The ongoing debate about the ethics of enhancement can be followed in the pages of academic journals including *Bioethics, The Hastings Center Report*, the *American Journal of Bioethics* and the *Journal of Medicine and Philosophy*.

I present the method of moral images as a means of making moral choices about enhancement without recourse to principles. Philosophers have appealed to a wide variety of principles for guidance on the kinds of people that cloning and genetic engineering might make. Some philosophers have applied these principles to the question of the morality of enhancement directly. Buchanan et al. (2000) extend Rawls's political philosophy to encompass questions of human enhancement. Harris (1998a) takes an explicitly consequentialist approach to these issues. O'Neill (2002) presents her arguments within the context of Kant's morality, arguing that liberals push the idea of reproductive autonomy beyond its proper limits.

References

Anderson, Mike, 1992. *Intelligence and Development: A Cognitive Theory.* New York: Basil Blackwell.

Archard, David, 2003. *Children, Family and the State.* Aldershot: Ashgate.

Atwood, Margaret, 2003. *Oryx and Crake.* London: Bloomsbury.

Beckwith, Jon and Alper, Joseph, 2002. Genetics of human personality: social and ethical implications. In J. Benjamin, R. Ebstein and R. Belmaker (eds), *Molecular Genetics and the Human Personality*, pp. 315–32. Washington, DC: American Psychiatric Publishing.

Benjamin, J., Ebstein, R. and Belmaker, R. H., 2002. *Molecular Genetics and Human Personality.* Washington, DC: APA Press.

Berlin, Isaiah, 1990. Two concepts of liberty. In *Four Essays on Liberty.* Oxford: Oxford University Press.

Black, Edwin, 2003. *War Against the Weak: Eugenics and America's Campaign to Create a Master Race.* New York: Four Walls Eight Windows.

Bostrom, Nick, 2003. Human genetic enhancements: a transhumanist perspective. *Journal of Value Inquiry* 37(4): 493–506.

Brock, Dan, 1998a. Enhancements of human function: some distinctions for policy makers. In E. Parens (ed.), *Enhancing Human Traits: Conceptual Complexities and Ethical Implications*, pp. 48–69. Washington, DC: Georgetown University Press.

Brock, Dan, 1998b. Cloning human beings: an assessment of the ethical issues pro and con. In M. Nussbaum and C. Sunstein (eds), *Clones and Clones: Facts and Fantasies about Human Cloning*, pp. 141–64. New York: W. W. Norton.

Buchanan, Allen, Brock, Dan, Daniels, Norman and Wikler, Daniel, 2000. *From Chance to Choice: Genetics and Justice.* Cambridge: Cambridge University Press.

Carina, Dennis, Gallagher, Richard and Watson, James, 2002. *The Human Genome.* London: Palgrave Macmillan.

Caspi, Avshalom, McClay, Joseph, Moffitt, Terrie E., Mill, Jonathan, Martin, Judy, Craig, Ian W., Taylor, Alan and Poulton, Richie, 2002. Role of genotype in the cycle of violence in maltreated children. *Science* 297: 851–4.

Chorney, M. J. K., Seese, N., Owen, M. J., Daniels, J., McGuffin, P., Thompson, L. A., Detterman, D. K., Benbow, C., Lubinski, D., Eley, T. and Plomin, R., 1998. A quantitative trait locus associated with cognitive ability in children. *Psychological Science* 9(3): 159–66.

Churchill, R. Paul, 1999. The obligation of parents to raise their children as altruists. In L. Houlgate (ed.), *Morals, Marriage, and Parenthood: An Introduction to Family Ethics*, pp. 242–51. Belmont, CA: Wadsworth.

Conway, Gordon, 2002. Open letter to Greenpeace. In M. Ruse and D. Castle (eds), *Genetically Modified Foods*, pp. 63–4. Amherst, NY: Prometheus Books.

Crouch, Martha, 2001. From golden rice to terminator technology: agricultural biotechnology will not feed the world or save the environment. In B. Tokar (ed.), *Redesigning Life: The Worldwide Challenge to Genetic Engineering.* Johannesburg: University of Witwatersrand Press.

Dawkins, Richard, 1989. *The Extended Phenotype.* Oxford: Oxford University Press.

Devlin, Bernie, Fienberg, Stephen E., Resnick, Daniel P. and Roeder, Kathryn, 1997. *Intelligence, Genes, and Success: Scientists Respond to the Bell Curve: Statistics for Social Science and Public Policy.* New York: Springer Verlag.

Dworkin, Gerald, 1988. Is more choice better than less? In *The Theory and Practice of Autonomy.* Cambridge: Cambridge University Press.

Elkind, David, 1988. *The Hurried Child: Growing Up Too Fast, Too Soon.* New York: Perseus.

Elliot, Robert, 1993. Identity and the ethics of gene therapy. *Bioethics* 7(1): 27–40.

Elliot, Robert, 1997. Genetic therapy, person-regarding reasons and the determination of identity. *Bioethics* 11(2): 151–9.

Elliott, Carl, 2003. *Better than Well: American Medicine Meets the American Dream.* New York: W. W. Norton.

Feinberg, Joel, 1980. The child's right to an open future. In W. Aiken and H. L. Follette (eds), *Whose Child? Children's Rights, Parental Authority, and State Power*, pp. 124–53. Totowa, NJ: Littlefield, Adams.

Fodor, Jerry, 1983. The present status of the innateness controversy. In *RePresentations: Philosophical Essays on the Foundations of Cognitive Science.* Cambridge, MA: MIT Press.

Fukuyama, Francis, 1992. *The End of History and the Last Man.* New York: Free Press.

Fukuyama, Francis, 2002. *Our Posthuman Future: Consequences of the Biotechnology Revolution.* New York: Farrar, Straus & Giroux.

Galton, Francis, 1973. *Inquiries into Human Faculty and its Development.* New York: AMS Press.

Gardner, Howard, 1983. *Frames of Mind: The Theory of Multiple Intelligences.* New York: Basic Books.

Gardner, Howard, 1993. *Multiple Intelligences: The Theory in Practice.* New York: Basic Books.

Goodman, Nelson, 1972. Seven strictures on similarity. In *Problems and Projects.* Indianapolis, IN: Bobbs-Merrill.

Gould, Stephen J., 1996. *The Mismeasure of Man.* New York: W. W. Norton.

Graham, Gordon, 2002. *Genes: A Philosophical Enquiry.* London: Routledge.

Graham, Robert, 1970. *The Future of Man.* North Quincy: Christopher Publishing House.

Gray, John, 2002. *Straw Dogs: Thoughts on Humans and Other Animals.* London: Granta.

Greenpeace, 2002. Genetically engineered 'golden rice' is fool's gold. In M. Ruse and D. Castle (eds), *Genetically Modified Foods*, pp. 52–4. Amherst, NY: Prometheus Books.

Habermas, Jürgen, 2003. *The Future of Human Nature.* Cambridge: Polity Press.

Haldane, J. B. S., 1963. Biological possibilities in the next ten thousand years. In G. Wolstenholme (ed.), *Man and his Future*, pp. 337–61. Boston, MA: Little, Brown.

Hall, Stephen, 2003. *Merchants of Immortality: Chasing the Dream of Human Life Extension.* Boston, MA: Houghton Mifflin.

Hamer, Dean, 2002. Genetics of sexual behavior. In J. Benjamin, R. Ebstein and R. Belmaker (eds), *Molecular Genetics and the Human Personality*, pp. 257–72. Washington, DC: American Psychiatric Publishing.

Hamer, Dean, and Copeland, Peter, 1994. *The Science of Desire: The Search for the Gay Gene and the Biology of Behavior.* New York: Simon and Schuster.

Hamer, Dean, Hu, S., Magnuson, V. and Pattatucci, A., 1993. A linkage between DNA markers on the X chromosome and male sexual orientation. *Science* 261: 321–7.

Harris, John, 1998a. *Clones, Genes, and Immortality: Ethics and the Genetic Revolution.* Oxford: Oxford University Press.

Harris, John, 1998b. Rights and reproductive choice. In J. Harris and S. Holm (eds), *The Future of Human Reproduction: Ethics, Choice, and Reproduction*, pp. 5–37. Oxford: Clarendon Press.

Herrnstein, Richard, and Murray, Charles, 1994. *The Bell Curve: Intelligence and Class Structure in American Life.* New York: Free Press.

Heyd, David, 1994. *Genethics: Moral Issues in the Creation of People.* Berkeley, CA: University of California Press.

Hill, Linzy, Chorney, Michael, Lubinski, David, Thompson, Lee and Plomin, Robert, 2002. A qualitative trait locus not associated with cognitive ability in children: a failure to replicate. *Psychological Science* 13(6): 561–2.

Holm, Soren, 2002. The role of informed consent in genetic experimentation. In J. Burley and J. Harris (eds), *A Companion to Genethics*, pp. 82–91. Oxford: Blackwell Publishers.

Horton, Richard, 2002. *Second Opinion: Doctors, Diseases and Decisions*. London: Granta Books.

Hume, David, 1973. *A Treatise on Human Nature*. Oxford: Clarendon Press.

Huxley, Aldous, 1998. *Brave New World*. New York: Perennial Classics.

Jamison, Kay, 1996. *Touched with Fire: Manic Depressive Illness and the Artistic Temperament*. New York: Touchstone Books.

Jefferson, Thomas, 1944. *The Life and Selected Writings of Thomas Jefferson*. New York: Modern Library.

Juengst, Eric, 1998. What does enhancement mean? In E. Parens (ed.), *Enhancing Human Traits: Conceptual Complexities and Ethical Implications*, pp. 29–47. Washington, DC: Georgetown University Press.

Kaplan, Jonathan, 2000. *The Limits and Lies of Human Genetic Research: Dangers for Social Policy*. London: Routledge.

Kass, Leon, 1971. Babies by means of in vitro fertilization: unethical experiments on the unborn? *New England Journal of Medicine* 285: 1174–79.

Kass, Leon, 1997. The wisdom of repugnance: Why we should ban the cloning of humans. In *The New Republic*, 2 June 1997, pp. 17–26.

Kass, Leon, 2002a. *Life, Liberty and the Defense of Dignity: The Challenge for Bioethics*. San Francisco, CA: Encounter Books.

Kass, Leon, 2002b. *Human Cloning and Human Dignity: The Report of the President's Council on Bioethics*. New York: Public Affairs.

Kevles, Daniel, 1995. *In the Name of Eugenics: Genetics and the Uses of Human Heredity*. Berkeley, CA: University of California Press.

Kitcher, Philip, 1996. *The Lives to Come: The Genetic Revolution and Human Possibilities*. New York: Simon and Schuster.

Kitcher, Philip, 2000. Human cloning. In G. McGee (ed.), *The Human Cloning Debate*. Berkeley, CA: Berkeley Hills Books.

Kolata, Gina, 1998. *Clone: The Road to Dolly, and the Path Ahead*. New York: Penguin.

Krauthammer, Charles, 2002. Crossing lines: A secular argument against research cloning. In *The New Republic*, 29 April 2002, pp. 20–3.

Kripke, Saul, 1972. *Naming and Necessity*. Cambridge, MA: Harvard University Press.

Kuhse, Helga, and Singer, Peter, 1995. Of genes, embryos, human individuals and future persons. *Bioethics* 9(1): iii–vi.

Lesch, K., Greenberg, B. D., Higley, J. D., Bennett, A. and Murphy, D. L., 2002. Serotonin transporter, personality, and behavior. In J. Benjamin, R. Ebstein and R. Belmaker (eds), *Molecular Genetics and the Human Personality*, pp. 109–35. Washington, DC: American Psychiatric Publishing.

Lewontin, Richard, 1972. The apportionment of human diversity. *Evolutionary Biology* 6: 381–98.

Little, Margaret Olivia, 1998. Cosmetic surgery, suspect norms, and the ethics of complicity. In E. Parens (ed.), *Enhancing Human Traits: Conceptual Complexities and Ethical Implications*, pp. 162–76. Washington, DC: Georgetown University Press.

Marquis, Don, 1989. Why abortion is immoral. *Journal of Philosophy* 86(4):183–202.

Marteau, Theresa M. and Lerman, Caryn, 2001. Genetic risk and behavioural change. *British Medical Journal* 322: 1056–59.

McCloskey, H. J., 1957. An examination of restricted utilitarianism. *Philosophical Review* 66: 466–85.

McGee, Glenn, 2000. *The Human Cloning Debate*. Berkeley, CA: Berkeley Hills Books.

McKibben, Bill, 2003. *Enough: Staying Human in an Engineered Age*. New York: Times Books.

McMahan, Jeff, 1998. Wrongful life: paradoxes in the morality of causing people to exist. In J. Coleman and C. Morris (eds), *Rational Commitment and Social Justice: Essays for Gregory Kavka*, pp. 208–47. New York: Cambridge University Press.

Midgley, Mary, 2000. Biotechnology and monstrosity: why we should pay attention to the 'yuk factor'. *Hastings Center Report* 30(5): 7–15.

Miller, Henry, and Conko, Gregory, 2002. Precaution without principle. In M. Ruse and D. Castle (eds), *Genetically Modified Foods*, pp. 292–7. Amherst, NY: Prometheus Books.

Mortensen, Erik, Michaelson, Kim, Saunders, Stephanie and Reinisch, June, 2002. The association between duration of breastfeeding and adult intelligence. *Journal of the American Medical Association* 287(18): 2365–71.

Murray, Thomas, 1996. *The Worth of a Child*. Berkeley, CA: University of California Press.

Nasar, Sylvia, 1998. *A Beautiful Mind*. New York: Touchstone Books.

Noonan, John, 1994. An almost absolute value in history. In T. Beauchamp and L. Walters (eds), *Contemporary Issues in Bioethics*, pp. 279–82. Belmont, CA: Wadsworth.

Nozick, Robert, 1974. *Anarchy, State, and Utopia*. New York: Random House.

Nussbaum, Martha, 1999. *Sex and Social Justice*. Oxford: Oxford University Press.

Nussbaum, Martha and Sunstein, Cass, 1998. *Clones and Clones: Facts and Fantasies about Human Cloning*. New York: W. W. Norton.

Olson, Eric, 1997. Was I ever a fetus? *Philosophy and Phenomenological Research* 57(1): 95–109.

O'Neill, Onora, 2002. *Autonomy and Trust in Bioethics*. Cambridge: Cambridge University Press.

Parens, Erik, 1998. Is better always good? The enhancement project. In E. Parens (ed.), *Enhancing Human Traits: Ethical and Social Implications.* Washington, DC: Georgetown University Press.

Parfit, D., 1984. *Reasons and Persons.* Oxford: Oxford University Press.

Paul, Diane, 1995. *Controlling Human Heredity: 1865 to the Present.* New Jersey: Humanities Press.

Pence, Gregory, 1998. *Who's Afraid of Human Cloning?* Lanham, MD: Rowman and Littlefield.

Pence, Gregory, 2002. *Designer Food: Mutant Harvest or Breadbasket of the World?* Lanham, MD: Rowman and Littlefield.

Persson, Ingmar, 1995. Genetic therapy, identity and the person-regarding reasons. *Bioethics* 9(1): 16–31.

Pinker, Steven, 2002. *The Blank Slate: The Modern Denial of Human Nature.* New York: Viking.

Pinker, Steven, 2003. Session 3: Human Nature and its Future: Address to Council on Bioethics: http://www.bioethics.gov/transcripts/march03/session3.html.

Potrykus, Ingo, 2002. Golden rice and the Greenpeace dilemma. In M. Ruse and D. Castle (eds), *Genetically Modified Foods*, pp. 55–7. Amherst, NY: Prometheus Books.

Rawls, John, 1971. *A Theory of Justice.* Cambridge, MA: Harvard University Press.

Rice, George, Anderson, Carol, Risch, Neil and Ebers, George, 1999. Male homosexuality: absence of linkage to microsatellite markers at Xq28. *Science* 284: 665–7.

Ridley, Mark, 2000. *Mendel's Demon: Gene Justice and the Complexity of Life.* London: Phoenix.

Ridley, Matt, 1999. *Genome: The Autobiography of a Species in 23 Chapters.* London: Fourth Estate.

Ridley, Matt, 2003. *Nature via Nuture: Genes, Experience and What Makes Us Human.* London: Fourth Estate.

Robertson, John, 1994. *Children of Choice: Freedom and the New Reproductive Technologies.* Princeton, NJ: Princeton University Press.

Ruddick, William, 1999. Parenthood: three concepts and a principle. In L. Houlgate (ed.), *Morals, Marriage, and Parenthood: An Introduction to Family Ethics*, pp. 242–51. Belmont, CA: Wadsworth.

Sellers, Edward M., Kaplan, Howard L. and Tyndale, Rachel F., 2000. Inhibition of cytochrome P450 2A6 increases nicotine's oral bioavailability and decreases smoking. *Clinical Pharmacology & Therapeutics* 68(1):35–43.

Sen, Amartya, 1999. *Development as Freedom.* New York: Alfred A. Knopf.

Shiva, Vandana, 2002. Golden rice hoax: When public relations replace science. In M. Ruse and D. Castle (eds), *Genetically Modified Foods*, pp. 58–62. Amherst, NY: Prometheus Books.

Shoemaker, Sydney and Swinburne, Richard, 1984. *Personal Identity.* Oxford: Basil Blackwell.

Silver, Lee, 1997. *Remaking Eden: Cloning and Beyond in a Brave New World.* New York: Avon Books.

Singer, Peter, 1993. *Practical Ethics.* Sydney: Federation Press.

Smart, J. J. C. and Williams, Bernard, 1973. *Utilitarianism: For and Against.* Cambridge: Cambridge University Press.

Sober, Elliot, 2000. The meaning of genetic causation. In Allen Buchanan, Dan Brock, Norman Daniels and Daniel Wikler (eds), *From Chance to Choice: Genetics and Justice.* New York: Cambridge University Press.

Solter, D., and McGrath, J., 1984. Inability of mouse blastomere nuclei transferred to enucleated zygotes to support development in vitro. *Science* 226: 1317–19.

Stock, Gregory, 2002. *Redesigning Humans: Our Inevitable Genetic Future.* Boston, MA: Houghton Mifflin.

Tang, Ya-Ping, Shimzu, Eiji, Dube, Gilles R., Rampon, Claire, Kerchner, Geoffrey A., Zhou, Min, Liu, Guosong and Tsien, Joe Z., 1999. Genetic enhancement of learning and memory in mice. *Nature* 401: 63–9.

Tanzi, Rudolph, and Parson, Ann, 2000. *Decoding Darkness: The Search for the Genetic Causes of Alzheimer's Disease.* Cambridge, MA: Perseus Publishing.

The President's Council on Bioethics, 2002. *Human Cloning and Human Dignity.* New York: Public Affairs Reports.

Thornhill, Randy, and Palmer, Craig, 2000. *A Natural History of Rape: Biological Bases of Sexual Coercion.* Cambridge, MA: MIT Press.

Tooley, Michael, 1972. Abortion and infanticide. *Philosophy and Public Affairs* 2: 37–65.

Travis, Cheryl Brown, 2003. *Evolution, Gender, and Rape.* Cambridge, MA: MIT Press.

Unger, Peter, 1990. *Identity, Consciousness, and Value.* New York: Oxford University Press.

Unger, Peter, 1996. *Living High and Letting Die: Our Illusion of Innocence.* Oxford: Oxford University Press.

Wachbroit, Robert, 2003. Normal humans, human nature, and genetic lessons. In V. Gehring (ed.), *Genetic Prospects: Essays on Biotechnology, Ethics, and Public Policy,* pp. 51–60. Lanham, MD: Rowman and Littlefield.

Wade, Nicholas, 2001. *Life Script: The Genome and the New Medicine.* London: Free Press.

Wasserman, David, 2001a. Personal identity and the moral appraisal of prenatal genetic therapy. In Lisa S. Parker and Rachel A. Ankeny (eds), *Mutating Concepts, Evolving Disciplines: Genetics, Medicine, and Society,* pp. 235–64. Dordrecht: Kluwer.

Wasserman, David, 2001b. *Genetics and Criminal Behavior.* New York: Cambridge University Press.

Wasserman, David, 2003. 'My fair baby': What's wrong with parents genetically enhancing their children? In V. Gehring (ed.), *Genetic Prospects: Essays on Biotechnology, Ethics, and Public Policy*, pp. 99–110. Lanham, MD: Rowman and Littlefield.

Wei, F., Wang, G.-D., Kerchner, G. A., Kim, S. J., Xu, H.-M., Chen, Z.-F. and Zhuo, M., 2001. Genetic enhancement of inflammatory pain by forebrain NR2B overexpression. *Nature Neuroscience* 4(2): 164–9.

Williams, Bernard, 1981. *Moral Luck.* Cambridge: Cambridge University Press.

Wilmut, Ian, Campbell, Keith and Tudge, Colin, 2000. *The Second Creation: The Age of Biological Control by the Scientists Who Cloned Dolly.* London: Headline.

Wilson, E. O., 1978. *On Human Nature.* Cambridge, MA: Harvard University Press.

Winston, Mark, 2002. *Travels in the Genetically Modified Zone.* Cambridge, MA: Harvard University Press.

Woodward, James, 1986. The non-identity problem. *Ethics* 96: 804–31.

Wright, Lawrence, 1997. *Twins and What They Tell Us about Who We Are.* New York: Wiley.

Zohar, Noam, 1991. Prospects for 'genetic therapy' – can a person benefit from being altered? *Bioethics* 5(4): 275–88.

Index

normal functioning
   protecting of, 81–4
Nozick, Robert
   Anarchy, State and Utopia, 136
NR2B genes, 10, 11, 23, 31, 90, 95, 159,
   166–7, 173
nurture, moral image of, 111–31, 142
nurture principle, 113, 114
Nussbaum, Martha, 103

objectivist biological theory of disease, 80,
   81
Olson, Eric, 70
O'Neill, Onora, 33
oocytes, 54
organ transplantation, 169–70, 171,
   175
ought-implies-is fallacy, 153–4

Palmer, Craig, 91
parenting
   enhancement and bad, 121–4
   see also children
Pence, Gregory, 58
Pennsylvania Old Order Amish community
   see Amish
Pinker, Steven, 23–4, 33
'playing God' argument, 88
Plomin, Robert, 30, 31, 114
Plotz, David, 2
pluralism, and human flourishing, 101–3,
   104
polarization, 134–5, 136, 146, 157
positional goods, 126–7
positional value
   and enhancement, 126–8
   regulating pursuit of, 128–31
posthumanity, 16–19, 90, 95, 132
pragmatic optimism, 34–8, 46, 66–7, 107,
   125, 133, 149, 158
Pre-implantation Genetic Diagnosis (PGD),
   10, 27–8, 33, 68
Precautionary Principle, 159–63, 169
preference utilitarians, 41
prejudice, 151, 155, 156–7
   and enhancement, 148–50

al Qaeda, 45

racism, 148, 149, 155, 156, 157
Raël, 44
Raelians, 9, 22, 24–5, 35, 37, 42, 44
Rawls, John, 101, 137
Repository for Germinal Choice, 1–2, 4, 9,
   12, 23, 106
reproductive cloning, 24–6, 33, 34–5, 42,
   51–2, 61, 166, 172
   and CLONAID *see* CLONAID
   Kass's criticism of, 139
   and large offspring syndrome, 25
   opponents of, 25
   reasons for, 8–9
   'yuck' argument against, 58
   'research cloning', 52–3; *see also* therapeutic
      cloning
Ridley, Matt, 30
Robertson, John, 5–6, 103, 112
Ruddick, William, 105, 123

Santayana, George, 5
Schwarzenegger mice, 10–11
SCID (Severe Combined Immune
   Deficiency), 65–6, 67–8, 167
Sen, Amartya, 103, 104–5
Severe Combined Immune Deficiency *see*
   SCID
sexual orientation, 109–10
sexual-orientation gene, 72, 73, 74, 109,
   125, 148, 156–7
Shiva, Vandana, 60, 152, 153
Shockley, William, 4
Silver, Lee, 17, 134, 136, 137–8
Singer, Peter, 41, 44
skin colour, 148–9, 155, 156, 157
social arrangements
   impact of enhancement technologies on,
      132–57
social constructivists
   and defining disease, 79–80
Solter, Davor, 33
somatic cell nuclear transfer, 7, 9,
   16, 20, 24, 25, 26, 33–6, 51,
   53, 54